About this book

This exclusive Marks and Spencer cookery book, now in paperback, explains all the basic techniques of cooking for the average family, and provides a complete range of easy-to-follow everyday recipes, as well as more advanced dishes for special occasions.

   Every recipe has been tested and approved by Marks and Spencer's cookery experts. We hope that you will find this book useful and enjoy trying any or all of the delicious dishes.

The *St Michael* All Colour
COOKERY
BOOK

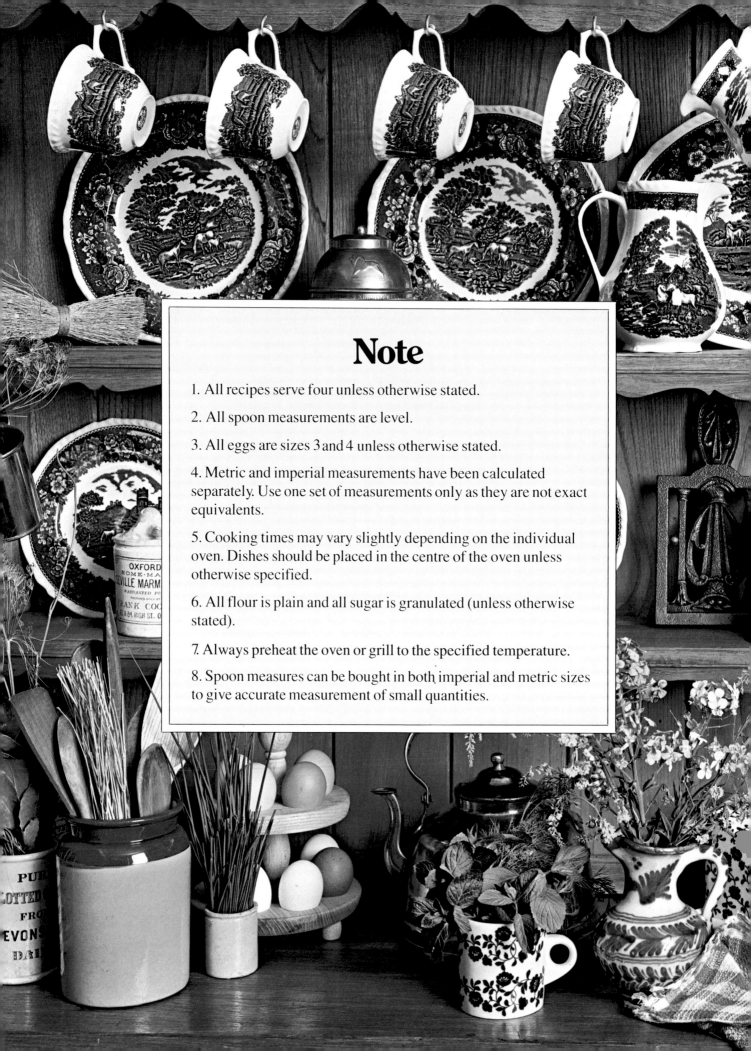

Note

1. All recipes serve four unless otherwise stated.

2. All spoon measurements are level.

3. All eggs are sizes 3 and 4 unless otherwise stated.

4. Metric and imperial measurements have been calculated separately. Use one set of measurements only as they are not exact equivalents.

5. Cooking times may vary slightly depending on the individual oven. Dishes should be placed in the centre of the oven unless otherwise specified.

6. All flour is plain and all sugar is granulated (unless otherwise stated).

7. Always preheat the oven or grill to the specified temperature.

8. Spoon measures can be bought in both imperial and metric sizes to give accurate measurement of small quantities.

The All Colour Cookery Book

Jeni Wright

Contents

First published in 1976 in hardback
by Sundial Publications Limited
59 Grosvenor Street, London W.1.

This edition first published in 1980
Thirteenth impression, paperback edition, 1984

© 1976 Hennerwood Publications Limited

ISBN 0 906320 69 0

Printed in Hong Kong

Convenience in the kitchen

Every good, modern cook should have a convenient kitchen. This means adequate working surfaces at a comfortable height (90 cm./3 ft. is about right for the average-sized person) and in a useful position in relation to the cooker, sink and electric plugs. It means adequate lighting, both natural and artificial, directed onto work surfaces, cooker and sink. Convenient storage space is essential too, for store-cupboard foods, fresh foods and kitchen equipment. Ideally, a cool larder or pantry could house all of these items; however, in most compact modern homes this is usually out of the question and the housewife must rely on cupboard space. For storing foodstuffs, cupboards should be cool which means locating them as far away from central heating boilers, heaters and cookers as possible.

A well-equipped kitchen need not be large or even spacious, but it should be a convenient, safe and pleasant place in which to work.

Your collection of kitchen equipment should be built up gradually. Choose the items that suit you and your kitchen best, that suit the kind of cooking you do – and the size of home and family you have. Most important of all, buy the best quality equipment you can afford: cheap equipment – utensils in particular – is false economy because it will need to be replaced more often.

Automatic chopper for chopping herbs, nuts, vegetables

Baking sheets minimum of two; heavy; made of a good conductor of heat

Balloon whisk ideal for egg whites, cream

Board or marble slab for bread- and pastry-making to protect work surfaces; marble preferable for pastry

Bottle/can opener wall-mounted if available

Bread board for slicing bread; to protect work surfaces and to ensure strong-tasting foods will not contaminate

Brushes two – one for oiling baking sheets, etc.; one for brushing water/milk/egg on pastry, etc.

Bun tins one tray; for individual cakes, buns and Yorkshire pudding

Cake tins set of three deep 17.5 cm./7 in., 20 cm./8 in., 22.5 cm./9 in.; round or square; two shallow 17.5 cm./7 in. sandwich tins; one loose-bottomed 20 cm./8 in. cake tin (round or square) or one 20 cm./8 in. cake tin with sloping sides (moule-à-manqué)

Carving fork with finger guard

Casserole dishes flameproof; two sizes – small, round and large oval; heavy-based, preferably of cast iron

Cherry pitter for easy removal of stones in fruit

Chopping boards minimum of two; to protect work surfaces; separate board for garlic, onions, etc.

Cocktail sticks wooden; to secure food, e.g. Angels on Horseback

Colander for draining; nylon or metal

Corkscrew

Dariole (castle) pudding moulds four to six individual moulds; for sponge puddings, custards, mousses, etc.

Deep-fat fryer with wire basket; for all deep-fat frying – fish, croquettes, potatoes, doughnuts, etc.

Deep-frying thermometer

Double boiler/steamer for delicate sauces, suet-based and sponge puddings, etc.

Egg poacher

Fish slice/spatula to remove fish and other flat food easily from pans, plates, etc.

Flan rings two 17.5 cm./7 in. (one plain, one fluted); two 20 cm./8 in. (one plain, one fluted); for tarts, flans, quiches

Flour and sugar sifters one of each

Frying pan all-purpose; 25 cm./10 in. is a useful size; preferably heavy-based, of cast iron with or without non-stick finish

Hand grater straight sides; metal; for grating lemon and orange rind, etc.

Jelly mould aluminium/glass/copper; attractive shape for jellies, mousses, creams, etc.

Kebab skewers set of six; for barbecue cooking or grilling meat, fish, etc..

Kitchen scales Metric and Imperial weights/dial

Kitchen scissors preferably poultry scissors to cut through bones

Kitchen timer clockwork; for accurate timing; fitted on most modern cookers

Knife sharpener/carborundum

Knives carving knife; bread knife; two French cooks knives (12.5 cm./5 in. and 15 cm./6 in.) of stainless or carbon steel; all-purpose for chopping, filleting; French vegetable knife (10 cm./4 in. pointed blade); serrated-edge knife for cutting fruit and vegetables; grapefruit knife; palette knife

Lemon squeezer

Loaf tins two 1 kg./2 lb. tins; for baking bread, pâtés, tea breads, etc.

Mandoline for fine slicing of potatoes, carrots, etc.

Measuring jug 600 ml./1 pint Metric and Imperial; heatproof

Measuring spoons two sets – Metric and Imperial

Mincer hand-operated; for meat, poultry, etc.

Mixing bowls minimum set of three, varying sizes

Mortar and pestle for pounding, crushing spices, garlic, etc.

Mouli grater hand-operated rotary grater for fine grating of cheese, chocolate, etc.

9

Mouli-Légumes food mill; for purées

Omelet/pancake pans one of each; keep exclusively for cooking omelets/pancakes; preferably of cast iron/aluminium

Pastry cutters set with different sizes from 1.25 cm./½ in. to 7.5 cm./3 in.

Pie dishes ovenproof, 600 ml./1 pint capacity; 1,200 ml./2 pint capacity; for sweet and savoury pies and puddings

Pie funnel to allow steam to escape from pies; to pour jellied stock into savoury pies to be served cold

Pie plates ovenproof glassware, ceramic or aluminium; 17.5 cm./7 in.; 20 cm./8 in.; 22.5 cm./9 in.; for fruit plate pies, etc.

Piping (forcing) bag washable nylon with small and large nozzles, plain or rose; for piping cream, icing, potato, etc.

Potato masher for softer mashed vegetables

Pressure cooker for cooking casseroles, stews, dumplings, basic stocks, pulse-based dishes, suet- and sponge-based puddings very quickly

Pudding basins set of three – 600 ml./1 pint, 900 ml./1½ pint, 1,200 ml./2 pint; set of four to six individual pudding basins 150 ml./¼ pint; for sponge- and suet-based puddings and individual moulds

Ramekin dishes set of six

Ring mould aluminium; 20 cm./8 in. – 22.5 cm./9 in.; for jellies, rice dishes, savarins, etc.

Roasting tin large; for roasting joints, poultry, Yorkshire pudding, etc.

Rolling pin

Rotary beater hand-operated

Rubber spatula for scraping bowls and pans clean

Salt and pepper mills for coarse sea salt and black and white peppercorns

Saucepans minimum set of three, plus milkpan (preferably non-stick) with pouring lip

Scoop for ice cream, potatoes, etc.

Sieves nylon and/or metal; small and large; for draining, particularly for sauces

Slotted spoon for easy draining

Soufflé dishes set of two straight-sided, ovenproof dishes – 12.5 cm./5 in. or 600 ml./1 pint capacity and 17.5 cm./7 in. or 1,200 ml./2 pint capacity; for sweet and savoury soufflés, cooked or uncooked

Soup ladle

Tongs to remove food easily from pans

Trussing needle and strings for trussing poultry and game, boned and rolled joints of meat, etc.

Vegetable brush for scrubbing vegetables, e.g. celery

Vegetable peeler for easy peeling of potatoes and all root vegetables; also cores apples

Wire rack round and square; to cool cakes, biscuits, buns, etc.

Wooden spatulas two – one for sweet, one for savoury

Wooden spoons two small and two large; one set for sweet and one for savoury

Electrical equipment in the kitchen

To be efficient – and to save time and effort – a good cook will appreciate a collection of electrical gadgets and appliances. As with basic equipment in the kitchen, the choice of electrical items will reflect personal taste, needs and circumstances.

Make sure that there are plenty of electric points in the kitchen. These should be situated above work surfaces (as far away from the sink as possible), and spaced conveniently apart. Ideally, there should be a socket for each electrical appliance, so that in the case of items such as mixers, blenders and toasters, these can stand on the work surface ready for use. (Appliances and gadgets in cupboards and drawers are often neglected.)

Here is a list of some of the most useful electrical appliances for the kitchen – ones which are used most often in the recipes in this book.

Automatic oven on most modern cookers; invaluable aid for busy cook who is not at home for long periods during the day

Blender/liquidiser either free-standing with two attachments – blender/liquidiser and grinder – or a blender/grinder attachment to fit a mixer appliance

Deep-fat fryer portable

Frypan portable; can be used for cooking complete meals in one pan

Freezer

Grill/griddle-waffle iron for steaks, chops, toasted sandwiches, waffles; portable

Mixer either free-standing or portable hand-held model

Toaster useful if grill is occupied

Convenience foods and the store cupboard

Convenience foods are exactly what their name suggests, and no sensible cook would be without them – to a certain degree. Used wisely, and with discretion, they can make life in the kitchen much, much easier – and they can add zest and interest to everyday meals.

Convenience foods are essential to cooks who either have little time to spend in the kitchen or who dislike spending hours preparing and cooking meals.

Your choice of convenience foods is obviously a very personal one, dictated by the tastes and habits of you as the cook – and your family, friends and guests. However, there are certain basic foodstuffs in the store cupboard which are essential if the kitchen is to run smoothly, and meals – whether they be grand affairs or simple snacks – are to be made without too much fuss and too many expeditions to the shops. A well-stocked cupboard is a must for successful, impromptu entertaining, and family meals in moments.

Obviously, for the happy owners of freezers, life is much simpler: whole meals, either cooked or uncooked, can be frozen away for some future date, and many basic fresh items may be put in the freezer and stored for weeks or months. However, a well-stocked store cupboard is still useful.

Dried foods, seasonings, etc.

For the best flavour in all dishes fresh **herbs** should be used, but at certain times of year these are not readily available, and the dried variety is useful to have on hand. However, remember that dried herbs and spices should be renewed every two to three months. Parsley and chives can be grown indoors throughout the year; the dried equivalents are not really worth using. In general, use half as much dried herbs as the fresh ones stated in any recipe.

Stock cubes should be used with caution. Wherever possible, use homemade stocks, as these will add far more flavour to a dish. Stock cubes are fine if you are in a hurry, but they do tend to be salty and make dishes taste alike. Powdered bouillon has a far better flavour than a stock cube.

Stuffing mixes are like stock cubes, fine if time is limited, but obviously the homemade variety is preferable (recipes are given in Chapters 5 and 6). Stuffing mixes can be made far more palatable if fresh ingredients are added: chop an onion, fry in butter and add to sage and onion stuffing mix with 1 × 15 ml./1 tablespoon freshly chopped sage and plenty of black pepper. Or add freshly chopped parsley and thyme with the finely grated rind and juice of 1 medium lemon to a packet of parsley and thyme stuffing. Season well with freshly ground black pepper.

Different kinds of **pasta, rice** and **pulses** (beans) are also very useful to have on hand.

Canned vegetables

Tomatoes are the most versatile of all canned foods, especially in winter when fresh tomatoes are expensive and rather tasteless; use in dishes such as Spaghetti Bolognese, Lasagne, Navarin de Mouton.

Sweetcorn, also available frozen (on the cob/kernels), adds colour and flavour, especially to rice-based dishes, soups and chowders; also available with chopped red peppers.

French beans could be served cold in salads with a tangy French dressing.

Red kidney beans should be drained and refreshed under cold running water before using; quick to use in dishes such as Chili con Carne and Minestrone Soup.

Potatoes are a good winter standby; can be used in salads with mayonnaise and/or cream, snipped chives and plenty of freshly ground black pepper; use for Potato and Mushroom Sauté, a quick vegetable accompaniment; can also be fried in butter and oil.

Canned **petits pois** are quite good cooked in butter (not water) with freshly chopped mint, chopped spring onions, sugar, salt and freshly ground black pepper.

Mushrooms canned in brine are expensive, but good as a standby vegetable to use in casseroles, soups and stuffings, etc.

11

Canned meat

Cooked meats make quick tasty meals; canned pâté de foie is useful for stuffings and fillings.

Stewing beef and minced steak can be used for impromptu meals like Chili con Carne, Steak and Kidney Pudding, curries, etc.; must be seasoned well with herbs and/or spices to taste, adding fresh or frozen vegetables wherever possible.

Chopped ham/corned beef, etc. for fritters, deep-frying, pies, sandwiches, corned beef hash, salads, etc; good standby for children's teas and weekend snacks, picnics; also can be diced and combined with a well-seasoned sauce for vol-au-vents.

Canned fish

Tuna canned in oil is good in salads (see Tuna and Bean Salad and Salad Niçoise); mixed with mayonnaise, lemon juice and a sprinkling of cayenne pepper, tuna fish is good in fish cocktails, makes a good sandwich filling, or quick starter served on shredded lettuce or watercress.

Anchovies in olive oil should be drained and soaked in milk for at least 30 minutes before using, to remove excess salt; anchovies are good with meat – use them in pâtés, terrines and stuffings to add extra bite and to bring out flavour; also good in summer salads and on toast (see Anchoïade).

Mackerel either smoked or in tomato sauce makes good sandwich fillings combined with mayonnaise; especially good for open sandwiches.

Salmon red or pink can be used for sandwich and vol-au-vent fillings, either mixed with mayonnaise or well-seasoned béchamel sauce. Also useful for quick supper dishes, such as Kedgeree.

Sardines in olive oil or tomato sauce may be used as salmon.

Prawns/shrimps are a good standby to use for sauces, fish cocktails, avocado with prawns, rice-based dishes, canapé toppings, sandwich and vol-au-vent fillings.

Crab is handy for cocktails, sandwiches and vol-au-vent fillings and rice-based dishes.

Soups

Cans, packets, cubes; immense variety available, though in general cans have fresher flavour; add freshly chopped herbs to tomato, oxtail, minestrone, asparagus; fresh or soured cream to any creamed soup, e.g. mushroom, asparagus, tomato. Wherever possible, float fresh ingredients in individual bowls of soup, e.g. seeded and chopped tomato for tomato soup, garnished with freshly grated orange rind; a few sliced mushroom caps sautéed in butter for mushroom soup. Sherry gives a kick to canned consommé or oxtail, grated Gruyère to canned French onion soup.

Canned fruit

Cherries, particularly Black Morello, are good for trifles and sauces, or combined with kirsch to taste and the finely grated rind and juice of an orange. Chill and serve with sweetened whipped cream or vanilla ice-cream for a luscious dessert.

Prunes may be served for breakfast and make delicious fillings for open flans. They also can be used as a garnish for roast pork and for other pork dishes (see Pork Fillet with Prunes and Sweet and Sour Spareribs). Stoned dried prunes are also used in cakes, sweet loaves, etc.

Raspberries/strawberries/loganberries/blackberries etc. in syrup can be used for trifles, flans, soufflés, etc.

Pineapple, available in rings, pieces or crushed, can be used in rice-based dishes and salads as a garnish for ham, bacon and pork.

Soups

Homemade soups are among the easiest of foods to make, and canned, packet and cube soups have nothing like the flavour and texture of their homemade counterparts. Virtually any ingredient, from vegetables and even fruit, to meat and poultry, or a mixture of these, can be used. To achieve the best flavour, good stock is the most important ingredient of all. Stock cubes, although convenient to use, should be avoided in soup-making as they tend to be bland and salty. Wherever possible, if stock is stated in a recipe, use homemade.

Broths are the sustaining soups, often meals in themselves. They are best made in winter with the cheaper cuts of meat and lots of root vegetables. Broths need long slow cooking. Serve with fresh bread or toast and cheese or pâté for a hearty lunch or welcome-home supper.

Cream soups are thickened by puréeing vegetables and stock in a sieve, electric blender or Mouli-légumes and then enriched with a little cream. Serve in 300 ml./½ pint bowls with fresh bread for lunches and snacks, 150 ml./¼ pint quantity for the first course of a lunch or dinner party.

Iced soups are summer soups, perfect for entertaining on hot balmy nights. They should be served as cold as possible; be sure to chill several hours in the refrigerator before serving. Chill the soup tureen and soup bowls at the same time. Delicately coloured iced soups benefit from being garnished with freshly chopped herbs and swirls of cream.

Chowders are thick substantial soups, ideal for supper meals. The name 'chowder' originates from the French word *chaudière* which was the cooking vessel used in France for soups and stews. Nowadays, chowders often contain fish or shellfish and are particularly popular in the United States.

Soups with a difference, from the rich colourful beetroot soup known as borshch in the U.S.S.R. to the less familiar Greek avgolemono, a subtle combination of chicken stock, eggs and lemon juice are the foreign soups that complete the chapter. These soups are an easy way to give an international flavour to your everyday cooking.

Beef stock

For broths and meat and vegetable soups. Also used in casseroles and stews, etc. Ask the butcher to chop the bones in easy-to-handle pieces.

METRIC	IMPERIAL
Approx. ¾–1 kg. marrow and shin bones	*Approx. 1½–2 lb. marrow and shin bones*
Salt	*Salt*
1 onion, peeled and quartered	*1 onion, peeled and quartered*
2 carrots, peeled and chopped	*2 carrots, peeled and chopped*
1 bouquet garni	*1 bouquet garni*
6 black peppercorns	*6 black peppercorns*

Put the bones in a large saucepan. Cover with water (about 2 l./2 quarts) and add 1 x 1.25 ml. spoon/¼ teaspoon salt for each quart of water. Bring to the boil, skimming off any scum with a slotted spoon. Half cover with a lid and simmer gently for 2 hours, skimming occasionally.

Add the vegetables, bouquet garni and peppercorns and continue simmering a further 1½ to 2 hours, adding more water if the level drops below that of the bones. Remove from the heat and strain. Leave to cool, then skim off fat with a spoon or absorbent kitchen paper. Use immediately or keep in the refrigerator.

NOTE: homemade stock deteriorates quickly; therefore, it should not be kept for any length of time – a maximum of three days in the refrigerator. However, stock does freeze and will keep for about two months if stored in the freezer.

Ham stock

Make as for Beef Stock, substituting a ham (knuckle or shank) bone for the marrow and shin bones.

White stock

Use for delicately flavoured and pale-coloured soups. Make as for Beef Stock, substituting blanched veal bones for the marrow and shin bones.

Chicken stock

Make as for Beef Stock, substituting a whole chicken carcass for the bones. After straining stock, pick over the carcass and remove any meat still on the bones. Add to the stock. Duck and Turkey Stock can be made in the same way.

Fish stock

For use in all fish soups, chowders, fish stews, etc.

METRIC	IMPERIAL
Approx. ½ kg. fish heads, bones, tails, etc. (cod, haddock, whiting, plaice, etc.)	Approx. 1 lb. fish heads, bones, tails, etc. (cod, haddock, whiting, plaice, etc.)
1 x 2.5 ml. spoon salt	½ teaspoon salt
2 celery stalks with the leaves, scrubbed and chopped	2 celery stalks with the leaves, scrubbed and chopped
1 onion, peeled and quartered	1 onion, peeled and quartered
1 parsley sprig	1 parsley sprig
1 bay leaf	1 bay leaf
6 black peppercorns	6 black peppercorns

Put the fish trimmings in a saucepan. Cover with water and stir in the remaining ingredients. Bring to the boil, skimming off any scum with a slotted spoon. Lower the heat, half cover with a lid and simmer gently for 30–40 minutes, skimming occasionally if necessary. Remove from the heat and strain. Cool, then chill in the refrigerator. Use the same day.

Garnishes and accompaniments

Simple garnishes and accompaniments give a professional finish to soup and make it look more inviting.

Fresh herbs

Parsley: should be finely chopped. Allow 2 × 15 ml. spoons/2 tablespoons for four soup bowls and sprinkle onto the centre of each. Suitable for most broths and purées and for soups which lack natural colour.

Chives: snip finely with scissors. Use as an alternative to parsley. Particularly good as a garnish for iced soups.

Cream: fresh single cream or soured cream makes an attractive garnish if swirled in individual bowls (soured cream will need thinning down with a little top of the milk). Cream cheese can also be thinned and used. For a special garnish, swirl cream or cream cheese and sprinkle over parsley in each bowl.

Cheese: grated cheese – Cheddar, Parmesan, Gruyère – can be sprinkled over individual flameproof bowls and put under a preheated hot grill until bubbling; good with soups such as Tomato Chowder or French Onion. Cheese can also be grated onto toast for a garnish. Toast thin slices of bread, crusts removed, on one side only, then butter untoasted sides and sprinkle thickly with grated cheese and a little cayenne or paprika pepper. Grill under a preheated hot grill until melted and browned, then cut into small cubes or triangles and float on top of individual soup bowls. Good with most meat or vegetable soups.

Croûtons: especially good with cream and purée soups as they provide a crunchy contrast in texture to the smoothness of the soup. Hand separately in small bowls.

For Fried Croûtons: cut stale bread, crusts removed, into small cubes or triangles and fry in equal quantities of hot oil and butter until crisp and golden-brown. Drain on absorbent kitchen paper and serve immediately, or keep hot until serving time.

For Toasted Croûtons: toast bread, crusts removed, on both sides, then cut into small cubes or triangles.

For Potato Croûtons: parboil 1 or 2 potatoes for 10 minutes, leave to cool, then skin and dice. Fry and drain as for Fried Croûtons.

Vegetables: make attractive garnishes for vegetable soups, e.g. sliced raw or sautéed mushrooms on mushroom soup, young celery leaves for celery soup, thin strips of cucumber for iced cucumber soup, grated raw carrot for carrot soup, etc.

Cream and purée soups

Cream of tomato soup

Cream of tomato soup

Summer tomatoes are best for this soup as they will give it most flavour. If the fat, juicy continental variety are available, then so much the better. When neither is available, use a 396 g./14 oz. can of tomatoes.

METRIC	IMPERIAL
Butter for frying	Butter for frying
1 medium-sized onion, peeled and finely chopped	1 medium-sized onion, peeled and finely chopped
2 streaky bacon rashers, rinds removed and diced	2 streaky bacon rashers, rinds removed and diced
1 × 15 ml. spoon flour	1 tablespoon flour
½ kg. fresh tomatoes, halved and seeded	1 lb. fresh tomatoes, halved and seeded
600 ml. chicken stock	1 pint chicken stock
Salt and freshly ground black pepper	Salt and freshly ground black pepper
1 × 5 ml. spoon chopped fresh basil or 1 × 2.5 ml. spoon dried basil	1 teaspoon chopped fresh basil or ½ teaspoon dried basil
Pinch of sugar	Pinch of sugar
Lemon juice to taste	Lemon juice to taste

To finish:

4 × 15 ml. spoons fresh single cream	4 tablespoons fresh single cream
Chopped fresh basil or snipped chives	Chopped fresh basil or snipped chives

Melt a knob of butter in a saucepan. Add the onion and bacon, cover and cook gently for 5 minutes. Stir in the flour and cook for 1 minute, stirring constantly. Add the tomatoes and gradually stir in the stock. Bring to the boil. Lower the heat, season to taste and add the basil and sugar. Half cover and simmer gently for 20 minutes.

Remove the pan from the heat and rub the soup through a sieve or Mouli-légumes. Return the soup to the rinsed-out pan and reheat. Adjust seasoning and add lemon juice. Pour the soup into bowls, swirl a spoon of cream on top of each and sprinkle with basil or chives.

Watercress and potato soup

Watercress makes a hot, spicy soup. The beautiful creamy texture comes from the potatoes which act as a thickening agent.

METRIC	IMPERIAL
Butter for frying	Butter for frying
1 small onion, peeled and finely chopped	1 small onion, peeled and finely chopped
2 bunches of watercress, washed and finely chopped	2 bunches of watercress, washed and finely chopped
¼ kg. potatoes, peeled and diced	½ lb. potatoes, peeled and diced
400 ml. milk	¾ pint milk
400 ml. chicken stock	¾ pint chicken stock
Salt and freshly ground black pepper	Salt and freshly ground black pepper
Few reserved watercress leaves to finish	Few reserved watercress leaves to finish

Watercress and potato soup

Melt a knob of butter in a saucepan. Add the vegetables, cover and cook gently for 5 minutes. Stir in the milk and stock, bring to the boil and add seasoning. Lower the heat, half cover and simmer gently for 30 minutes, stirring occasionally.

Purée the soup in an electric blender or work through a sieve or Mouli-légumes. Return to the rinsed-out pan and reheat. Before serving adjust seasoning and float a few leaves of watercress on each soup bowl.

Cream of mushroom soup

Cream of mushroom soup

A soup with a superb flavour, this makes an ideal dinner party starter.

METRIC	IMPERIAL
Butter for frying	Butter for frying
1 small onion, peeled and finely chopped	1 small onion, peeled and finely chopped
¼ kg. mushrooms, cleaned and finely chopped	½ lb. mushrooms, cleaned and finely chopped
2 × 15 ml. spoons flour	2 tablespoons flour
1¼ l. chicken stock	2 pints chicken stock
Salt and freshly ground black pepper	Salt and freshly ground black pepper
Pinch of grated nutmeg	Pinch of grated nutmeg
1 bay leaf	1 bay leaf

To finish:
150–300 ml. fresh single cream	¼–½ pint fresh single cream
Chopped fresh parsley	Chopped fresh parsley

Melt a knob of butter in a saucepan. Add the onion and mushrooms, cover and cook gently for 5 minutes. Stir in the flour and continue cooking for a further 2 minutes, stirring constantly. Gradually add the chicken stock and bring to the boil, stirring. Add the seasonings. Lower the heat, half cover and simmer gently for 20 minutes.

Before serving, remove the bay leaf and adjust seasoning. Stir in cream to taste and top each bowl of soup with a good sprinkling of parsley.

Courgette Soup

This soup is best made at the end of summer when home grown courgettes and tomatoes are in abundance.

METRIC	IMPERIAL
25 g. butter	1 oz. butter
1 small onion, peeled and finely chopped	1 small onion, peeled and finely chopped
½ kg. courgettes, finely sliced	1 lb. courgettes, finely sliced
½ kg. tomatoes, roughly chopped	1 lb. tomatoes, roughly chopped
1 × 15 ml. spoon flour	1 tablespoon flour
900 ml. chicken stock	1½ pints chicken stock
1 × 1.25 ml. spoon turmeric powder	¼ teaspoon turmeric powder
Pinch of salt	Pinch of salt
Salt and freshly ground black pepper	Salt and freshly ground black pepper
Grated Parmesan cheese, to serve	Grated Parmesan cheese, to serve

Melt the butter in a saucepan. Add the onion and courgettes, cover and cook gently for 5 minutes, shaking the pan occasionally. Add the tomatoes, then stir in the flour and continue cooking for a further 2 minutes. Stir in the remaining ingredients and bring to the boil. Lower the heat, half cover and simmer gently for 20 minutes.

Purée in an electric blender, then work through a sieve. Return to the rinsed-out pan and reheat. Taste and adjust seasoning. Serve hot with grated Parmesan handed separately. **Serves 4 to 6**

Courgette soup

Potage bonne femme

Potage bonne femme

A good winter standby, this soup makes a wholesome supper when served with cheese or pâté on toast.

METRIC	IMPERIAL
Butter for frying	*Butter for frying*
3 medium-sized carrots, peeled and chopped	*3 medium-sized carrots, peeled and chopped*
3 medium-sized leeks, washed and sliced	*3 medium-sized leeks, washed and sliced*
3 medium-sized potatoes, peeled and diced	*3 medium-sized potatoes, peeled and diced*
1¼ l. chicken stock	*2 pints chicken stock*
Salt and freshly ground black pepper	*Salt and freshly ground black pepper*
1 × 5 ml. spoon sugar	*1 teaspoon sugar*
Milk (if necessary)	*Milk (if necessary)*

To finish:	**To finish:**
Chopped fresh parsley or fried croûtons	*Chopped fresh parsley or fried croûtons*

Melt a knob of butter in a saucepan. Add the vegetables, cover and cook gently for 5 minutes. Add the stock, seasoning and sugar, stir well and bring to the boil. Lower the heat, half cover and simmer for 20 to 30 minutes or until the vegetables are tender.

Blend to a smooth purée in an electric blender or work through a sieve or Mouli-légumes. The soup should have the consistency of double cream, so if it is too thick, stir in a little milk. Return the soup to the rinsed-out pan and reheat. Adjust seasoning and serve sprinkled with chopped parsley or fried croûtons.

Broths

Cock-a-leekie

In Scotland this soup is traditionally served on Burns Night. Once an old cock rooster would have been used, but today a boiling fowl will be more readily available.

METRIC	IMPERIAL
1 boiling fowl (about 1¼ – 1½ kg.), trussed, with the giblets (except liver and gall bladder)	*1 boiling fowl (about 2½ – 3 lb.), trussed, with the giblets (except liver and gall bladder)*
1 bouquet garni	*1 bouquet garni*
Salt and freshly ground black pepper	*Salt and freshly ground black pepper*
6 leeks, washed, halved and sliced lengthways	*6 leeks, washed, halved and sliced lengthways*
4 – 6 prunes, soaked overnight, halved and stoned	*4 – 6 prunes, soaked overnight, halved and stoned*

Put the fowl and bouquet garni in a large saucepan, season well and cover with water. Bring to the boil then lower the heat, half cover and simmer very gently for 2 hours, skimming with a slotted spoon from time to time if necessary to remove the scum.

Add the leeks and more water to cover the fowl if required and continue to simmer, uncovered, for a further 1 hour or until both fowl and leeks are tender. The prunes should be added 30 minutes before the end of cooking time.

To serve, remove the fowl and discard the giblets and bouquet garni. Skim the broth and adjust seasoning. The fowl can be carved and some of the meat returned to the soup and reheated before serving or eaten separately as a main course. **Serves 4 to 6.**

Cock-a-leekie

Chicken broth

This is a fine soup for using up the leftover carcass of a roasted chicken.

METRIC	IMPERIAL
1 chicken carcass and any leftover chicken, diced	1 chicken carcass and any leftover chicken, diced
1 × 2.5 ml. spoon salt	½ teaspoon salt
6 peppercorns, finely crushed	6 peppercorns, finely crushed
1 bay leaf	1 bay leaf
1 bouquet garni	1 bouquet garni
2 carrots, peeled and sliced	2 carrots, peeled and sliced
3 celery stalks, scrubbed and chopped	3 celery stalks, scrubbed and chopped
50 g. long-grain rice	2 oz. long-grain rice

To finish:
Chopped fresh parsley
50 g. chopped almonds

To finish:
Chopped fresh parsley
2 oz. chopped almonds

Put the chicken carcass and any meat in a large saucepan, cover with water and add the remaining ingredients. Bring to the boil. Lower the heat, cover and simmer gently for 2 hours, skimming with a slotted spoon when necessary to remove any scum. Add more water if the liquid in the pan becomes low.

To serve, remove the carcass from the pan, making sure that every scrap of meat is in the broth. Skim well to remove any fat using a spoon or absorbent kitchen paper. Discard the bay leaf and bouquet garni, adjust seasoning and serve the broth piping hot, topped with plenty of parsley and the almonds.

Oxtail soup

Oxtail soup

An oxtail makes a cheap nourishing winter soup. Get your butcher to chop through the oxtail as this can be difficult to do at home.

METRIC	IMPERIAL
Lard or beef dripping for frying	Lard or beef dripping for frying
1 large onion, peeled and chopped	1 large onion, peeled and chopped
1 oxtail, chopped and excess fat removed	1 oxtail, chopped and excess fat removed
2 – 3 carrots, peeled and chopped	2 – 3 carrots, peeled and chopped
2 – 3 celery stalks, scrubbed and chopped	2 – 3 celery stalks, scrubbed and chopped
1 bay leaf	1 bay leaf
6 peppercorns	6 peppercorns
Salt	Salt

Melt a knob of lard or dripping in a large saucepan. Add the onion and oxtail and fry until brown. Add remaining ingredients and cover with water. Salt lightly. Bring to the boil, then lower the heat, cover and simmer gently for 3 to 4 hours or until the oxtail is thoroughly tender and the meat is falling from the bone. Add more water during cooking if the liquid level becomes rather low.

Take the pan from the heat. Remove the oxtail and take the meat off the bone with a sharp knife. Skim the stock well to remove any fat using a spoon or absorbent kitchen paper. Return the meat to the soup, discarding the bone and bay leaf, and purée the soup in an electric blender. Thin with a little water if the soup is too thick and adjust seasoning. Return to the rinsed-out pan and reheat before serving.

Serves 4 to 6.

Chicken broth

Pot-au-feu

Pot-au-feu

Sometimes referred to as the national soup of France, Pot-au-feu makes a substantial meal in itself for cold wintry days. In France the meat is usually served separately.

METRIC
1 kg. clod or shin of beef
 with bones, excess fat
 removed
1 × 5 ml. spoon salt
6 peppercorns, finely
 crushed
1 onion, peeled and stuck
 with a few cloves
1 bouquet garni
1 garlic clove, finely
 chopped
2 carrots, peeled and
 quartered

IMPERIAL
2 lb. clod or shin of beef
 with bones, excess fat
 removed
1 teaspoon salt
6 peppercorns, finely
 crushed
1 onion, peeled and stuck
 with a few cloves
1 bouquet garni
1 garlic clove, finely
 chopped
2 carrots, peeled and
 quartered

2 celery stalks, scrubbed and
 chopped
2 leeks, washed and sliced
½ kg. potatoes, peeled and
 diced
Chopped fresh parsley to
 finish

2 celery stalks, scrubbed and
 chopped
2 leeks, washed and sliced
1 lb. potatoes, peeled and
 diced
Chopped fresh parsley to
 finish

Put the meat and bones in a large saucepan. Cover with water, add the salt and bring slowly to the boil. Skim off the scum with a slotted spoon. Lower the heat, add the peppercorns, onion, bouquet garni and garlic and half cover. Simmer very gently for 2½ hours or until the meat is just tender, skimming from time to time if necessary. Add more water if the liquid level in the pan becomes rather low.

Remove the bones and the bouquet garni and onion, then add the vegetables. Continue to simmer gently for a further 1 hour when both the meat and vegetables will be tender. Before serving, bring the soup quickly to the boil, skim well to remove any fat, adjust seasoning and sprinkle with plenty of chopped parsley. **Serves 4 to 6.**

Lentil and ham soup

A traditional British recipe, this hearty soup is very filling and makes a satisfying meal in itself. Make the ham stock the day before. Cut some of the ham off the shank, dice it and add to the soup after blending.

METRIC	IMPERIAL
1 large onion, peeled and roughly chopped	*1 large onion, peeled and roughly chopped*
4 large celery stalks, scrubbed and roughly chopped	*4 large celery stalks, scrubbed and roughly chopped*
2 large carrots, peeled and chopped	*2 large carrots, peeled and chopped*
75 g. split yellow lentils	*3 oz. split yellow lentils*
1 large fresh parsley sprig or 1 × 2.5 ml. spoon dried parsley	*1 large fresh parsley sprig or ½ teaspoon dried parsley*
Few celery leaves	*Few celery leaves*
Salt and freshly ground black pepper	*Salt and freshly ground black pepper*
2 cloves, crushed	*2 cloves, crushed*
1 l. homemade ham stock	*2 pints homemade ham stock*
Cooked diced ham	*Cooked diced ham*
Chopped fresh parsley to finish	*Chopped fresh parsley to finish*

Put all the ingredients, except the ham, with 600 ml./1 pint of the stock in a large saucepan. Bring to the boil, then lower the heat, cover and simmer very gently for 1 to 1½ hours or until everything is soft and mushy. Purée in an electric blender or work through a sieve or Mouli-légumes. Return to the rinsed-out pan. Add the remaining stock and pieces of ham. Reheat gently. Adjust seasoning. Stir in plenty of chopped parsley and serve. **Serves 4 to 6.**

Lentil and ham soup

Iced soups

Chilled avocado soup

Chilled avocado soup

Quick and easy to make, this soup is unusual in that it is uncooked – a boon to busy cooks on hot summer days. Do not leave it for longer than 1 hour after mixing because the avocados will cause it to discolour.

METRIC	IMPERIAL
2 ripe avocados	*2 ripe avocados*
2 × 5 ml. spoons lemon juice	*2 teaspoons lemon juice*
1 celery stalk, scrubbed and very finely chopped	*1 celery stalk, scrubbed and very finely chopped*
1 × 15 ml. spoon tomato purée	*1 tablespoon tomato purée*
3 × 141 g. cartons unsweetened natural yogurt	*3 × 5 oz. cartons unsweetened natural yogurt*
Salt and freshly ground black pepper	*Salt and freshly ground black pepper*
300 – 400 ml. chicken stock, skimmed of fat	*½ – ¾ pint chicken stock, skimmed of fat*
Dash of Tabasco sauce	*Dash of Tabasco sauce*
Snipped chives to garnish	*Snipped chives to garnish*

Halve the avocados, remove the stones and scoop out the flesh into a bowl. Add the lemon juice to the flesh and mash with a fork until smooth. Stir in the remaining ingredients, with seasoning to taste, adding enough stock to make a pouring consistency. Taste for seasoning. Chill in the refrigerator for 30 minutes, standing the bowl in a bowl of ice cubes. Serve in well-chilled bowls and garnish the soup with plenty of snipped chives.

Iced cucumber soup

Iced cucumber soup is beautifully refreshing on a summer evening.

METRIC
Butter for frying
1 small onion, peeled and finely chopped
2 cucumbers, peeled, halved, seeded and chopped
1 × 15 ml. spoon flour
600 ml. hot milk
300 ml. chicken stock
Salt and ground white pepper
1 × 2.5 ml. spoon grated nutmeg

To finish:
Few drops green food colouring
150 ml. fresh single cream
2 × 15 ml. spoons chopped fresh mint

IMPERIAL
Butter for frying
1 small onion, peeled and finely chopped
2 cucumbers, peeled, halved, seeded and chopped
1 tablespoon flour
1 pint hot milk
½ pint chicken stock
Salt and ground white pepper
½ teaspoon grated nutmeg

To finish:
Few drops green food colouring
¼ pint fresh single cream
2 tablespoons chopped fresh mint

Melt a knob of butter in a saucepan. Add the onion and cucumbers, cover and cook gently for 5 minutes. Stir in the flour and cook for a further 2 minutes, stirring constantly.

Remove the pan from the heat and gradually stir in the hot milk. Pour in the stock. Return the pan to the heat and bring to the boil, stirring. Season with salt, pepper and nutmeg. Lower the heat, half cover and simmer gently for 20 minutes.

Purée the soup in an electric blender or work through a sieve or Mouli-légumes. The soup should be the consistency of single cream, so if it is too thick, add a little more milk. Cool, then chill in the refrigerator until quite cold. Adjust seasoning and add a few drops of green food colouring, mixing well. Pour into chilled serving bowls, swirl with cream and top with chopped mint.

Vichyssoise

Vichyssoise is a simple leek and potato soup. Be sure to purée it well in the blender or sieve as its velvety smoothness adds to its appeal.

METRIC
Butter for frying
½ kg. leeks, white and pale green part, washed and chopped
½ kg. potatoes, peeled and diced
1 medium-sized onion, peeled and finely chopped
900 ml. jellied homemade chicken stock, skimmed of fat
Salt and ground white pepper

To finish:
150 ml. fresh single cream
Snipped chives

IMPERIAL
Butter for frying
1 lb. leeks, white and pale green part, washed and chopped
1 lb. potatoes, peeled and diced
1 medium-sized onion, peeled and finely chopped
1½ pints jellied homemade chicken stock, skimmed of fat
Salt and ground white pepper

To finish:
¼ pint fresh single cream
Snipped chives

Melt a knob of butter in a saucepan. Add the leeks, potatoes and onion, cover and cook gently for 5 minutes. Stir in the stock, bring to the boil, then lower the heat. Season to taste, half cover and simmer for 20 to 25 minutes or until the vegetables are tender.

Purée in an electric blender or work several times through a sieve or Mouli-légumes until the soup is very smooth. Adjust seasoning. Swirl in the cream with a metal spoon to achieve a marbled effect, then chill in the refrigerator for at least 3 hours. Serve topped with snipped chives.

Gazpacho

There are many different recipes for this Spanish soup, but all should be served in true Spanish style with the small bowls of accompaniments – finely chopped onions, cucumbers, tomatoes, green or red peppers.

Purée all the ingredients, except the oil and seasoning, in an electric blender. Put the soup in a soup tureen or serving bowl and beat in the olive oil. Add enough water to make the soup a fairly runny consistency – true Gazpacho is a thin soup – and season well. Stand the tureen or bowl in a bowl of ice cubes and chill in the refrigerator for at least 3 hours. Serve with the accompaniments.

METRIC	IMPERIAL
¼ kg. ripe tomatoes, skinned, seeded and chopped	½ lb. ripe tomatoes, skinned, seeded and chopped
1 large Spanish onion, peeled and chopped	1 large Spanish onion, peeled and chopped
1 garlic clove, chopped, or 1 × 5 ml. spoon garlic granules	1 garlic clove, chopped, or 1 teaspoon garlic granules
1 large green or red pepper, cored, seeded and chopped	1 large green or red pepper, cored, seeded and chopped
50 g. fine fresh white breadcrumbs, soaked in 1 × 15 ml. spoon wine vinegar	2 oz. fine fresh white breadcrumbs, soaked in 1 tablespoon wine vinegar
2 × 15 ml. spoons olive oil	2 tablespoons olive oil
Salt and freshly ground black pepper	Salt and freshly ground black pepper

Iced cucumber soup; Vichyssoise; Gazpacho

Chowders

Tomato chowder

Sweet and spicy in flavour, this colourful chowder makes good use of canned foods.

METRIC	IMPERIAL
1 × 298 g. can condensed tomato soup, undiluted	1 × 10½ oz. can condensed tomato soup, undiluted
400 ml. milk	¾ pint milk
1 × 396 g. can tomatoes, sieved	1 × 14 oz. can tomatoes, sieved
1 × 326 g. can sweetcorn, drained	1 × 11½ oz. can sweetcorn, drained
1 × 15 ml. spoon Worcestershire sauce	1 tablespoon Worcestershire sauce
1 × 5 ml. spoon sugar	1 teaspoon sugar
Salt and freshly ground black pepper	Salt and freshly ground black pepper
100 g. grated Cheddar cheese to finish	4 oz. grated Cheddar cheese to finish

Combine all the ingredients with seasoning to taste in a large saucepan and bring slowly to the boil, stirring constantly. Pour into a hot serving bowl or individual bowls and sprinkle the top with the grated cheese. Put under a preheated hot grill for 5 minutes or until the cheese melts and is bubbling. Serve immediately. **Serves 4 to 6.**

Chicken and corn chowder

Chicken and corn chowder

Use leftovers from a roast chicken to make this soup. The chicken carcass can be used to make the stock.

METRIC	IMPERIAL
Butter for frying	Butter for frying
1 large onion, peeled and finely chopped	1 large onion, peeled and finely chopped
1 green or red pepper, cored, seeded and chopped	1 green or red pepper, cored, seeded and chopped
2 × 15 ml. spoons flour	2 tablespoons flour
400 ml. hot milk	¾ pint hot milk
400 ml. well-flavoured chicken stock, skimmed of fat	¾ pint well-flavoured chicken stock, skimmed of fat
Salt and freshly ground black pepper	Salt and freshly ground black pepper
¼ kg. leftover cooked chicken, shredded	½ lb. leftover cooked chicken, shredded
½ kg. potatoes, peeled and diced	1 lb. potatoes, peeled and diced
1 × 326 g. can sweetcorn, drained	1 × 11½ oz. can sweetcorn, drained

Melt a knob of butter in a large saucepan. Add the onion and pepper and fry gently until soft. Stir in the flour and cook for a further 2 minutes, stirring constantly. Remove the pan from the heat and gradually stir in the hot milk and stock. Return to the heat and slowly bring to the boil, stirring. Season to taste and add the remaining ingredients. Lower the heat, cover and simmer gently for 20 to 25 minutes or until the potatoes are tender. Adjust seasoning and serve. **Serves 4 to 6.**

Tomato chowder

Fish chowder

This soup makes a substantial meal in itself, served with fresh French bread and butter.

METRIC	IMPERIAL
Olive oil for frying	*Olive oil for frying*
1 medium-sized onion, peeled and finely chopped	*1 medium-sized onion, peeled and finely chopped*
1 garlic clove, crushed with 1 × 2.5 ml. spoon salt	*1 garlic clove, crushed with ½ teaspoon salt*
1 × 396 g. can tomatoes, sieved	*1 × 14 oz. can tomatoes, sieved*
1 carrot, peeled and chopped	*1 carrot, peeled and chopped*
1 celery stalk, scrubbed and chopped	*1 celery stalk, scrubbed and chopped*
¼ kg. potatoes, peeled and diced	*½ lb. potatoes, peeled and diced*
½ kg. white fish (cod, haddock, whiting), skinned, filleted and cut into bite-sized pieces	*1 lb. white fish (cod, haddock, whiting), skinned, filleted and cut into bite-sized pieces*
600 ml. water	*1 pint water*
Freshly ground black pepper	*Freshly ground black pepper*
300 ml. milk	*½ pint milk*
Chopped fresh parsley to finish	*Chopped fresh parsley to finish*

Heat 2 spoons of oil in a large fish kettle or saucepan. Add the vegetables, except the potatoes, and cook gently, stirring occasionally, for 5 minutes, or until the oil is absorbed into the vegetables. Add the potatoes, fish and water and bring slowly to the boil, skimming off any scum with a slotted spoon. Lower the heat, add pepper to taste, cover the kettle or pan and simmer gently for 20 to 30 minutes or until the fish and vegetables are quite tender. Be careful not to over-cook or they will disintegrate. Add the milk and reheat gently. Adjust seasoning, stir in plenty of chopped parsley and serve. **Serves 4 to 6.**

Fish chowder

Foreign soups

Potage Crécy

Potage Crécy

Creamy French carrot soup is one of the nicest homemade soups there is, both for a homely winter's snack with hot toast or a special dinner party.

METRIC	IMPERIAL
Butter for frying	*Butter for frying*
1 medium-sized onion, peeled and finely chopped	*1 medium-sized onion, peeled and finely chopped*
½ kg. carrots, peeled and chopped	*1 lb. carrots, peeled and chopped*
1 large potato, peeled and diced	*1 large potato, peeled and diced*
900 ml. chicken stock, skimmed of fat	*1½ pints chicken stock, skimmed of fat*
Salt and freshly ground black pepper	*Salt and freshly ground black pepper*
1 × 15 ml. spoon chopped fresh parsley	*1 tablespoon chopped fresh parsley*
1 × 5 ml. spoon sugar	*1 teaspoon sugar*
To finish:	**To finish:**
4 × 15 ml. spoons fresh single cream	*4 tablespoons fresh single cream*
Fried croûtons	*Fried croûtons*

Melt a knob of butter in a saucepan. Add the vegetables, cover and cook gently for 5 minutes. Gradually stir in the chicken stock. Bring to the boil, add the seasoning, parsley and sugar, lower the heat and half cover. Simmer gently for 20 to 30 minutes or until the carrots are tender.

Purée the soup in an electric blender or work through a sieve or Mouli-légumes. Return to the rinsed-out pan, reheat gently and adjust seasoning. Pour into warmed bowls for serving. Swirl a spoonful of cream in each bowl and top with fried croûtons. **Serves 4 to 6.**

French onion soup

This is a warming soup on cold nights. Traditionally, a spoonful of cognac was stirred in before serving.

METRIC	IMPERIAL
Butter for frying	*Butter for frying*
½ kg. Spanish onions, peeled and sliced into rings	*1 lb. Spanish onions, peeled and sliced into rings*
2 × 15 ml. spoons flour	*2 tablespoons flour*
1¼ l. well-flavoured homemade beef stock, skimmed of fat	*2 pints well-flavoured homemade beef stock, skimmed of fat*
Salt and freshly ground black pepper	*Salt and freshly ground black pepper*

To finish:

4 slices of French bread, buttered	*4 slices of French bread, buttered*
4 large slices of Gruyère or Cheddar cheese	*4 large slices of Gruyère or Cheddar cheese*

Melt a knob of butter in a saucepan. Add the onions and fry gently until soft and golden. Stir in the flour and cook gently for a further 2 minutes, stirring constantly. Gradually stir in the stock and bring to the boil. Season with salt and plenty of black pepper, then lower the heat and simmer for 20 to 25 minutes or until the onions are soft. Adjust seasoning.

Pour the soup into individual warmed soup bowls. Float a slice of bread on each and top with a slice of cheese. Sprinkle with black pepper and put under a preheated hot grill for 5 minutes or until the cheese melts and is bubbling. Serve immediately.

Minestrone

A favourite in Italian restaurants, real minestrone is a hearty vegetable soup which can easily be made at home.

METRIC	IMPERIAL
Olive oil for frying	*Olive oil for frying*
100 g. streaky bacon, rinds removed and chopped	*4 oz. streaky bacon, rinds removed and chopped*
1 green pepper, cored, seeded and finely chopped	*1 green pepper, cored, seeded and finely chopped*
1 large onion, peeled and finely chopped	*1 large onion, peeled and finely chopped*
1 garlic clove, crushed with 1 × 5 ml. spoon salt	*1 garlic clove, crushed with 1 teaspoon salt*
3 celery stalks, scrubbed and chopped	*3 celery stalks, scrubbed and chopped*
1 × 396 g. can tomatoes	*1 × 14 oz. can tomatoes*
2 medium-sized carrots, peeled and finely chopped	*2 medium-sized carrots, peeled and finely chopped*
2 courgettes, finely chopped	*2 courgettes, finely chopped*

Minestrone; Avgolemono; French onion soup

100 g. small pasta shells or bows	4 oz. small pasta shells or bows
Freshly ground black pepper	Freshly ground black pepper
1 × 5 ml. spoon dried oregano or basil	1 teaspoon dried oregano or basil
1 × 5 ml. spoon sugar	1 teaspoon sugar
1 × 15 ml. spoon tomato purée	1 tablespoon tomato purée
1½ l. chicken stock, skimmed of fat	2½ pints chicken stock, skimmed of fat
1 × 432 g. can red kidney beans, drained and refreshed under cold running water	1 × 15¼ oz. can red kidney beans, drained and refreshed under cold running water
100 g. freshly grated Parmesan cheese to finish	4 oz. freshly grated Parmesan cheese to finish

Heat 2 spoons of olive oil in a large saucepan. Add the bacon, pepper, onion and garlic and fry gently for 5 to 10 minutes or until the onions are golden and the bacon is crisp. Stir in the remaining vegetables (except the kidney beans) and pasta. Add pepper and stir in the oregano or basil, sugar, tomato purée and stock. Bring to the boil, stirring constantly. Lower the heat, cover and simmer gently for 20 minutes, stirring occasionally. Add the kidney beans and simmer for 10 minutes or until all the vegetables are tender.

Adjust seasoning and serve piping hot with grated Parmesan cheese handed separately.   **Serves 6 to 8.**

Borshch

Avgolemono

Popular in Greece and Cyprus and in many parts of the Middle East, this piquant lemon-flavoured soup is a good way to use leftover chicken. The carcass will make an excellent chicken stock and any leftover meat can be cut into small dice and added to the soup at the finish.

METRIC	IMPERIAL
1¼ l. well-flavoured chicken stock, skimmed of fat	2 pints well-flavoured chicken stock, skimmed of fat
50 g. long-grain rice	2 oz. long-grain rice
juice of 1–2 lemons (approx. 90 ml.)	juice of 1–2 lemons (approx. 3 fl. oz.)
2 eggs	2 eggs
Salt and freshly ground black pepper	Salt and freshly ground black pepper
Snipped chives to finish	Snipped chives to finish

Put the stock and rice in a saucepan. Bring to the boil, stir once and cover, then lower the heat and simmer gently for 20 minutes. Beat the lemon juice and eggs together in a bowl then beat in a few spoonfuls of the hot stock. Blend into the remaining stock and rice and reheat very gently. Do not allow the soup to boil or it will curdle. Adjust seasoning and serve immediately sprinkled with snipped chives.

Borshch

Although eaten every day throughout the U.S.S.R. and Eastern Europe, borshch is an unusual soup for British palates. It is a marvellous way of using cooked beetroot.

METRIC	IMPERIAL
Butter for frying	Butter for frying
1 large onion, peeled and sliced	1 large onion, peeled and sliced
1 large carrot, peeled and shredded	1 large carrot, peeled and shredded
2 large cooked beetroots, sliced	2 large cooked beetroots, sliced
½ small red cabbage, shredded	½ small red cabbage, shredded
1¼ l. beef stock, skimmed of fat	2 pints beef stock, skimmed of fat
1 × 15 ml. spoon tomato purée	1 tablespoon tomato purée
1 × 15 ml. spoon malt vinegar	1 tablespoon malt vinegar
1 × 15 ml. spoon sugar	1 tablespoon sugar
Salt and freshly ground black pepper	Salt and freshly ground black pepper
2 × 150 ml. cartons soured cream to finish	2 × 5 fl. oz. cartons soured cream to finish

Melt a knob of butter in a large saucepan. Add the vegetables, cover and cook gently for 5 minutes. Stir in the remaining ingredients and bring to the boil. Lower the heat, cover and simmer gently for 20 to 30 minutes or until the vegetables are tender and the soup has a soft consistency. Adjust seasoning and serve with the soured cream, handed round in a separate bowl.

Starters

Starters are an important part of any meal, whether the occasion be grand or informal. Not only should a starter set the mood for the meal to come, it should also create a good impression and marry well with the following courses.

Always choose the starter bearing in mind the courses that are to follow. If, for example, you have decided to serve Kipper Pâté or Shellfish Cocktail as a first course, do not follow with a fish main dish. A meat or liver pâté would be more suitable. Try to balance the courses well, choosing light starters such as Grilled Spiced Grapefruit with heavy main courses and rich desserts. Vary colours, textures and types of sauces, too.

It is worth taking time and thought in choosing and preparing the first course. If possible, it helps if this part of the meal is prepared in advance; this allows time for last-minute finishing touches to the main course (often the trickiest part of the meal from the point of view of timing).

Above all, attractive presentation is essential: garnish with freshly chopped parsley or snipped chives, twisted lemon slices, watercress sprigs, tomato slices or whatever suits the dish best. An attractively-garnished starter always looks good placed on the table just before the guests sit down.

Dips and Dunks

A good way to whet your guests' appetites, dips should be creamy and full of flavour. Above all, they should be light in texture: if they are too substantial, they will be too filling. Serve with sticks of celery, carrot, diced cucumber and cubes of pineapple on cocktail sticks, savoury biscuits, cheese straws and crisps.

Cheese dip

METRIC	IMPERIAL
225 g. Danish Blue or Gorgonzola cheese, softened	*½ lb. Danish Blue or Gorgonzola cheese, softened*
300 ml. whipping cream	*½ pint whipping cream*
1 × 15 ml. spoon Worcestershire sauce	*1 tablespoon Worcestershire sauce*
Salt and freshly ground black pepper	*Salt and freshly ground black pepper*

Mix the cheese and cream together with a wooden spoon, then beat vigorously. Stir in the Worcestershire sauce and seasoning to taste. Spoon into a serving bowl and chill in the refrigerator before serving.

Fish dip

METRIC
225 g. cream cheese
150 ml. fresh single cream
1 × 50 g. can anchovies in
  olive oil, drained and
  soaked in milk for 30
  minutes
Freshly ground black
  pepper

IMPERIAL
½ lb. cream cheese
¼ pint fresh single cream
1 × 2 oz. can anchovies in
  olive oil, drained and
  soaked in milk for 30
  minutes
Freshly ground black
  pepper

Beat the cheese and cream together until light and fluffy with
a wooden spoon or electric or rotary beater. Drain the
anchovies, pat dry with absorbent kitchen paper and chop
finely. Add to the cheese and cream mixture with black
pepper to taste. Spoon into a serving bowl and chill in the
refrigerator before serving.

Devilled dip

METRIC
225 g. cottage cheese
150 ml. thick homemade
  mayonnaise
100 g. mixed nuts and
  raisins, finely chopped
1 green pepper, cored,
  seeded and finely chopped
1 red pepper, cored, seeded
  and finely chopped
1 × 5 ml. spoon Tabasco
  sauce
Pinch of cayenne pepper
Salt and freshly ground
  black pepper

IMPERIAL
½ lb. cottage cheese
¼ pint thick homemade
  mayonnaise
4 oz. mixed nuts and raisins,
  finely chopped
1 green pepper, cored,
  seeded and finely chopped
1 red pepper, cored, seeded
  and finely chopped
1 teaspoon Tabasco sauce
Pinch of cayenne pepper
Salt and freshly ground
  black pepper

Mix the cottage cheese and mayonnaise together in a bowl.
Stir in the remaining ingredients and season to taste. Spoon
into a serving bowl and chill in the refrigerator before serving. Good with potato crisps and sticks.

Vol-au-vents

Vol-au-vents

Frozen puff pastry is excellent for these savouries which should be so light that they literally melt in the mouth. Offer a selection of different fillings on one serving platter, to tempt your guests' appetites.

METRIC	IMPERIAL
1 × 405 g. packet frozen puff pastry, thawed	1 × 14.3 oz. packet frozen puff pastry, thawed
1 egg, beaten	1 egg, beaten

For sauce base:

40 g. butter	1½ oz. butter
40 g. flour	1½ oz. flour
400 ml. hot milk	¾ pint hot milk
Salt and ground white pepper	Salt and ground white pepper

Roll out the dough thinly on a floured board and stamp into 20 to 24 7.5 cm./3 in. rounds with a pastry cutter. Place on dampened baking sheets. Brush with beaten egg. Using a 5 cm./2 in. pastry cutter, stamp circles on the pastry rounds, without cutting right through. Bake in a fairly hot oven (200°C/400°F or Gas Mark 6) for about 10 to 15 minutes or until well-risen and golden-brown. Allow to cool slightly,

then remove the tops with a sharp knife and reserve. Scoop out any soft pastry with a teaspoon. If serving hot, spoon hot fillings into the vol-au-vents, replace the tops and serve immediately. If serving cold, allow the pastry cases to become quite cold before spooning in cold fillings.

To make the sauce base, melt the butter in a saucepan. Stir in the flour and cook for 2 minutes, stirring constantly. Remove the pan from the heat and gradually add the hot milk, stirring vigorously with a wooden spoon. Return to the heat and bring slowly to the boil, stirring constantly. Season to taste and simmer for 5 minutes or until the sauce is thick and smooth. This sauce forms the base for the vol-au-vent fillings. Mix with any of the following combinations and use to fill pastry cases. **Makes 20 to 24 vol-au-vents.**

Ham and Parmesan
Chop 100 g./4 oz. cooked ham very finely and mix into the sauce with 2 × 15 ml. spoons/2 tablespoons grated Parmesan cheese.

Shrimp and cayenne
Drain 1 × 128 g./4½ oz. can peeled shrimps and mix into the sauce with 1 × 2.5 ml. spoons/½ teaspoon cayenne pepper.

Mushroom and anchovy
Clean and chop finely 100 g./4 oz. button mushrooms. Sauté for 1 to 2 minutes in 25 g./1 oz. butter. Drain. Mix into the sauce with 2 × 5 ml. spoons/2 teaspoons anchovy essence.

Angels and devils on horseback

These are classic cocktail appetisers to serve with drinks on special occasions. The 'angels' are in fact oysters and the 'devils' are prunes. As oysters can be rather expensive, make a selection of both 'angels' and 'devils' and mix the two together on a serving platter, garnished with watercress. If you like, put the 'angels' and 'devils' on fried bread triangles.

Angels

METRIC	IMPERIAL
4 oysters, shelled	4 oysters, shelled
4 × 5 ml. spoons lemon juice	4 teaspoons lemon juice
Salt	Salt
Cayenne pepper	Cayenne pepper
4 streaky bacon rashers, rinds removed	4 streaky bacon rashers, rinds removed
4 wooden cocktail sticks	4 wooden cocktail sticks

To finish:

1 bunch of watercress	1 bunch of watercress
Juice of ½ lemon	Juice of ½ lemon

Dip the oysters in the lemon juice and sprinkle with salt and cayenne pepper. Stretch the bacon with the blade of a knife then wrap each oyster in a rasher. Secure with cocktail sticks. Cook under a preheated hot grill for 5 to 10 minutes or until the bacon is golden and crisp. Arrange on a serving platter garnished with watercress, sprinkle with lemon juice and serve immediately.

Devils

METRIC	IMPERIAL
4 large prunes, soaked overnight in water and drained	*4 large prunes, soaked overnight in water and drained*
4 blanched almonds	*4 blanched almonds*
Salt and freshly ground black pepper	*Salt and freshly ground black pepper*
4 streaky bacon rashers, rinds removed	*4 streaky bacon rashers, rinds removed*
4 wooden cocktail sticks	*4 wooden cocktail sticks*

Slit the skins of the prunes with a sharp knife and carefully remove the stones. Put one almond in each prune and close up. Season well with salt and pepper. Stretch the bacon rashers with the blade of a knife then wrap each stuffed prune in a rasher. Secure with cocktail sticks. Grill as for Angels on Horseback above, arranging the two together on the serving platter.

Angels and devils on horseback

Cheese straws

Cheese straws

With a subtle cheese flavour, these pastry 'straws' are as light as air. They are good to serve with drinks before a meal as they are not too filling.

METRIC	IMPERIAL
100 g. flour	*4 oz. flour*
Salt	*Salt*
Pinch of cayenne pepper	*Pinch of cayenne pepper*
50 g. butter	*2 oz. butter*
50 g. Cheddar cheese, finely grated	*2 oz. Cheddar cheese, finely grated*
1 egg yolk, beaten	*1 egg yolk, beaten*

Sift the flour and seasonings together in a mixing bowl. Add the butter in pieces and rub together with the fingertips until the mixture resembles fine breadcrumbs. Stir in the grated cheese and the egg yolk. Draw together with the fingertips to form a smooth dough, using a little cold water if the mixture is too dry. Chill in the refrigerator for at least 30 minutes.

Roll out the dough thinly on a floured board and cut into strips about 12.5 cm./5 in. long and 0.5 cm./¼ in. wide. Place on baking sheets and bake in a fairly hot oven (200°C/400°F or Gas Mark 6) for 10 to 15 minutes or until golden. Remove from the oven, allow to cool slightly, then transfer to a wire rack to cool completely. Store in an airtight tin.

Makes approx. 40 cheese straws.

Stuffed tomatoes

Stuffed tomatoes

Bright and eye-catching, stuffed tomatoes make an attractive addition to an hors d'oeuvre tray.

METRIC	IMPERIAL
4 large firm tomatoes, skinned	4 large firm tomatoes, skinned
100 g. cream cheese	4 oz. cream cheese
2 × 15 ml. spoons fresh double cream	2 tablespoons fresh double cream
1 small bunch of spring onions, topped, tailed and finely chopped	1 small bunch of spring onions, topped, tailed and finely chopped
Salt and freshly ground black pepper	Salt and freshly ground black pepper

For the dressing:

3 × 15 ml. spoons salad oil	3 tablespoons salad oil
1 × 15 ml. spoon wine vinegar	1 tablespoon wine vinegar
1 × 1.25 ml. spoon dry mustard	¼ teaspoon dry mustard
1 × 5 ml. spoon sugar	1 teaspoon sugar

Slice the tops off the tomatoes and reserve. Scoop out the seeds and core and discard. Blend together the cheese and cream and fold in the chopped onions. Season well. Spoon the filling into the tomato cases, piling it up, and replace the tops on a slant.

To make dressing, beat the oil and vinegar together in a bowl with a fork, then beat in the mustard and sugar. Spoon the dressing over the tomatoes and chill in the refrigerator for at least 30 minutes before serving.

Grilled spiced grapefruit

Grapefruit is always a welcome starter as it stimulates the appetite, but it can be rather boring if served plain. This method of serving grapefruit is more unusual, and definitely more tasty.

METRIC	IMPERIAL
2 large grapefruit	2 large grapefruit
4 × 15 ml. spoons soft brown sugar	4 tablespoons soft brown sugar
2 × 15 ml. spoons butter, softened	2 tablespoons butter, softened
2 × 15 ml. spoons sweet sherry, vermouth or rum	2 tablespoons sweet sherry, vermouth or rum
1 × 2.5 ml. spoon ground cinnamon	½ teaspoon ground cinnamon

Cut the grapefruit in half, loosen the segments with a grapefruit knife and remove any pips. Mix the remaining ingredients together in a bowl and spread over the top of each grapefruit half. Place under a preheated hot grill and cook for 5 minutes or until the tops are bubbling and browned. Transfer to individual serving bowls and serve immediately.

Grilled spiced grapefruit

Anchoïade

Delicious with a glass of chilled white or sparkling wine, anchoïade may also be served as an after-dinner savoury.

METRIC	IMPERIAL
4 slices brown bread, crusts removed	*4 slices brown bread, crusts removed*
Unsalted butter	*Unsalted butter*
1 × 50 g. can anchovies in olive oil, drained and soaked in milk for 30 minutes	*1 × 2 oz. can anchovies in olive oil, drained and soaked in milk for 30 minutes*
1 garlic clove, crushed	*1 garlic clove, crushed*
Freshly ground black pepper	*Freshly ground black pepper*

Toast the bread on one side only and butter the untoasted side. Cut into fingers. Drain the anchovies and pound to a paste with the garlic in a mortar and pestle. Season with pepper to taste and spread onto the buttered toast fingers.

Place on a baking sheet and bake in a fairly hot oven (200°C/400°F or Gas Mark 6) for 10 minutes or until hot and crisp. Serve immediately.

Anchoïade

Mushrooms à la grecque

Mushrooms à la Grecque

A cool summer hors d'oeuvre, Mushrooms à la grecque will improve in flavour if well chilled in the refrigerator before serving. It can be made the day before.

METRIC	IMPERIAL
Olive oil for frying	*Olive oil for frying*
1 small onion, peeled and finely chopped	*1 small onion, peeled and finely chopped*
1 garlic clove, crushed with 1 × 2.5 ml. spoon salt	*1 garlic clove, crushed with ½ teaspoon salt*
4 tomatoes, skinned, seeded and finely chopped	*4 tomatoes, skinned, seeded and finely chopped*
½ kg. button mushrooms, cleaned and coarsely chopped	*1 lb. button mushrooms, cleaned and coarsely chopped*
1 × 15 ml. spoon tomato purée	*1 tablespoon tomato purée*
1 wineglass dry white wine	*1 wineglass dry white wine*
4 × 15 ml. spoons freshly chopped parsley	*4 tablespoons freshly chopped parsley*
Freshly ground black pepper	*Freshly ground black pepper*

Heat 2 spoons of oil in a frying pan. Add the onion and garlic and fry gently for 5 minutes or until golden. Add the tomatoes and mushrooms and cook for a further 5 minutes, stirring occasionally.

Mix the tomato purée with the wine and add to the pan. Bring just to boiling point, then remove immediately from the heat and add half the chopped parsley and plenty of pepper. Stir well and leave to cool.

Chill for at least 2 hours before serving. Adjust seasoning and top with the remaining parsley.

Egg mayonnaise

Egg mayonnaise

There is nothing better than a simple, well-made egg mayonnaise. The secret of making good mayonnaise lies in the temperature of the kitchen and the utensils used – they must be cool. Do not try to hurry the addition of the oil, this will only result in the mayonnaise curdling. If it should curdle, start again with a fresh egg yolk and seasoning, adding the curdled mayonnaise drop by drop to the fresh yolk and then continuing with the remaining oil.

METRIC	IMPERIAL
4 hard-boiled eggs, shelled	4 hard-boiled eggs, shelled
4 lettuce leaves	4 lettuce leaves
Salt and freshly ground black pepper	Salt and freshly ground black pepper
For the mayonnaise:	**For the mayonnaise:**
2 egg yolks	2 egg yolks
1 × 2.5 ml. spoon dry mustard	½ teaspoon dry mustard
300 ml. corn or olive oil	½ pint corn or olive oil
1 × 15 ml. spoon wine, tarragon or cider vinegar or lemon juice	1 tablespoon wine, tarragon or cider vinegar or lemon juice

Slice the eggs in half lengthways. Place a lettuce leaf on each serving plate, sprinkle with salt and pepper and lay two egg halves on each, cut side down.

To make mayonnaise, place the egg yolks in a cool mixing bowl with the mustard and salt and pepper to taste. Beat together with a wooden spoon, electric whisk or rotary beater. Add the oil, drop by drop at first, beating constantly. As the yolks begin to thicken the oil can be added faster until finally being added in a thin steady stream. If the mayonnaise becomes too thick to work, thin with a little of the vinegar or lemon juice, then continue adding the oil. Finish the mayonnaise by beating in the remaining vinegar or lemon juice. This makes a thick mayonnaise suitable for coating – if a thinner mayonnaise is liked, it can be diluted by adding more vinegar or lemon juice or single cream.

Spoon the mayonnaise over the eggs. Serve with brown bread and butter.

Celeriac rémoulade

Celeriac rémoulade

Celeriac is a little-known vegetable in this country, yet its subtle aniseed-like flavour is quite delicious.

METRIC	IMPERIAL
4 lettuce leaves	4 lettuce leaves
Salt and freshly ground black pepper	Salt and freshly ground black pepper
1 head celeriac (about ¼ kg.), washed, peeled and coarsely grated	1 head celeriac (about ½ lb.), washed, peeled and coarsely grated
½ small onion, peeled and finely chopped	½ small onion, peeled and finely chopped
225 ml. thick homemade mayonnaise	8 fl. oz. thick homemade mayonnaise
2 × 5 ml. spoons lemon juice	2 teaspoons lemon juice
1 × 15 ml. spoon French mustard	1 tablespoon French mustard
1 × 15 ml. spoon snipped chives to finish	1 tablespoon snipped chives to finish

Place a lettuce leaf on each serving plate and sprinkle with salt and pepper to taste. Combine the remaining ingredients together in a mixing bowl, ensuring that the vegetables are thoroughly coated in the mayonnaise. Season to taste. Spoon onto the lettuce and sprinkle with snipped chives.

Guacamole

Guacamole

Serve this hot, spicy Mexican dip with slices of hot buttered wholemeal toast, Melba toast or crisps. If it is to be made in advance, store it in the refrigerator with the avocado stones buried in the mixture, and keep the dish well covered so the guacamole will not discolour.

METRIC	IMPERIAL
2 ripe avocados	2 ripe avocados
Juice of 1 lemon	Juice of 1 lemon
2 × 15 ml. spoons olive oil	2 tablespoons olive oil
1 small onion, peeled and finely chopped	1 small onion, peeled and finely chopped
1 garlic clove, crushed with 1 × 2.5 ml. spoon salt	1 garlic clove, crushed with ½ teaspoon salt
¼ kg. tomatoes, skinned, seeded and finely chopped	½ lb. tomatoes, skinned, seeded and finely chopped
Dash of Tabasco sauce	Dash of Tabasco sauce
Freshly chopped parsley to finish	Freshly chopped parsley to finish

Cut the avocados in half with a sharp, stainless steel knife. Remove the stones and scoop out the flesh into a bowl. Mash the lemon juice into the flesh with a fork. Add the remaining ingredients and blend well together until the guacamole is quite smooth. Transfer to a serving dish and top with plenty of freshly chopped parsley before serving.

Farmhouse pâté

This is a coarse-textured, moist pâté, which makes a substantial first course when served with toast. It is equally good for lunch or supper if served with French bread and red wine.

METRIC	IMPERIAL
350 g. boneless belly pork, rinds removed and minced	¾ lb. boneless belly pork, rinds removed and minced
350 g. pig's liver, cleaned and minced	¾ lb. pig's liver, cleaned and minced
¼ kg. boned pork loin, minced	½ lb. boned pork loin, minced
100 g. pork fat, diced	4 oz. pork fat, diced
150 ml. red wine	¼ pint red wine
1 × 50 g. can anchovies in olive oil, drained and chopped	1 × 2 oz. can anchovies in olive oil, drained and chopped
1 garlic clove, crushed	1 garlic clove, crushed
6 juniper berries, crushed	6 juniper berries, crushed
6 black peppercorns, crushed	6 black peppercorns, crushed
1 × 15 ml. spoon dried mixed herbs	1 tablespoon dried mixed herbs
8 streaky bacon rashers, rinds removed	8 streaky bacon rashers, rinds removed

To garnish:
Watercress sprigs
Tomato wedges

To garnish:
Watercress sprigs
Tomato wedges

In a large mixing bowl mix together the meats, liver and fat. Add the remaining ingredients, except the bacon. Stir well.

Stretch the bacon rashers with the blade of a knife and use to line the base and sides of a 1 kg./2 lb. loaf tin, reserving two bacon rashers for the top of the pâté. Spoon in the pâté mixture and place the two reserved rashers on the top. Stand the tin in a bain marie of hot water and bake in a cool oven (150°C/300°F or Gas Mark 2) for 1½ to 2 hours or until the juices are just faintly pink and the pâté has shrunk away from the sides of the tin. When cooked, remove from the bain marie, pour off the excess fat and allow to cool in the tin. Place a weight on a plate or greaseproof paper on top of the pâté to help press the meats together. Chill for at least 8 hours or overnight. Before serving, turn out onto a serving platter, cut into six to eight slices and garnish with watercress sprigs and tomato wedges. **Serves 6 to 8.**

Farmhouse pâté

35

Taramasalata

Served with hot pitta – a type of unleavened bread – this soft, mild creamy fish pâté is a famous Greek and Turkish speciality. Pitta can be bought at some Middle Eastern speciality shops in this country, but if unavailable Melba toast is a good substitute.

METRIC	IMPERIAL
2 slices white bread, crusts removed	2 slices white bread, crusts removed
50 g. smoked cod's roe, skinned	2 oz. smoked cod's roe, skinned
1 garlic clove, crushed	1 garlic clove, crushed
150 ml. vegetable, olive or corn oil	¼ pint vegetable, olive or corn oil
4 × 15 ml. spoons lemon juice	4 tablespoons lemon juice
1 × 15 ml. spoon hot water	1 tablespoon hot water
Freshly ground black pepper	Freshly ground black pepper
Few parsley sprigs to finish	Few parsley sprigs to finish

Put the bread in a small bowl, cover with cold water and leave to soak for 10 minutes. Squeeze dry.

Using an electric or rotary beater, beat the cod's roe until smooth. Beat in the soaked bread and garlic, then work in the oil drop by drop, beating well as for mayonnaise. As the taramasalata becomes thicker, the oil can be added faster. If the pâté separates, crumble in a little more white bread to absorb the oil. Beat constantly until all the oil is incorporated, then stir in the lemon juice and hot water. Spoon the taramasalata into a serving dish and chill in the refrigerator for at least 2 hours before serving. Sprinkle with pepper. Garnish with a few parsley sprigs.

Kipper pâté

Kipper pâté

Serve this creamy pâté with Melba toast or brown bread and butter as a starter or as part of a salad lunch.

METRIC	IMPERIAL
Unsalted butter for frying	Unsalted butter for frying
225 g. kipper fillets	½ lb. kipper fillets
225 g. cream cheese	½ lb. cream cheese
½ garlic clove, crushed	½ garlic clove, crushed
Juice of ½ lemon	Juice of ½ lemon
Freshly ground black pepper	Freshly ground black pepper
Lemon slices to garnish	Lemon slices to garnish

Melt a knob of butter in a frying pan. Add the kipper fillets and cook gently for 10 minutes or until the fish is soft. Remove the fillets from the pan and allow to cool slightly, then remove the skin and any large bones.

Put the kipper flesh in a bowl and mash with a fork. Beat in the cream cheese with a wooden spoon or pound it with a pestle. Add the garlic, lemon juice, and pepper to taste, and continue beating until the pâté is quite smooth.

Spoon the pâté into a serving dish and smooth the top with the prongs of a fork. Sprinkle with more black pepper and garnish with twisted lemon slices. **Serves 4 to 6.**

Taramasalata

Pâté en croûte

Pâté encased in a puff pastry case makes a spectacular start to any meal. The pastry trimmings can be used to make an attractive decoration on the top and sides – flowers and leaves look especially attractive.

METRIC
½ kg. streaky bacon
¼ kg. chicken livers,
  cleaned
1 onion, peeled and finely
  chopped
1 garlic clove, crushed with 1
  × 2.5 ml. spoon salt
2 × 15 ml. spoons fresh
  white breadcrumbs
3 × 15 ml. spoons brandy
1 × 5 ml. spoon grated
  nutmeg
Freshly ground black
  pepper

IMPERIAL
1 lb. streaky bacon
½ lb. chicken livers, cleaned
1 onion, peeled and finely
  chopped
1 garlic clove, crushed with
  ½ teaspoon salt
2 tablespoons fresh white
  breadcrumbs
3 tablespoons brandy
1 teaspoon grated nutmeg
Freshly ground black
  pepper

To finish:
1 × 212 g. packet frozen
  puff pastry, thawed
1 egg, beaten

To finish:
1 × 7½ oz. packet frozen
  puff pastry, thawed
1 egg, beaten

Remove and discard the rinds from all but six rashers of the bacon, reserving these for lining the pâté tin. Mince the rindless bacon together with the chicken livers then transfer to a mixing bowl. Stir in the remaining ingredients with black pepper to taste. Stretch the reserved bacon rashers with the blade of a knife and use to line the base and sides of a 1 kg./2 lb. loaf tin or 1 l./2 pint terrine or pâté dish, reserving two rashers for the top. Spoon in the pâté mixture and place the two reserved rashers on the top. Cover with foil. Stand the tin in a bain marie of hot water and bake in a moderate oven (180°C/350°F or Gas Mark 4) for 45 minutes, or until the juices are just faintly pink and the pâté has shrunk away from the sides of the tin. Pour off the excess fat. Remove the pâté from the bain marie and leave to cool for 15 minutes.

Meanwhile, roll out the dough thinly. Remove the pâté from the tin or dish, brush with some of the beaten egg and cover the pâté with the dough, sealing the edges well with beaten egg. Use the dough trimmings to decorate the top and sides. Brush all over the pastry case with the remaining beaten egg, place on a dampened baking sheet and bake in a fairly hot oven (200°C/400°F or Gas Mark 6) for a further 30 minutes or until the pastry is golden-brown. Remove from the oven, transfer to a serving platter and allow to become completely cold before serving.

Pâté en croûte

Avocado with prawns

Avocado with prawns

Prawns coated in a garlic-flavoured dressing provide an added touch of luxury to avocados for a special occasion.

METRIC
2 ripe avocados
Juice of ½ lemon
300 ml. cooked and shelled prawns

IMPERIAL
2 ripe avocados
Juice of ½ lemon
½ pint cooked and shelled prawns

For the dressing:
150 ml. fresh double cream
2 × 15 ml. spoons wine vinegar
1 × 5 ml. spoon Dijon-style mustard
1 × 5 ml. spoon sugar
1 garlic clove, crushed with 1 × 2.5 ml. spoon salt
Cayenne pepper to finish

For the dressing:
¼ pint fresh double cream
2 tablespoons wine vinegar
1 teaspoon Dijon-style mustard
1 teaspoon sugar
1 garlic clove, crushed with ½ teaspoon salt
Cayenne pepper to finish

Cut the avocados in half with a sharp, stainless steel knife and remove the stones. Brush the cut surfaces of the flesh with the lemon juice.

To make the dressing, whisk the cream and vinegar together in a bowl with a fork. Add the remaining ingredients and whisk until thoroughly combined. Alternatively, put all the ingredients in a jar with a screw lid, cover and shake.

In a mixing bowl combine the prawns with the dressing, ensuring that the prawns are thoroughly coated. Spoon into the avocado halves, sprinkle the top of each with a little cayenne pepper and serve immediately with brown bread and butter.

Quick chicken liver pâté

This pâté can be made very quickly as it is not baked. It makes an ideal starter for a dinner party at short notice.

METRIC
Butter for frying
1 small onion, peeled and finely chopped
1 garlic clove, crushed with 1 × 2.5 ml. spoon salt
¼ kg. chicken livers, cleaned and chopped
1 × 5 ml. spoon dried thyme
2 × 15 ml. spoons brandy or sherry
Salt and freshly ground black pepper
Melba toast to serve

IMPERIAL
Butter for frying
1 small onion, peeled and finely chopped
1 garlic clove, crushed with ½ teaspoon salt
½ lb. chicken livers, cleaned and chopped
1 teaspoon dried thyme
2 tablespoons brandy or sherry
Salt and freshly ground black pepper
Melba toast to serve

Melt a knob of butter in a frying pan. Add the onion, garlic, livers and thyme and fry gently for about 5 to 10 minutes or until the juices of the liver are only faintly pink. Remove from the heat and leave to cool slightly.

Mince the mixture finely or purée in an electric blender until smooth. Work in another knob of butter and the brandy or sherry with a wooden spoon, then season to taste. Press firmly into a serving dish and refrigerate before serving with Melba toast.

Quick chicken liver pâté

Shellfish cocktail

A time-honoured favourite, every good cook should know how to make a shellfish cocktail. Any fresh or frozen shellfish can be used, depending on the season of year and personal preference. If you like, decorate each glass with a whole unshelled prawn.

METRIC
¼ kg. shelled and prepared shellfish (prawns, crab, lobster, mussels, etc.)
150 ml. thick homemade mayonnaise
2 × 5 ml. spoons lemon juice
1 × 15 ml. spoon tomato purée
2 × 5 ml. spoons Worcestershire sauce
Salt and freshly ground black pepper

IMPERIAL
½ lb. shelled and prepared shellfish (prawns, crab, lobster, mussels, etc.)
¼ pint thick homemade mayonnaise
2 teaspoons lemon juice
1 tablespoon tomato purée
2 teaspoons Worcestershire sauce
Salt and freshly ground black pepper

To finish:
1 lettuce, shredded
Cayenne pepper
4 slices of lemon

To finish:
1 lettuce, shredded
Cayenne pepper
4 slices of lemon

Flake or cut the fish into bite-sized pieces and put in a mixing bowl. Lightly fold in the remaining ingredients and season well to taste. Ensure the shellfish is thoroughly coated in the mayonnaise.

Divide the lettuce equally between four glasses and sprinkle with salt. Spoon the fish mixture carefully into the glasses, sprinkle the top of each with a little cayenne pepper and arrange a slice of lemon on the side of each glass. Serve with thinly sliced brown bread and butter.

Shellfish cocktail

Fish

Not only is fish a versatile food in that there are numerous different varieties available in this country all year round, either fresh, frozen, canned, smoked or pickled; it is also a valuable ingredient in that there are scores of ways it can be prepared and cooked. In addition, fish is a highly nutritious food, rich in protein, vitamins and a number of minerals.

Basically, the fish available may be divided into four main categories: oily, white, shellfish and smoked or pickled. The methods of dealing with each of these are covered in the charts. Wherever possible, ask your fishmonger to clean and gut the fish you buy from him; he may even fillet or dress certain fish for you and, even if he charges a little extra for this service, you will probably find it is well worth it. The information given in the chart applies to fresh fish; for frozen fish, follow the recommendations given on the packet.

Always be sure that the fish you are buying is absolutely fresh (look for firm flesh, moist shiny scales and bright eyes), and cook it as soon as possible. Fresh fish deteriorates quickly and, therefore, should be eaten the day it is bought. Do not keep, even in the refrigerator, where its smell would be likely to affect other food.

Tartare sauce

For deep-fried fish. Serve in separate sauceboat.

METRIC	IMPERIAL
150 ml. thick homemade mayonnaise	¼ pint thick homemade mayonnaise
2 hard-boiled egg yolks, sieved	2 hard-boiled egg yolks, sieved
1 × 5 ml. spoon capers, chopped	1 teaspoon capers, chopped
1 × 5 ml. spoon chopped gherkins	1 teaspoon chopped gherkins
1 × 5 ml. spoon freshly chopped parsley	1 teaspoon freshly chopped parsley
1 × 5 ml. spoon snipped chives	1 teaspoon snipped chives
1 × 15 ml. spoon lemon juice	1 tablespoon lemon juice

Put all the ingredients in a mixing bowl and stir well to combine.

Anchovy sauce

Serve with herring or mackerel. Make basic white sauce as above. Stir in 2 × 5 ml. spoons/2 teaspoons anchovy essence and 1 × 5 ml. spoon/1 teaspoon lemon juice before serving. If liked, a few drops of red food colouring may be added.

Caper sauce

Serve with herring or mackerel. Make basic white sauce as above. Stir in 1 × 15 ml. spoon/1 tablespoon chopped capers with an equal quantity of their juice before serving.

Parsley sauce

Serve with any white fish. Make basic white sauce as above. Stir in 2 × 15 ml. spoons/2 tablespoons freshly chopped parsley before serving.

Mustard sauce

Serve with herring or mackerel. Make basic white sauce as above. Stir in 1 × 2.5 ml. spoon/½ teaspoon dry English mustard, 2 × 5 ml. spoons/2 teaspoons lemon juice or wine vinegar and 1 × 2.5 ml. spoon/½ teaspoon sugar before serving.

Shrimp sauce

Serve with any white fish, particularly plaice. Make basic white sauce as above. Substitute pinch of cayenne pepper for grated nutmeg. Stir in 50 g./2 oz. cooked and shelled shrimps, chopped, before serving.

Maître d'hôtel butter

METRIC	IMPERIAL
100 g. unsalted butter, softened	4 oz. unsalted butter, softened
1 × 15 ml. spoon freshly chopped parsley	1 tablespoon freshly chopped parsley
1 × 5 ml. spoon lemon juice	1 teaspoon lemon juice
Salt and freshly ground black pepper	Salt and freshly ground black pepper

Put the butter in a mixing bowl and gradually work in the remaining ingredients, with salt and pepper to taste, until evenly distributed. Flatten the butter and place between two sheets of greaseproof paper or foil. Chill in the refrigerator until firm before using.

Mustard butter

Prepare as for Maître d'Hôtel butter above, substituting 2 × 5 ml. spoons/2 teaspoons dry English mustard for the parsley.

Shrimp butter

Prepare as for Maître d'Hôtel butter above, substituting 50 g./2 oz. cooked and shelled shrimps, finely chopped, for the parsley.

Anchovy butter

Prepare as for Maître d'Hôtel butter above, substituting 1 can (50 g./2 oz.) anchovies in olive oil (drained and soaked for 30 minutes in milk), drained and pounded with a mortar and pestle for the parsley. Omit salt.

Chive butter

Prepare as for Maître d'Hôtel butter above, substituting 2 × 15 ml. spoons/2 tablespoons snipped chives for parsley.

Basic white sauce

METRIC	IMPERIAL
25 g. butter	1 oz. butter
25 g. flour	1 oz. flour
150 ml. hot poaching liquid	¼ pint hot poaching liquid
150 ml. hot milk	¼ pint hot milk
Pinch of grated nutmeg	Pinch of grated nutmeg
Salt and freshly ground black pepper	Salt and freshly ground black pepper

Melt the butter in a saucepan. Stir in the flour and cook for 1 to 2 minutes, stirring constantly. Remove from the heat and gradually add the hot liquid and milk, stirring vigorously. When all the liquid and milk are incorporated, return the pan to the heat and bring to the boil, stirring constantly. Lower the heat, add the seasonings and simmer gently until the sauce thickens.

Coatings for frying fish

Prepared whole fish or fillets can be fried in a number of ways:
1. Coated in flour seasoned with salt and pepper to taste and shallow-fried in butter or oil or equal quantities of both.
2. Coated in seasoned flour, then dipped in beaten egg and coated with dried breadcrumbs (1 egg and 100 g./4 oz. breadcrumbs is generally enough for four fillets). Shallow-fry as above.
3. Coat in batter (see below) and deep-fry in hot oil.

Drain fried fish thoroughly on absorbent kitchen paper and serve immediately with lemon quarters, parsley sprigs and tomato wedges, if liked. Tartare Sauce is also a good accompaniment to fried fish.

Coat cod steaks in seasoned flour, egg and breadcrumbs before frying

Court bouillon

Court bouillon is a mixture of water, or water and wine, herbs and seasonings, used for poaching fish. It gives flavour and colour to the flesh of the fish and therefore to the finished dish.

METRIC	IMPERIAL
Approx. 1 l. water or water and dry white wine, mixed	*Approx. 2 pints water or water and dry white wine, mixed*
1 × 15 ml. spoon lemon juice	*1 tablespoon lemon juice*
1 carrot, peeled and sliced	*1 carrot, peeled and sliced*
1 onion, peeled and sliced	*1 onion, peeled and sliced*
1 celery stalk, scrubbed and chopped	*1 celery stalk, scrubbed and chopped*
1 bouquet garni	*1 bouquet garni*
6 black peppercorns	*6 black peppercorns*
1 × 2.5 ml. spoon salt	*½ teaspoon salt*

Put all the ingredients in a large pan, bring to the boil, then lower the heat. Cover with a lid and simmer gently for about 30 minutes. Strain before using.

Batter for deep-frying fish

METRIC	IMPERIAL
100 g. flour	*4 oz. flour*
1 × 1.25 ml. spoon salt	*¼ teaspoon salt*
1 × 15 ml. spoon cooking oil	*1 tablespoon cooking oil*
approx. 150 ml. tepid water	*approx. ¼ pint tepid water*
2 egg whites	*2 egg whites*
vegetable oil for frying	*vegetable oil for frying*

Sift the flour and salt into a mixing bowl. Make a well in the centre and stir in the oil and enough water to form a smooth batter that coats the back of the spoon. Beat the egg whites until stiff, then fold into the batter with a metal spoon. Use immediately.

To clean, split and bone out

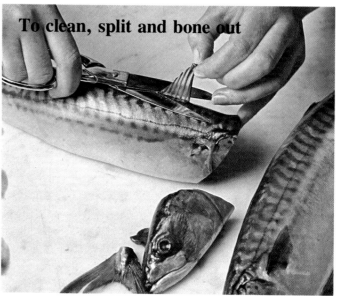

1. Wash in cold water. Scrape off scales with the back of a knife, working from tail towards head.
2. Cut off fins and trim tail with scissors. Cut off head just below the gills with a sharp knife.

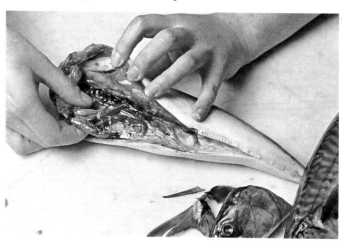

3. Cut fish open from head to vent along the underside and carefully scrape out the entrails, membranes and blood with a sharp knife, using the flat of the blade. Wash under cold running water and pat dry on absorbent kitchen paper. Sprinkle the flesh with a little salt – this makes it less slippery and therefore easier to bone out.

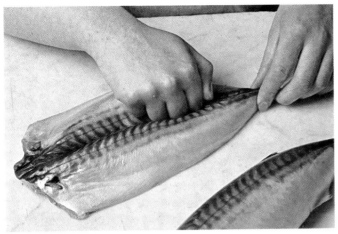

4. Put fish, opened out flat with skin side uppermost, on flat working surface or board and push down firmly along the backbone with the fist to flatten the fish and loosen the bone.

5. Turn fish over and lift bone out in one piece using the flat of the knife.
6. Wash thoroughly under cold running water and pat dry with absorbent kitchen paper.

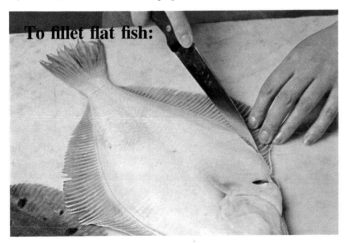

To fillet flat fish:

1. Wash in cold water and remove scales as before, for cleaning and gutting. Lay the fish flat on a working surface or board, white side up, with the head away from you.
2. With a sharp knife, cut between fins and edge of fish, under the head and down the centre line which is visible along the underside; this way the fillets will be outlined.

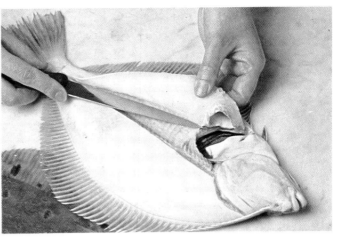

3. Working from the backbone outwards, and from head to tail, using long strokes, remove the left hand fillet. Keep the blade of the knife flat on the bone.
4. Turn fish round so that the head is facing towards you. Remove second fillet in same way as first.

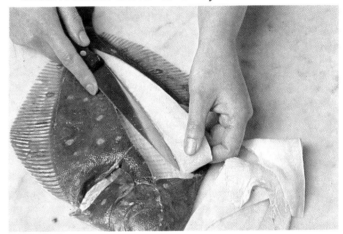

5. Turn fish over to the side with the black skin. Cut outline of fillets with a sharp knife and remove fillets as for white side above.

6. Remove black skin by gripping the tail end of the fillets and sawing along the skin with the blade of the knife pointing away from you. Rub the fish all over with a little salt to make this easier.
7. Wash fillets thoroughly under cold running water and pat dry with absorbent kitchen paper.

Oily Fish

PREPARATION	POACHING	GRILLING
Herring (season: all year round; best – June to December) Clean and leave whole, bone out or fillet.	Poach whole or filleted in fish kettle, large saucepan on top of stove or in cool oven. Cover with Court Bouillon, poach, covered, for 10 to 15 mins. or until fish flakes easily when tested with a fork. Drain, reserving poaching liquid for sauce.	Brush whole scored fish or fillets with melted butter or oil, sprinkle with lemon juice and salt and pepper to taste. Grill 4 to 5 minutes on each side for whole fish, 3 to 4 minutes on each side for fillets.
Mackerel (season: October to July; best in Spring) As Herring above	As Herring above, allowing slightly longer cooking time depending on size. See also Mackerel in cider sauce.	As Herring above, allowing slightly longer cooking time depending on size.
Salmon and Salmon Trout (season: February/March to August) Clean and leave whole or cut into thick steaks, depending on size.	Poach whole as Herring above, allowing 10 minutes to the ½ kg./1 lb. and 10 minutes over. Poach steaks as for Herring above for approx. 15 to 20 minutes depending on size.	Grill salmon steaks as Herring above, allowing approx. 15 to 20 minutes cooking time in all, depending on thickness of fish. Brush with melted butter during the cooking time.
Trout (season: February to September) Clean and leave whole or bone out: cut off fins with scissors. Cut off head with sharp knife. Slit along backbone, lay fish flat on working surface or board and carefully ease out bone with knife. Wash under cold running water. Pat dry with absorbent kitchen paper.	Poach whole as Herring above.	Remove skin or score and grill whole fish as for Herring above, allowing 5 minutes cooking time on each side, depending on size.
Sprats (season: November to March) **Whitebait** (season: May to July) Clean and leave whole. Clean sprats by slitting and squeezing out intestines, etc. Wash and pat dry with absorbent kitchen paper.		Sprats: cook under hot grill for approx. 5 to 10 minutes, turning once.

White Fish

PREPARATION	POACHING	GRILLING
Cod **Haddock** (season: all year round) Available whole, filleted or in steaks. Wash under cold running water and pat dry with absorbent kitchen paper.	Poach for approx. 15 to 20 minutes, depending on thickness of fish, on top of stove, or in moderate oven, in Court Bouillon or equal quantities of milk and water with seasonings to taste. Drain, reserving poaching liquid for sauce. Poach smoked cod and haddock in milk or milk and water and seasonings for 15 to 20 minutes. Drain.	Brush fillets or steaks with melted butter or oil, sprinkle with lemon juice and salt and pepper to taste. Grill fillets for 4 to 5 minutes on each side, and steaks for 7 to 10 minutes on each side, depending on thickness. Brush with melted butter during the cooking time.
Halibut (season: all year round; best August to April) Available filleted or in steaks. Sometimes whole if small. Wash under cold running water and pat dry with absorbent kitchen paper.	Poach as for Cod/Haddock above.	Grill fillets or steaks as for cod above.
Plaice (season: all year round) Leave whole and clean. Remove fins, scales and eyes (whole head if wished). Can also be filleted.	Poach whole or filleted fish as for Cod/Haddock above, allowing 10 minutes cooking time depending on thickness. Whole fish can be filleted after poaching before serving, if wished. See also Plaice with mushrooms and cream.	Grill whole fish or fillets as for Herring above, allowing 3 to 5 minutes cooking time on each side, depending on thickness of fish.

FRYING	BAKING	SERVING SUGGESTIONS
Coat fillets in seasoned flour or oatmeal and fry in hot oil or fat for 2 to 3 minutes on each side until golden. Drain on absorbent kitchen paper.	Whole fish boned out can be stuffed and baked with variety of stuffings.	Serve poached and coated in sauce made with poaching liquid. Grilled or fried with lemon quarters, parsley sprigs, Maître d'Hôtel, Anchovy or Mustard butters. Kippers and buckling (smoked herring) may be grilled or fried as fresh herring, or served cold in salads. See Kippers in lemon dressing.
As Herring above, in seasoned flour (not oatmeal). Allow longer cooking time depending on size.	Whole fish boned out can be stuffed and baked with variety of stuffings. See recipe for Mackerel with lemon stuffing.	As Herring above. Smoked mackerel may be grilled as fresh mackerel or served cold as a starter or in salads. See also Kippers in lemon dressing.
Fry salmon steaks coated in seasoned flour in hot butter. Allow 15 to 20 minutes cooking time in all. Drain on absorbent kitchen paper.	See recipe for Salmon herb parcels. Whole salmon may be baked in same way in warm oven. Same cooking time as for poaching.	Serve poached salmon with parsley sauce made with poaching liquid. Grilled or fried salmon with Maître d'Hôtel butter, lemon quarters and parsley sprigs. Salmon may also be served with Hollandaise sauce or cold with Mayonnaise. Smoked salmon is served thinly sliced as a starter with lemon quarters and cayenne pepper. Can also be used in fish cocktails or in quiches.
Coat whole fish with seasoned flour and fry in hot butter for 10 to 15 minutes or until flesh flakes easily when tested. Turn once during cooking time. Can also be coated in egg and breadcrumbs and shallow-fried for 10 to 15 minutes. See also Trout with Almonds.	Can be boned out and stuffed and baked with variety of stuffings: herbs, mushrooms, shellfish, spinach, etc., or baked in wine or wine and stock.	Serve grilled or fried trout as Herring above. Trout is also good served cold. Smoked trout is served as a starter with Horseradish sauce or lemon quarters.
See Deep-fried whitebait. Can also be shallow fried in hot butter or oil for approx. 5 to 10 mins.		Serve with lemon quarters, parsley sprigs and thinly sliced bread and butter. Can also be served with a devilled sauce.

FRYING	BAKING	SERVING SUGGESTIONS
Coat steaks or fillets in seasoned flour and fry as for Herring fillets and Salmon steaks above. Can also be coated in egg and breadcrumbs and shallow fried in hot butter or oil and butter for 2 to 3 minutes (fillets) or 4 to 5 minutes (steaks) on each side. Drain on absorbent kitchen paper. Or coat fillets in batter and deep-fry in hot oil. Drain as above.	Bake fillets or steaks in moderate oven for 15 to 20 minutes, either in wine or cider and seasonings to taste, or stuff steaks with any of numerous stuffings – mushroom, herb, lemon, tomato, anchovy, etc. See also Cod bake.	Poached, grilled or fried with garnishes as for Herring above. Serve deep-fried fish with Tartare Sauce and lemon wedges, garnished with parsley sprigs and tomatoes. Can also be used for pies. See Fisherman's pie and Fish cakes. Serve poached smoked fish topped with poached eggs. See also Smoked haddock kedgeree and Smoked haddock soufflé. Smoked cod's roe in Taramasalata.
Coat fillets or steaks in seasoned flour or egg and breadcrumbs and fry as for Herring Fillets and Salmon Steaks above.	Bake in moderate oven for approx. 20 minutes in wine, cider, cream and seasonings to taste, etc. See also Halibut Catalan.	Poached, grilled or fried fish with garnishes as for Herring above.
Coat fillets in egg and breadcrumbs. Shallow-fry in hot butter or butter and oil for approx. 10 minutes, turning once during cooking time. Drain on absorbent kitchen paper or coat in batter and deep-fry in hot oil. Drain as above.	Bake fillets as for Halibut above. Fillets can also be filled with lemon, herbs, mushroom, onion and tomato stuffings, etc., and rolled. Bake in moderate oven for approx. 20 minutes.	Poached, grilled or fried fish with garnishes as for Herring above.

PREPARATION	POACHING	GRILLING
Skate (season: September to April) Only the wings are eaten and are usually cut into strips before cooking. Is tough when very fresh; should be left 1 to 2 days before eating. Wash under cold running water and pat dry with absorbent kitchen paper.	Poach skate wings on top of stove or in moderate oven in Court Bouillon for 15 to 20 minutes or until tender. Drain. Dry well on absorbent kitchen paper before serving.	
Sole (season: all year round) Available whole. Clean and remove skin. Can also be filleted.	Poach whole or filleted fish as for Plaice above. See also Sole Dugléré.	Grill whole fish or fillets as for Herring above, allowing 3 to 5 minutes cooking time on each side, depending on thickness of fish.

Shellfish

PREPARATION	POACHING	GRILLING
Crab (season: all year round; best – May to September) Bought live or cooked. See Dressed Crab for cooking live crab.		
Lobster (season: all year round; best – April to October) Bought live or cooked. To kill lobster place in large pan, cover with cold water, add a little salt and bring slowly to the boil. Simmer for 20 minutes or until shell turns coral pink. Drain. Twist off large claws and take out meat. (Reserve small claws for garnish.) Cut off head, if liked. Split lobster from head to tail with a sharp knife. Discard stomach, intestine, gills, liver. Meat can be taken out of shell, according to recipe.		Prepare lobster leaving meat in shell. Brush with melted butter or oil, sprinkle with salt and freshly ground black pepper. Cook under hot grill for approx. 10 minutes or until meat is heated through.
Mussels (season: September to March) Bought live. Scrub well with stiff vegetable brush under cold running water. Remove beards. Discard any mussels which are open or which do not shut when tapped. Scrape away tufts from between shells with a sharp knife. Soak for approx. 1 hour in cold water. Drain.	Put mussels in a large saucepan with a little water and seasonings to taste. Cover with a tight-fitting lid and cook for approx. 10 mins. Drain and discard any mussels which have not opened. See Moules marinières.	Grill cooked mussels on half shells with garlic, parsley or herb butter for approx. 5 minutes or until butter is bubbling.
Prawns/Scampi/Shrimps (season: all year round) Bought either cooked or uncooked in shell or cooked and shelled. Wash under cold running water and pat dry with absorbent kitchen paper.	If uncooked, poach in gently simmering Court Bouillon to cover for 4 to 10 minutes, depending on size. Drain and shell. Poaching liquid can be used for making sauce.	
Scallops (season: October to March) Bought cleaned and uncooked in open shell. Remove from shell, wash under cold running water and pat dry with absorbent kitchen paper. Scrub shells and reserve for serving.	Poach in Court Bouillon or wine and seasonings for 5 to 10 mins. or until tender. Drain. Reserve cooking liquid for making sauce.	Can be marinated in oil, lemon juice and seasoning to taste. Thread on skewers and grill as for kebabs for approx. 10 minutes, turning and basting continually. Poached scallops can be returned to shell with sauce and seasonings, topped with breadcrumbs and/or cheese and browned under hot grill.

FRYING	BAKING	SERVING SUGGESTIONS
Coat poached, drained skate in egg and breadcrumbs and shallow fry for 4 to 5 minutes on each side. Or coat in batter and deep-fry in hot oil. Drain on absorbent kitchen paper.		Serve with Black butter. Serve crumbed and deep-fried fish with lemon quarters and parsley sprigs.
Fry fillets as for Plaice above.	Bake fillets as for Halibut above.	Serve poached, grilled and fried fish as for Cod/Haddock above.

FRYING	BAKING	SERVING SUGGESTIONS
	Can be combined with other ingredients – cheese, mushrooms, breadcrumbs, tomatoes, onions, etc., and baked in shell in hot oven for 10 to 15 minutes.	Serve cold as starter in shell. Crab meat can be used in salads, cocktails, with mayonnaise, in vol-au-vents, quiches, mousses, soufflés, rice-based dishes. As a stuffing for avocados, aubergines, peppers, etc. Also in soup.
Lobster meat can be gently fried with other ingredients and added to a rich sauce.		Serve as for Crab above. Also delicious served as a starter with Vinaigrette dressing.
Remove cooked mussels from shells and fry in butter or oil or equal quantities of both, and herbs or garlic to taste. Mussels can also be coated in batter and deep-fried in hot oil. Drain.	Remove cooked mussels from shells and bake in wine, tomatoes, cream, herbs, etc., in moderate oven for approx. 10 minutes.	Cold cooked mussels can be served in salads, rice-based dishes, etc. Hot mussels in soups, pies, pasta dishes. Serve grilled and fried mussels with lemon wedges and parsley sprigs, also herb, garlic and Maître d'hôtel butters.
Coat cooked shellfish in batter and deep-fry in hot oil. Drain.		Use shelled in numerous different recipes. Cold – as for Crab. Hot – Serve fried shellfish with Tartare sauce, lemon wedges, parsley sprigs; also in curries, sauces, stuffings, mousses, rice-based dishes, etc.
Coat poached and drained scallops in egg and breadcrumbs and shallow-fry in butter or oil or equal quantities of both until golden brown, or in batter and deep-fry in hot oil. Drain.	Poached and drained scallops can be returned to shells with sauce and seasonings to taste. Bake in fairly hot oven for approx. 10 minutes. See also Scallops with cream and wine sauce.	Serve grilled or fried scallops with lemon wedges and parsley sprigs. Also serve cold in salads, etc.

Oily fish

Mackerel in cider sauce

Mackerel in cider sauce

Use a medium-dry cider to make a fairly sharp sauce. This will contrast well with the rich definite flavour of fish such as mackerel.

METRIC	IMPERIAL
Butter for frying	*Butter for frying*
½ onion, peeled and very finely chopped	*½ onion, peeled and very finely chopped*
1 × 15 ml. spoon flour	*1 tablespoon flour*
400 ml. medium-dry or dry cider	*¾ pint medium-dry or dry cider*
Salt and freshly ground black pepper	*Salt and freshly ground black pepper*
4 mackerel (about 175 g. each), filleted	*4 mackerel (about 6 oz. each), filleted*
2 small eating apples, peeled, cored and finely sliced	*2 small eating apples, peeled, cored and finely sliced*
Freshly chopped parsley	*Freshly chopped parsley*

Melt a knob of butter in a large frying pan. Add the onion and fry gently for 5 minutes or until golden and soft. Stir in the flour and cook for a further 2 minutes, stirring constantly.

Stir in the cider gradually. Season to taste and add the mackerel fillets. Cover the pan and simmer gently for 15 minutes or until the mackerel is quite tender. Test with a fork: the flesh should flake easily.

Transfer the mackerel to a hot serving platter and keep warm. Add the apples to the pan, increase the heat slightly and simmer for 5 minutes or until the sauce is reduced to the consistency of double cream and the apples are glazed. Adjust seasoning. Pour over the fish, sprinkle with parsley and serve immediately with creamed potatoes and a seasonal green vegetable.

Mackerel with lemon stuffing

A substantial supper dish for the family, lemon-stuffed mackerel could be served with a diced cucumber salad and boiled new potatoes tossed in parsley butter.

METRIC	IMPERIAL
4 mackerel (about 175 g. each), split and boned out	*4 mackerel (about 6 oz. each), split and boned out*
Juice of ½ lemon	*Juice of ½ lemon*
Salt and freshly ground black pepper	*Salt and freshly ground black pepper*
1 bay leaf, crushed	*1 bay leaf, crushed*
For the stuffing:	**For the stuffing:**
Butter for frying	*Butter for frying*
1 small onion, peeled and finely chopped	*1 small onion, peeled and finely chopped*
75 g. fresh white breadcrumbs	*3 oz. fresh white breadcrumbs*
Finely grated rind and juice of 1 lemon	*Finely grated rind and juice of 1 lemon*
1 × 15 ml. spoon freshly chopped parsley	*1 tablespoon freshly chopped parsley*
½ egg, beaten	*½ egg, beaten*

First prepare stuffing. Melt a knob of butter in a pan. Add the onion and fry gently for 5 minutes or until golden. Transfer to a mixing bowl and combine with the remaining stuffing ingredients.

Lay the mackerel flat on a board and sprinkle the flesh with lemon juice, and salt and pepper to taste. Spoon the prepared stuffing into the fish and reshape. Place in an oven-proof casserole, barely cover the bottom of the dish with water and add the bay leaf and more salt and pepper to taste.

Cover the casserole with a lid, or greased greaseproof paper or foil and poach in a warm oven (160°C/325°F or Gas Mark 3) for 15 to 20 minutes or until the fish feels tender when pierced with a skewer. Drain and serve immediately.

Herrings in mustard sauce

Mustard sauce is one of the classic accompaniments for fish and it goes especially well with the richness of herrings.

METRIC	IMPERIAL
4 herrings, split and boned out	*4 herrings, split and boned out*
Juice of 1 lemon	*Juice of 1 lemon*
Salt and freshly ground black pepper	*Salt and freshly ground black pepper*

For the mustard sauce:
50 g. butter
50 g. flour
600 ml. hot milk
1 × 5 ml. spoon dry English
    mustard and 1 × 15 ml.
    spoon wine or vinegar, or
    1 × 15 ml. spoon
    Dijon-style mustard
1 × 5 ml. spoon sugar

For the mustard sauce:
2 oz. butter
2 oz. flour
1 pint hot milk
1 teaspoon dry English
    mustard and 1 tablespoon
    wine or vinegar, or 1
    tablespoon Dijon-style
    mustard
1 teaspoon sugar

Lay the herrings flat on a board and sprinkle the flesh with the lemon juice and salt and black pepper to taste. Put under a preheated hot grill and cook until tender, about 8 minutes each side.

Meanwhile, make the sauce. Melt the butter in a pan, stir in the flour and cook for 2 minutes, stirring constantly. Remove the pan from the heat and gradually add the hot milk, stirring vigorously. When all the milk has been incorporated, add the mustard, sugar and salt and pepper to taste. Return the pan to the heat and bring slowly to the boil, stirring constantly. Lower the heat and simmer gently for 1 to 2 minutes or until the sauce thickens.

Transfer the grilled herrings to a hot serving platter, coat with the mustard sauce and serve immediately.

Mackerel with lemon stuffing; Herrings in mustard sauce

49

Trout with almonds

Trout with almonds

A classic dish which combines the soft succulent texture of trout with the crisp crunchy bite of fried almonds, Trout with almonds makes an ideal luncheon dish or fish course for a formal dinner party.

METRIC	IMPERIAL
4 trout, gutted and cleaned, with the heads on	*4 trout, gutted and cleaned, with the heads on*
Flour for coating	*Flour for coating*
Salt and freshly ground black pepper	*Salt and freshly ground black pepper*
Butter for frying	*Butter for frying*
50 g. flaked blanched almonds	*2 oz. flaked blanched almonds*
Juice of 1 lemon	*Juice of 1 lemon*

To finish:	**To finish:**
4 lemon wedges	*4 lemon wedges*
Few parsley sprigs	*Few parsley sprigs*

Coat the fish in the flour seasoned with salt and pepper.

Melt a knob of butter in a large frying pan. Add the almonds and fry gently, stirring, for 2 to 3 minutes or until golden-brown, being careful that the butter does not begin to burn. Remove the almonds from the pan with a slotted spoon. Drain on absorbent kitchen paper and keep warm.

Wipe the pan clean with kitchen paper and add another knob of butter. When it has melted, add the trout and cook gently for 5 to 8 minutes on each side or until the trout is tender. Test with a fork: the flesh should flake easily.

Transfer the fish to a hot serving platter, sprinkle with the almonds and lemon juice and serve immediately garnished with lemon wedges and parsley sprigs.

Salmon herb parcels

By wrapping the salmon in 'parcels' of foil, the flavour and goodness of the fish are sealed in and not lost in the cooking process. Salmon herb parcels may be served with parsley sauce, minted green peas and potato croquettes.

METRIC	IMPERIAL
4 salmon steaks	*4 salmon steaks*
50 g. butter	*2 oz. butter*
2 bay leaves, halved	*2 bay leaves, halved*
4 parsley sprigs	*4 parsley sprigs*
4 onion slices	*4 onion slices*
4 slivers of lemon rind	*4 slivers of lemon rind*
4 thyme sprigs or 1 × 5 ml. spoon dried thyme	*4 thyme sprigs or 1 teaspoon dried thyme*
Salt and freshly ground black pepper	*Salt and freshly ground black pepper*
Watercress sprigs to finish	*Watercress sprigs to finish*

Place each salmon steak on a square of foil, large enough to enclose the whole steak. Place a knob of butter on each steak and top with ½ bay leaf, 1 parsley sprig, 1 onion slice, 1 sliver of lemon rind and 1 thyme sprig or sprinkling of dried thyme. Season to taste. Wrap the steaks in the foil then place in an ovenproof dish. Barely cover the bottom of the dish with water and bake in a moderate oven (180°C/350°F or Gas Mark 4) for 15 to 20 minutes or until the salmon is tender. Test with a fork: the flesh should flake easily. Remove the 'parcels' from the dish, unwrap and discard the herbs and seasonings before serving, garnished with watercress.

Deep-fried whitebait

Whitebait make an excellent light starter to a meal with a substantial main course of meat. Serve with thinly-sliced brown bread and butter and a glass of chilled white wine.

METRIC	IMPERIAL
½ kg. whitebait, washed	*1 lb. whitebait, washed*
Flour for coating	*Flour for coating*
Salt and freshly ground black pepper	*Salt and freshly ground black pepper*
Vegetable oil for frying	*Vegetable oil for frying*
Lemon slices to finish	*Lemon slices to finish*

Coat the fish in the flour seasoned with salt and pepper. Heat the oil gently in a deep-fat fryer until it is hot enough to turn a stale bread cube golden in 20 to 30 seconds (180–190°C/350–375°F on a deep-frying thermometer). Using a frying basket, add about one-quarter of the fish. Increase the heat and fry until golden, about 2 to 3 minutes. Shake the basket occasionally to ensure the fish do not stick together during cooking.

Remove the fish from the pan, drain on absorbent kitchen paper and keep warm on a hot serving platter until all the fish are fried. Garnish the platter with lemon slices and serve immediately.

White fish

Deep-fried whitebait; Salmon herb parcels

Plaice with mushrooms and cream

This is a rich dish which requires few accompaniments. Serve with chopped spinach or a fresh green salad tossed in a sharp vinaigrette dressing.

METRIC	IMPERIAL
Butter for frying	Butter for frying
¼ kg. button mushrooms, cleaned and sliced	½ lb. button mushrooms, cleaned and sliced
4 plaice fillets, skinned	4 plaice fillets, skinned
Flour for coating	Flour for coating
Salt and freshly ground black pepper	Salt and freshly ground black pepper
150 ml. dry white wine	¼ pint dry white wine
150 ml. fresh single cream	¼ pint fresh single cream
1–2 × 15 ml. spoons freshly chopped parsley to finish	1–2 tablespoons freshly chopped parsley to finish

Melt a knob of butter in a large frying pan. Add the mushrooms and fry gently for 2 to 3 minutes. Remove from the pan and keep hot.

Coat the plaice in flour seasoned with salt and pepper. Melt another knob of butter in the pan and add the fish. Fry quickly until golden on both sides. Add the wine and simmer gently for 10 minutes or until the fish is tender, turning once during the cooking time. Test with a fork: the flesh should flake easily.

Return the mushrooms to the pan. Stir in the cream and heat gently. Do not allow to boil or the cream will separate.

Transfer the fish to a hot serving platter and pour the sauce over. Sprinkle with chopped parsley and serve immediately.

Plaice with mushrooms and cream

Cod bake

Spinach and cheese go well with fish, especially with the somewhat bland flavour of cod. Serve this fish casserole as a family supper dish with potato croquettes.

METRIC	IMPERIAL
¾ kg. fresh spinach or 1 × 283 g. packet frozen chopped spinach	1½ lb. fresh spinach or 1 × 10 oz. packet frozen chopped spinach
Salt and freshly ground black pepper	Salt and freshly ground black pepper
1 × 1.25 ml. spoon grated nutmeg	¼ teaspoon grated nutmeg
50 g. butter	2 oz. butter
4 cod steaks	4 cod steaks

For the cheese sauce:

25 g. butter	1 oz. butter
25 g. flour	1 oz. flour
400 ml. hot milk	¾ pint hot milk
100 g. Cheddar cheese, grated	4 oz. Cheddar cheese, grated

Cod bake; Fish cakes

Wash the fresh spinach and place in a large saucepan with salt to taste. Heat gently until juices flow from the spinach, then cover the pan with a lid and cook gently for 5 to 10 minutes or until the spinach is tender. Drain well and chop finely or purée in an electric blender. If using frozen spinach, cook according to packet directions.

Season the cooked spinach with plenty of black pepper and the nutmeg and stir in half of the butter. Place in the bottom of a shallow ovenproof dish.

Fry the cod steaks in the remaining butter for 2 to 3 minutes on each side, then place on top of the spinach in the dish.

To prepare the cheese sauce, melt the butter in a pan. Stir in the flour and cook for 2 to 3 minutes, stirring constantly. Remove the pan from the heat and add the milk gradually, stirring vigorously. When all the milk has been incorporated, return the pan to the heat. Bring slowly to the boil, stirring constantly. Lower the heat, add 50 g./2 oz. of the grated cheese and cook for 2 to 3 minutes or until cheese melts in the sauce, stirring constantly.

Cover the fish with the cheese sauce and sprinkle with the remaining grated cheese. Bake in a fairly hot oven (190°C/375°F or Gas Mark 5) for 20 to 30 minutes or until the fish is cooked and the top of the casserole is lightly browned and bubbling. Test the fish with a fork: the flesh should flake easily. Serve immediately.

Fish cakes

Homemade fish cakes are quite delicious. Serve with lemon wedges and parsley butter.

METRIC	IMPERIAL
¼ kg. filleted white or smoked fish, cooked, skinned and flaked	½ lb. filleted white or smoked fish, cooked, skinned and flaked
¼ kg. potatoes, boiled and mashed	½ lb. potatoes, boiled and mashed
1 × 5 ml. spoon lemon juice	1 teaspoon lemon juice
1 × 15 ml. spoon freshly chopped parsley	1 tablespoon freshly chopped parsley
Salt and freshly ground black pepper	Salt and freshly ground black pepper
1 × 15 ml. spoon milk, if necessary	1 tablespoon milk, if necessary
Vegetable oil for frying	Vegetable oil for frying

To coat:
1 egg, beaten
50 g. dried breadcrumbs

To coat:
1 egg, beaten
2 oz. dried breadcrumbs

In a mixing bowl combine the fish, potatoes, lemon juice, parsley and seasoning to taste, binding the mixture with the milk if too dry. On a floured board, shape the mixture into four cakes. Dip the cakes into the beaten egg, ensuring that they are evenly coated, then coat in the breadcrumbs.

Heat the oil gently in a deep-fat fryer until it is hot enough to turn a stale bread cube golden in 20 to 30 seconds (180–190°C/350–375°F on a deep-frying thermometer). Lower the cakes, two at a time, into the hot oil, increase the heat and fry until golden-brown on all sides. Drain on absorbent kitchen paper and serve immediately.

The fish cakes may also be shallow fried in equal quantities of butter and oil for 5 to 7 minutes on each side or until golden brown. **Makes 4 cakes.**

Fisherman's pie

Fisherman's pie

Any thick white fish can be used for this super family dish.

METRIC	IMPERIAL
½ kg. filleted white fish (haddock, whiting, cod)	1 lb. filleted white fish (haddock, whiting, cod)
400 ml. milk	¾ pint milk
Salt and freshly ground black pepper	Salt and freshly ground black pepper
3 black peppercorns	3 black peppercorns
1 onion slice	1 onion slice
1 bay leaf	1 bay leaf
25 g. butter	1 oz. butter
25 g. flour	1 oz. flour
50 g. Cheddar cheese, grated	2 oz. Cheddar cheese, grated

For the topping:
2 hard-boiled eggs, sliced
½ kg. potatoes, boiled and mashed with 25 g. butter, 1 × 15 ml. spoon milk and 1 beaten egg

For the topping:
2 hard-boiled eggs, sliced
1 lb. potatoes, boiled and mashed with 1 oz. butter, 1 tablespoon milk and 1 beaten egg

Place the fish in an ovenproof dish with the milk, salt, peppercorns, onion and bay leaf. Cover with a lid or foil and bake in a moderate oven (180°C/350°F or Gas Mark 4) for 15 to 20 minutes or until the fish is tender and will flake easily with a fork.

Remove the fish from the dish and flake with a fork, discarding any skin. Keep warm. Strain the milk and cooking juices and reserve.

Melt the butter in a pan. Stir in the flour and cook for 2 minutes, stirring constantly. Remove the pan from the heat and gradually add the reserved cooking juices, stirring vigorously. When all the juices have been incorporated, return the pan to the heat and slowly bring to the boil, stirring constantly. Stir in the grated cheese and add salt and pepper to taste. Cook the sauce for 2 to 3 minutes or until the cheese melts into the sauce, stirring constantly.

Fold the flaked fish into the cheese sauce, then transfer to a deep ovenproof dish. Place the sliced hard-boiled eggs in a layer on top of the fish and the mashed potatoes on top of the eggs. Mark the potato with the back of a fork and bake on the top shelf of a fairly hot oven (200°C/400°F or Gas Mark 6) for 10 to 15 minutes or until the potato topping is golden-brown. Serve straight from the cooking dish.

Halibut Catalan

Around the Mediterranean they love to cook white fish in thick sauces, highly flavoured with tomatoes, onion and garlic. Halibut lends itself well to this particular combination of flavours.

METRIC	IMPERIAL
6 × 15 ml. spoons olive oil	6 tablespoons olive oil
Juice of 1 lemon	Juice of 1 lemon
Salt and freshly ground black pepper	Salt and freshly ground black pepper
4 slices filleted halibut or halibut steaks	4 slices filleted halibut or halibut steaks
1 small onion, peeled and finely chopped	1 small onion, peeled and finely chopped
1 garlic clove, crushed with 1 × 2.5 ml. spoon salt	1 garlic clove, crushed with ½ teaspoon salt
1 × 15 ml. spoon flour	1 tablespoon flour
¼ kg. tomatoes, skinned, seeded and chopped	½ lb. tomatoes, skinned, seeded and chopped
1 × 15 ml. spoon tomato purée	1 tablespoon tomato purée
300 ml. dry white wine	½ pint dry white wine

To finish:

50 g. finely chopped hazelnuts	2 oz. finely chopped hazelnuts
2 × 15 ml. spoons freshly chopped parsley	2 tablespoons freshly chopped parsley

Mix together 4 spoons of the oil, the lemon juice, and salt and pepper to taste. Leave the halibut to soak in this marinade for 1 to 2 hours before cooking, basting and turning occasionally.

Heat the remaining oil in a deep flameproof casserole. Add the onion and garlic and fry gently until golden. Stir in the flour, tomatoes, tomato purée and white wine. Slowly bring to the boil, stirring constantly. Add the marinated halibut, coating the fish with the sauce, and cover with a lid or foil. Transfer to a moderate oven (180°C/350°F or Gas Mark 4) and bake for about 20 minutes or until the fish is tender and will flake easily with a fork.

Remove from the oven and top with the chopped hazelnuts and parsley. Serve immediately with creamed potatoes.

Halibut Catalan

Sole dugléré

Sole dugléré

Although sole is used here, any filleted flat white fish can be cooked in the same way. The finished dish looks very good if you roll up the fish, securing the rolls with cocktail sticks, before frying.

METRIC	IMPERIAL
Butter for frying	Butter for frying
1 bunch of spring onions, topped and tailed and finely chopped	1 bunch of spring onions, topped and tailed and finely chopped
4 Dover soles, filleted and skinned	4 Dover soles, filleted and skinned
Flour for coating	Flour for coating
Salt and freshly ground black pepper	Salt and freshly ground black pepper
300 ml. dry white wine	½ pint dry white wine
300 ml. fish stock	½ pint fish stock
4 tomatoes, skinned, seeded and chopped	4 tomatoes, skinned, seeded and chopped
4 × 15 ml. spoons fresh single cream	4 tablespoons fresh single cream
2 × 15 ml. spoons freshly chopped parsley to finish	2 tablespoons freshly chopped parsley to finish

Melt a knob of butter in a large frying pan. Add the spring onions and fry gently for 5 minutes. Coat the sole fillets in flour seasoned with salt and pepper and add to the pan. Fry gently for a few minutes on all sides or until lightly coloured. Stir in the wine, fish stock and tomatoes and simmer gently for 15 to 20 minutes or until the sole is tender. Test with a fork: the flesh should flake easily. Pour in the cream and stir well. Serve immediately, sprinkled with the parsley.

Skate with black butter

This is the simplest way to cook skate and is delicious. Serve with boiled new potatoes tossed in butter and freshly chopped parsley.

METRIC	IMPERIAL
1-2 wings skate (about 1 kg.)	1–2 wings skate (about 2 lb.)
Court bouillon	Court bouillon
1 × 15 ml. spoon freshly chopped parsley to finish (optional)	1 tablespoon freshly chopped parsley to finish (optional)

For the black butter:	For the black butter:
50 g. butter	2 oz. butter
2 × 15 ml. spoons wine vinegar	2 tablespoons wine vinegar
1 × 15 ml. spoon capers	1 tablespoon capers
Salt and freshly ground black pepper	Salt and freshly ground black pepper

Poach the skate in a shallow pan in the court bouillon for 15 to 20 minutes or until just tender. Test with a fork: the flesh should flake easily. Remove from the pan, drain and dry well on absorbent kitchen paper. Transfer to a hot serving dish and keep warm.

Melt the butter in a pan and cook until a rich brown. Stir in the vinegar and capers and boil to reduce slightly. Adjust seasoning. Pour over the skate on the serving dish, sprinkle with the parsley (optional) and serve immediately.

Skate with black butter

Shellfish

Dressed crab

Although most fishmongers will generally dress crabs if given adequate notice, they will probably charge for this service. It is worth knowing how to dress a crab yourself in case you are lucky enough to be given one. Serve with thick homemade mayonnaise and thinly-sliced brown bread and butter.

METRIC	IMPERIAL
1 medium-sized crab	*1 medium-sized crab*
Court bouillon or water	*Court bouillon or water*
Salt and freshly ground black pepper	*Salt and freshly ground black pepper*
Juice of 1 lemon	*Juice of 1 lemon*
2 × 15 ml. spoons dried breadcrumbs	*2 tablespoons dried breadcrumbs*
1 × 15 ml. spoon freshly chopped parsley	*1 tablespoon freshly chopped parsley*
2 × 15 ml. spoons wine vinegar	*2 tablespoons wine vinegar*
Lettuce leaves to serve	*Lettuce leaves to serve*

Dressed crab

1. Twist off the legs and claws

2. Pull the body and shell apart

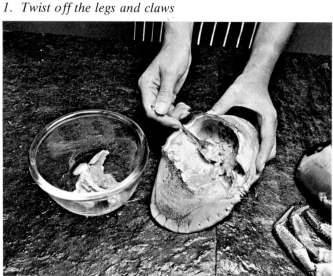

4. Scoop out the soft dark meat

5. Crack the claws with a hammer

If the crab is alive, put it in a large saucepan. Cover with court bouillon or salted water and bring slowly to the boil. Boil steadily for 10 to 15 minutes, then turn off the heat and leave to cool in the liquid.

When quite cold, remove the crab from the cooking liquid and lay on its back on a board. Twist off the legs and claws and set aside. Pull the body and shell apart with the hands.

Discard the stomach sac and any green matter in the outer shell part just below the head. Discard the 'dead men's fingers' – the pale-greyish coloured fronds – from the inner body part.

With a teaspoon or skewer, scoop out all the soft dark meat from the shell part and put in a bowl. Season well and stir in the lemon juice, dried breadcrumbs and parsley.

Knock away the shell around the dark rim and scrub and dry the shell. Pack the meat neatly around the sides of this prepared shell.

Remove all the white meat from the reserved inner body part of the crab. With nutcrackers or a heavy weight, crack the claws and take out the white meat with pincers or a skewer. Discard any cartilage. Flake the white meat carefully with a fork and mix with the wine vinegar. Pile into the centre of the shell.

To serve, lay the crab shell on the lettuce leaves and surround with the claws.

3. *Discard the stomach sac and green matter*

6. *Remove white meat from the claws*

Prawn curry

Prawn curry

For an informal supper or family meal, prawns make a good curry which can be made very quickly. Frozen prawns are quite suitable and can be kept in the freezer for impromptu entertaining.

METRIC	IMPERIAL
Vegetable oil for frying	Vegetable oil for frying
1 large onion, peeled and finely chopped	1 large onion, peeled and finely chopped
1 garlic clove, crushed with 1 × 2.5 ml. spoon salt	1 garlic clove, crushed with ½ teaspoon salt
1 × 2.5 ml. spoon turmeric	½ teaspoon turmeric
1 × 2.5 ml. spoon mustard seeds	½ teaspoon mustard seeds
1 × 5 ml. spoon ground ginger	1 teaspoon ground ginger
1 × 5 ml. spoon chilli powder	1 teaspoon chilli powder
1 × 396 g. can tomatoes, sieved	1 × 14 oz. can tomatoes, sieved
½ kg. shelled prawns	1 lb. shelled prawns
Juice of ½ lemon	Juice of ½ lemon
1 × 141 g. carton unsweetened natural yogurt	1 × 5 oz. carton unsweetened natural yogurt

Heat a spoon of oil in a frying pan. Add the onion and garlic and fry gently for 5 minutes or until golden. Stir in the spices and fry for 2 to 3 minutes. Stir in the tomatoes and cook for 10 minutes, then add the prawns and cook gently for 10 to 15 minutes. Stir in the lemon juice and yogurt. Serve on a bed of boiled rice with Cucumber Raita.

Chinese-style scampi

Scampi in a sweet and sour sauce is a piquant dish to serve with boiled noodles or rice. Prawns can be substituted if preferred.

METRIC	IMPERIAL
Vegetable oil for frying	*Vegetable oil for frying*
1 large onion, peeled and sliced into rings	*1 large onion, peeled and sliced into rings*
1 garlic clove, crushed with 1 × 2.5 ml. spoon salt	*1 garlic clove, crushed with ½ teaspoon salt*
1 × 5 ml. spoon ground ginger	*1 teaspoon ground ginger*
Freshly ground black pepper	*Freshly ground black pepper*
1 green pepper, cored, seeded and sliced into rings	*1 green pepper, cored, seeded and sliced into rings*
1 red pepper, cored, seeded and sliced into rings	*1 red pepper, cored, seeded and sliced into rings*
4 tomatoes, skinned, seeded and chopped	*4 tomatoes, skinned, seeded and chopped*
300 ml. chicken stock	*½ pint chicken stock*
½ kg. shelled scampi	*1 lb. shelled scampi*

For the sweet and sour sauce:	**For the sweet and sour sauce:**
2 × 15 ml. spoons soya sauce	*2 tablespoons soya sauce*
1 × 15 ml. spoon vinegar	*1 tablespoon vinegar*
1 × 15 ml. spoon soft brown sugar	*1 tablespoon soft brown sugar*
2 × 15 ml. spoons cornflour	*2 tablespoons cornflour*
1 × 5 ml. spoon vegetable oil	*1 teaspoon vegetable oil*

Heat 2 spoons of oil in a frying pan. Add the onion, garlic, ginger and black pepper and fry gently together until golden. Stir in the vegetables and stock. Mix together all the sauce ingredients and add to the pan. Bring to the boil, stirring constantly, then lower the heat and simmer gently for 10 minutes. Stir in the scampi and continue to cook for 5 to 10 minutes or until the sauce is glossy. Serve immediately.

Moules marinière

Serve Moules marinière in soup plates and let guests use forks or fingers to scoop the mussels out of their shells.

METRIC	IMPERIAL
Butter for frying	*Butter for frying*
4 shallots or onions, peeled and finely chopped	*4 shallots or onions, peeled and finely chopped*
1 garlic clove, crushed with 1 × 2.5 ml. spoon salt	*1 garlic clove, crushed with ½ teaspoon salt*
300 ml. dry white wine	*½ pint dry white wine*
1 bouquet garni	*1 bouquet garni*
Freshly ground black pepper	*Freshly ground black pepper*
4 dozen mussels, scrubbed, with beards removed	*4 dozen mussels, scrubbed, with beards removed*
2 × 15 ml. spoons freshly chopped parsley to finish	*2 tablespoons freshly chopped parsley to finish*

Melt a knob of butter in a large pan. Add the shallots or onions and garlic and fry gently for 5 minutes or until golden. Stir in the wine, bouquet garni, pepper and mussels. Cover the pan with a tight-fitting lid and cook the mussels for 5 to 10 minutes or until the shells open. Remove the top shells and place the mussels in individual soup bowls. Taste the sauce for seasoning and pour over the mussels.

If a thicker sauce is liked, the cooking juice may be thickened with beurre manié. Cream together 2 × 15 ml. spoons/2 tablespoons butter with 1 × 15 ml. spoon/1 tablespoon flour and stir into the juices in the pan after taking out the mussels. Bring slowly to the boil then simmer until sauce thickens.

Sprinkle with the chopped parsley and serve immediately.

Scallops with wine sauce

Scallops make an attractive starter with their flat open shells used for serving. This recipe coats them in a wine sauce and is quite rich, so be sure to follow with a light main course.

METRIC	IMPERIAL
4 scallops	4 scallops
150 ml. dry white wine	¼ pint dry white wine
1 small onion, peeled and chopped	1 small onion, peeled and chopped
1 bouquet garni	1 bouquet garni
Salt	Salt
3 black peppercorns	3 black peppercorns

For the sauce:

METRIC	IMPERIAL
25 g. butter	1 oz. butter
25 g. flour	1 oz. flour
150 ml. hot milk	¼ pint hot milk
Salt and freshly ground black pepper	Salt and freshly ground black pepper

To finish:

METRIC	IMPERIAL
2 × 15 ml. spoons grated Parmesan cheese	2 tablespoons grated Parmesan cheese
¼ kg. potatoes, boiled and mashed with 25 g. butter and 2 × 15 ml. spoons milk	½ lb. potatoes, boiled and mashed with 1 oz. butter and 2 tablespoons milk
4 parsley sprigs	4 parsley sprigs

Remove the scallops from the shells. Scrub and reserve the shells. Put the scallops in a pan and add the wine, onion, bouquet garni and seasoning. Simmer gently for 5 to 10 minutes or until the scallops are tender. Do not boil or the scallops will be tough. Take from the heat and allow scallops to cool slightly in the wine. Remove scallops from the wine. Strain and reserve. Cut the scallops into bite-sized pieces and arrange them in the reserved shells.

To make the sauce, melt the butter in a pan. Stir in the flour and cook for 2 minutes, stirring constantly. Remove the pan from the heat and gradually add the milk and the reserved cooking liquid, stirring vigorously. When all the liquid has been incorporated, return to the heat and bring slowly to the boil, stirring constantly. Season to taste. Cook for 1 to 2 minutes or until thick.

Coat the scallops with the sauce, sprinkle with the Parmesan cheese and pipe a border of potato around the edge of each scallop shell. Place on a baking sheet and bake in a fairly hot oven (200°C/400°F or Gas Mark 6) for 10 minutes or until the cheese browns slightly. Decorate with parsley sprigs and serve immediately.

Chinese-style scampi; Scallops with wine sauce; Moules marinière

Paella

Paella

Recipes for Paella vary widely from region to region in Spain. Any kind of fish or shellfish can be used, depending on availability and the time of year.

METRIC	IMPERIAL
Olive oil for frying	*Olive oil for frying*
1 large onion, peeled and finely chopped	*1 large onion, peeled and finely chopped*
1 garlic clove, crushed with 1 × 2.5 ml. spoon salt	*1 garlic clove, crushed with ½ teaspoon salt*
100 g. unsmoked bacon, rinds removed and diced	*4 oz. unsmoked bacon, rinds removed and diced*
1 green or red pepper, cored, seeded and finely chopped	*1 green or red pepper, cored, seeded and finely chopped*
225 g. long-grain rice	*½ lb. long-grain rice*
600 ml. hot chicken stock	*1 pint hot chicken stock*
Freshly ground black pepper	*Freshly ground black pepper*
1 × 1.25 ml. spoon powdered saffron	*¼ teaspoon powdered saffron*
¼ kg. filleted white fish, skinned and diced	*½ lb. filleted white fish, skinned and diced*
¼ kg. cooked chicken meat, diced	*½ lb. cooked chicken meat, diced*
100 g. prawns, shelled	*4 oz. prawns, shelled*

To finish:

8 unshelled prawns, cooked	*8 unshelled prawns, cooked*
8 mussels, cooked	*8 mussels, cooked*
4 lemon wedges	*4 lemon wedges*

Heat 2 spoons of oil in a deep flameproof casserole. Add the onion and garlic and fry gently for 5 minutes or until golden. Add the bacon and pepper and fry for a further 5 minutes. Add the rice and cook, stirring, for 1 to 2 minutes or until it is just beginning to change colour. Stir in the hot stock, add the black pepper and saffron and bring to the boil. Add the white fish, cover and bake in a fairly hot oven (190°C/375°F or Gas Mark 5) for 20 to 25 minutes or until the rice is tender and has absorbed most of the cooking liquid.

Add the chicken and prawns, cover and return to the oven for a further 10 minutes to heat through. Adjust seasoning, then transfer to a hot serving platter and arrange the prawns and mussels on top. Garnish with lemon wedges.

Smoked and pickled fish

Kippers in lemon dressing

A very simple dish to make, this is a refreshing summer starter, served with thinly-sliced brown bread and butter.

METRIC	IMPERIAL
1 large packet frozen kipper fillets, thawed and skinned	*1 large packet frozen kipper fillets, thawed and skinned*
6 × 15 ml. spoons olive oil	*6 tablespoons olive oil*
3 × 15 ml. spoons lemon juice	*3 tablespoons lemon juice*
Freshly ground black pepper	*Freshly ground black pepper*

To finish: **To finish:**

Thinly-sliced onion rings	*Thinly-sliced onion rings*
Lemon wedges	*Lemon wedges*

Cut the kipper fillets into thin slivers and place in a mixing bowl. Mix together the oil, lemon juice and plenty of black pepper and spoon over the kippers. Chill in the refrigerator, preferably overnight.

Arrange the kippers on a serving platter and spoon the dressing over. Top with onion rings and lemon wedges.

Soused herrings

Home-soused herrings make a tasty starter with soured cream and snipped chives, or try them as a snack.

METRIC	IMPERIAL
4 herrings, filleted	*4 herrings, filleted*
2 × 5 ml. spoons salt	*2 teaspoons salt*
6 peppercorns	*6 peppercorns*
6 allspice berries	*6 allspice berries*
1 bouquet garni	*1 bouquet garni*
1 onion, sliced	*1 onion, sliced*
Vinegar	*Vinegar*

Roll the herrings up from head end to tail end, secure with wooden cocktail sticks and pack tightly into an ovenproof dish. Add the seasonings and cover with equal parts of water and vinegar. Cover with a lid.

Bake in a cool oven (150°C/300°F or Gas Mark 2) for 1 hour. Leave to cool in the liquid before draining well.

Smoked haddock kedgeree

Traditionally served at breakfast time, this rice dish also makes a substantial luncheon or supper.

METRIC
¼ kg. smoked haddock,
  filleted
2 × 15 ml. spoons butter
225 g. long-grain rice,
  cooked
Freshly ground black
  pepper
1 × 5 ml. spoon garam
  masala or curry powder
2 hard-boiled eggs,
  quartered
2 tomatoes, quartered
Freshly chopped parsley to
  finish

IMPERIAL
½ lb. smoked haddock,
  filleted
2 tablespoons butter
½ lb. long-grain rice,
  cooked
Freshly ground black
  pepper
1 teaspoon garam masala or
  curry powder
2 hard-boiled eggs,
  quartered
2 tomatoes, quartered
Freshly chopped parsley to
  finish

Poach the haddock gently in water to cover until tender, about 10 to 15 minutes. Test with a fork: the flesh should flake easily. Drain, remove the skin and any bones, and flake with a fork.

Melt the butter in a frying pan. Add the rice and haddock and heat through, stirring gently. Season well with black pepper and the garam masala or curry powder. Transfer to a hot serving platter and garnish with quarters of egg and tomato. Sprinkle with the chopped parsley and serve immediately.

Smoked haddock kedgeree;
Kippers in lemon dressing;
Soused herrings

Meat

Meat is a valuable food in that it supplies protein, vitamins and minerals including iron. This chapter on cooking with meat is divided into five separate sections: Beef, Lamb, Pork, Veal and Offal. Basic cooking methods are given, followed by more unusual and advanced recipes using the various cuts. There is also a section on accompaniments to meat which gives the traditional stuffings and sauces.

When buying meat, choose between fresh, home-fed and killed produce – which is the most expensive – and chilled or frozen imported meat which is generally cheaper than British meat. Naturally enough, your choice will depend on personal taste and the amount of money you wish to spend.

Fresh meat should not be kept for any length of time – this rule applies particularly to minced meats and offal which should be eaten on the day of purchase. Other meats should be loosely wrapped and kept in the refrigerator for a maximum of two to three days. In general, beef is the best meat for keeping, whereas pork can deteriorate quickly, particularly in summertime or in warm conditions.

Chilled or frozen meat should be allowed to thaw out and come to room temperature before cooking. Once thawed, it should be stored and dealt with in exactly the same way as fresh meat.

Always cook meat according to recommended methods, temperatures and cooking times. These vary considerably from type of meat to type of cut, and the charts in this chapter offer guidelines for you to follow. Do not try to cut corners – or make a cut of meat something it isn't; this will only result in disappointing finished dishes.

Yorkshire pudding

Always served with roast beef. Can also be served as a sweet pudding with sweetened stewed fruit such as apples or rhubarb baked in the centre.

METRIC	IMPERIAL
100 g. flour	4 oz. flour
Pinch of salt	Pinch of salt
1 egg, beaten	1 egg, beaten
300 ml. milk	½ pint milk
25 g. dripping, lard or butter	1 oz. dripping, lard or butter

Sift the flour and salt into a mixing bowl. Make a well in the centre and pour in the egg and half the milk. Beat the mixture with a wooden spoon, gradually drawing the flour into the liquid from the sides. When all the flour is incorporated into the liquid and a thick batter is formed, gradually beat in the remaining milk until the batter is smooth and of a pouring consistency.

Put the fat into a baking or Yorkshire pudding tin or, if individual puddings are liked, divide the fat equally between a 12-hole bun tin. Put in a fairly hot oven (200°C/400°F or Gas Mark 6) and heat until very hot. Pour in the prepared batter and bake for 40 minutes for a large pudding, 20 minutes for individual ones, or until well-risen and golden-brown. Remove from the oven and serve immediately.

The recipes below are sufficient quantity to stuff a joint or bird for 4 people. If a larger joint or large bird such as goose or turkey is being stuffed, double the quantities given here.

Sage and onion stuffing

One of the most delicious of stuffings, sage and onion is traditionally used to stuff pork joints and duck and goose.

METRIC	IMPERIAL
Butter for frying	Butter for frying
2 large onions, peeled and finely chopped	2 large onions, peeled and finely chopped
100 g. fresh white breadcrumbs	4 oz. fresh white breadcrumbs
1 × 15 ml. spoon freshly chopped sage or 2 × 5 ml. spoons dried sage	1 tablespoon freshly chopped sage or 2 teaspoons dried sage
½–1 egg, beaten	½–1 egg, beaten
Salt and freshly ground black pepper	Salt and freshly ground black pepper

Melt a knob of butter in a small pan. Add the onions and fry until golden. Transfer to a mixing bowl and stir in the remaining ingredients, adding enough beaten egg to bind the mixture. Season to taste.

Horseradish sauce

A delicious accompaniment to roast beef and smoked fish, Horseradish sauce is best made with fresh horseradish when available.

METRIC	IMPERIAL
150 ml. soured cream, or fresh double cream and 1 × 5 ml. spoon lemon juice	¼ pint soured cream, or fresh double cream and 1 teaspoon lemon juice
2 × 15 ml. spoons grated horseradish	2 tablespoons grated horseradish
1 × 1.25 ml. spoon dry English mustard	¼ teaspoon dry English mustard
1 × 2.5 ml. spoon caster sugar	½ teaspoon caster sugar
Salt and freshly ground black pepper	Salt and freshly ground black pepper

Put all the ingredients in a mixing bowl with salt and pepper to taste. Stir well to combine thoroughly.

Apple sauce

The tangy bite of apple sauce makes an ideal contrast to rich meats such as pork, goose and sausages.

METRIC	IMPERIAL
½ kg. cooking apples, peeled, cored and chopped	1 lb. cooking apples, peeled, cored and chopped
2 × 15 ml. spoons water	2 tablespoons water
Juice of ½ lemon	Juice of ½ lemon
25 g. unsalted butter	1 oz. unsalted butter
Caster sugar (optional)	Caster sugar (optional)

Put the apples in a saucepan with the water, lemon juice and butter and simmer gently for 10 to 15 minutes or until very tender, depending on the variety and ripeness of the apples. Purée the apples in an electric blender, work through a sieve or beat with a wooden spoon until smooth. Taste the sauce: if too tart, stir in a little sugar.

Forcemeat stuffing

Forcemeat stuffing is basically a herb stuffing, sometimes made with the addition of veal and bacon. It is traditionally used for stuffing veal joints and for chicken and turkey. Forcemeat balls are coated in seasoned flour, fried in hot dripping or lard and roasted – usually around a game bird.

METRIC	IMPERIAL
100 g. fresh white breadcrumbs	4 oz. fresh white breadcrumbs
37.5 g. shredded beef suet	1½ oz. shredded beef suet
2 × 15 ml. spoons freshly chopped parsley	2 tablespoons freshly chopped parsley
1 × 2.5 ml. spoon dried mixed herbs	½ teaspoon dried mixed herbs
Finely grated rind and juice of ½ lemon	Finely grated rind and juice of ½ lemon
½–1 egg, beaten	½–1 egg, beaten
Salt and freshly ground black pepper	Salt and freshly ground black pepper

Put all the ingredients in a mixing bowl and stir well to combine thoroughly, adding enough egg to bind the mixture. Season to taste.

GRILLING	FRYING	ROASTING

Beef

Steaks – fillet (tournedos), rump, sirloin (porterhouse), T-bone.
Marinate (optional) in oil, lemon juice or wine vinegar and salt and freshly ground black pepper. Cook under preheated hot grill.

Grilling times:
(according to thickness and type of steak)
  6 – 8 minutes: Rare
  8 – 10 minutes: Medium-Rare
10 – 15 minutes: Well Done
       Turn once during cooking.

Steaks as for grilling. Fry in hot oil or equal quantities of hot oil and butter. Cooking times as for grilling.
See also Tournedos en croûte and Beef Stroganoff.
Other cuts of beef also fried to seal juices before pot roasting/braising/stewing, etc.
Minced beef is also fried with onions, vegetables and various sauces, seasonings, etc.

Popular cooking method for many cuts of beef: fillet, sirloin, wing, ribs, prime (fore) ribs, middle ribs, topside, aitchbone.
Season the joint and roast uncovered in roasting tin with dripping or lard.

Roasting Times:
Slow roasting in moderate oven (180°C/350°F or Gas Mark 4: 15 minutes to ½ kg./1 lb. plus 15 minutes over for rare meat; 20 minutes to ½ kg./1 lb. plus 20 minutes over for medium meat; 25 minutes to ½ kg./1 lb. plus 25 minutes over for well-done meat (for meat on the bone); 33 minutes to ½ kg./1 lb. plus 33 minutes over (for boned and rolled meat).
For stuffed joints, weigh after stuffing and allow 5 to 10 minutes to ½ kg./1 lb. extra cooking time.
Quick roasting in hot oven (220°C/425°F or Gas Mark 7): 20 minutes to ½ kg./1 lb. plus 20 minutes over (for meat on the bone); 25 minutes to ½ kg./1 lb. plus 25 minutes over (for boned and rolled meat).

GRILLING	FRYING	ROASTING

Lamb

Cutlets (best end of neck); noisettes (from best end of neck, without bone); chops (loin or chump) fillet (from leg or shoulder).
Brush lamb with oil or melted butter and seasonings to taste. Cook under preheated moderate grill for approx. 5 to 7 minutes on each side, according to taste – and thickness of meat. Baste occasionally and turn once during cooking time. Grilled lamb should be brown on the outside, pink in the middle when cut.
Fillet of lamb may be cut into cubes, marinated and threaded on oiled skewers. Cook on barbecue charcoal or under a hot grill for Shish kebab.
Mixed grill is usually made with lamb cutlets, kidneys, sausages, mushrooms, tomatoes, etc.

Cuts as for grilling. Fry in hot oil or equal quantities of hot oil and butter. Cooking times as for grilling. Cutlets and noisettes may be coated in egg and breadcrumbs and shallow- or deep-fried for 8 to 10 minutes or until golden brown on both sides. Cutlets and noisettes may be browned then covered in pastry (Shortcrust or Rough puff) and baked in a hot oven for 15 to 20 minutes or until golden brown.
See also Noisettes of lamb with pernod.
Other cuts of lamb also fried to seal juices before braising/stewing, etc.

Popular cooking method for many cuts: saddle, loin, leg, shoulder (with bone or boned and rolled), best end of neck (crown roast/carré d'agneau), breast (boned and rolled).
Season the joint and roast uncovered in roasting tin with dripping or lard.

Roasting Times:
As for beef, following well-done meat times. Shoulder, crown roast and breast of lamb are usually stuffed before roasting. Use any stuffings according to taste and roast according to cooking times for Beef, weighing joint after stuffing and allowing 5 to 10 minutes extra cooking time per ½ kg./1 lb.
See also Crown roast of lamb, Stuffed breast of lamb, French roast, Leg of lamb and Shoulder of Lamb à la Turque.

| BRAISING/POT ROASTING | STEWING/CASSEROLING | SERVING SUGGESTIONS |

Suitable for sirloin, topside, silverside, brisket, top ribs, aitchbone.
Coat meat in flour seasoned with salt and freshly ground black pepper. Fry quickly over high heat to brown meat on all sides. Put in saucepan or casserole dish on bed of fried diced root vegetables. Add stock and water or wine with seasonings to taste. Cover pan or casserole and simmer gently on top of stove or in warm oven (160°C/325°F or Gas Mark 3) for 2 to 2½ hours or until meat is tender. Check level of cooking liquid occasionally and add more if necessary.
See also Boeuf en daube.

Long, slow cooking, suitable for tougher, cheaper cuts of meat – flank, shin, clod, sticking, chuck, neck, blade, leg, skirt.
Cut meat into large cubes, coat in flour seasoned with salt and freshly ground black pepper and fry quickly over high heat to brown meat on all sides. Put in casserole dish with vegetables, stock, wine, seasonings, etc., to taste. Cover and cook in a warm oven (160°C/325°F or Gas Mark 3) for 2 to 3 hours or until meat is tender, depending on cut.
There are numerous stew and casserole recipes. See Carbonnade of beef and Boeuf bourguignon.
Also curries – see Sag gosht.
Stewing beef is also used for Steak and kidney pudding.

Serve grilled and fried steaks with Maître d'Hôtel/garlic butters, green or mixed salads, sauté, French-fried or Jacket baked potatoes, English or French mustard.
Roast beef is traditionally served with Roast potatoes, Yorkshire pudding, Horseradish sauce and gravy made in the roasting tin. Pour off most of the fat and sprinkle over enough flour to absorb it and the sediment. Cook until browned, then stir in hot stock or vegetable cooking liquid. Boil until thickened and season to taste.

| BRAISING/POT ROASTING | STEWING/CASSEROLING | SERVING SUGGESTIONS |

Suitable for loin, leg, and boned and rolled shoulder and breast.
As for braising/pot roasting beef above.

Suitable for tougher, cheaper cuts – middle neck, scrag end, boned shoulder and breast, also chump chops.
Coat chops or cubed meat in flour seasoned with salt and freshly ground black pepper and stew as for Beef above – cooking times will vary depending on cut of lamb.
Numerous recipes for stews and casseroles of lamb. See also Navarin de mouton and Lancashire hot pot.

Serve grilled or fried lamb with savoury butter to taste (see Chapter 4).
Other accompaniments include green or mixed salads, Sauté or French-fried potatoes, See also Chapter 7 for other accompaniments.
Roast lamb is traditionally served with Roast potatoes, mint sauce or sometimes an onion sauce.
Gravy is made in the roasting tin with cooking liquid from vegetables (see Beef).

GRILLING	FRYING	ROASTING

Pork

Loin and spare rib (English cut) chops are suitable for grilling. Marinate (optional) as for Beef steaks and cook under preheated moderate grill for at least 15 minutes until cooked through, basting occasionally and turning once during cooking time.

Pork fillet (tenderloin) may be cut into cubes, marinated and threaded on oiled skewers. Cook on barbecue charcoal or under a hot grill for kebabs for approx. 15 minutes, turning frequently. Baste during the cooking. See also Hot spiced pork.

Loin and spare rib chops as for grilling. Fry in hot oil or equal quantities of hot oil and butter. Cooking times as for griiling.

Can also be coated in egg and breadcrumbs and shallow- or deep-fried for 15 minutes or until golden brown on both sides.

Other cuts of pork also fried to seal juices before further cooking by other methods.

Cubes of cooked pork can also be coated in batter and deep-fried in hot oil. This is a popular Chinese dish, often served with a sweet and sour sauce. See Sweet and sour spare ribs.

Suitable roasting cuts: loin, leg, hand and spring, blade, crop or shoulder (spare rib).

Score the rind and brush with oil or melted dripping, sprinkle with salt. Season the joint and roast uncovered on rack in roasting tin with dripping or lard.

Roasting Times:
Roast in fairly hot oven 190°C/375°F or Gas Mark 5: 35 minutes to ½ kg./1 lb. plus 35 minutes over (for boned and rolled meat).

For stuffed joints, weigh after stuffing and allow 5 to 10 minutes to ½ kg./1 lb. extra cooking time.

See also Pork Alsacienne and Roast loin of pork with garlic.

Spare ribs (American cut) can also be roasted. See Sweet and sour spare ribs.

GRILLING	FRYING	ROASTING

Veal

Cutlets, loin and chump chops are suitable. Prepare and grill as for Lamb, basting frequently during cooking time as veal is a lean and therefore dry meat.

Fry cutlets, loin and chump chops as for Lamb in hot oil or equal quantities of hot oil and butter, also in egg and breadcrumbs. Veal escalopes (fillet of veal) are beaten thin, then coated in egg and breadcrumbs and shallow-fried for 2 to 3 minutes on each side. See also Wiener Schnitzel and Escalopes de veau à la crème.

Suitable roasting cuts are shoulder, leg, loin, fillet, best end of neck, breast.

All these joints are sold either on the bone or boned and rolled. The latter may be stuffed according to taste.

See also Veal Orloff.

Season the joint, put in roasting tin and cover with rashers of streaky bacon.

Roasting Times:
Slow roasting in moderate oven 180°C/350°F or Gas Mark 4.

35 minutes to ½ kg./1 lb. plus 35 minutes over (for meat on the bone).

40 minutes to ½ kg./1 lb. plus 40 minutes over (for boned and rolled meat).

For stuffed joints, weigh after stuffing and allow 5 to 10 minutes to ½ kg./1 lb. extra cooking time.

Quick roasting in hot oven 220°C/425°F or Gas Mark 7.

25 minutes to ½ kg./1 lb. plus 25 minutes over (for meat on the bone).

30 minutes to ½ kg./1 lb. plus 30 minutes over (for boned and rolled meat).

GRILLING	FRYING	BOILING

Bacon/Gammon/Ham

Cuts include: streaky bacon, gammon rashers, gammon steaks, gammon chops, middle cut. Rashers can be grilled according to taste. Bacon rashers can be rolled on to skewers or wrapped around sausages and grilled until crisp and cooked through.

As for grilling.

Bacon is often diced and fried as part of a dish such as Boeuf Bourguignonne, Coq au vin or Quiche Lorraine.

See also Jacket baked potatoes.

Suitable cuts: joints of streaky and collar bacon and middle, corner and hock gammon.

Soak in cold water to cover overnight. Drain and simmer in water to cover and seasonings. (See recipe for Glazed baked gammon.) Drain and serve boiled or drain and bake before serving.

Boiling Times:
20 to 25 minutes to ½ kg./1 lb. plus 20 minutes over for joints under 4½ kg./10 lb. For joints over this weight allow 15 to 20 minutes to ½ kg./1 lb. plus 15 minutes over.

BRAISING/POT ROASTING	STEWING/CASSEROLING	SERVING SUGGESTIONS
Suitable for fillet (tenderloin), loin or spare rib (either in form of chops or cubed meat). As for Braising /Pot Roasting Beef above. Allow approx. 1 hour cooking time for fillet; 1½ to 2 hours for loin or spare rib, depending on thickness of meat.	Also suitable for fillet (tenderloin), loin or spare rib cut into cubes and chops. Stew as for Beef above. Allow 1 hour cooking time for fillet, 1½ to 2 hours for cubed loin or spare rib. See also Pork with orange, Pork and apple hot pot and Pork fillet with prunes.	Serve grilled or fried pork with apple rings tossed in butter or with apple sauce. Other accompaniments include green or mixed salads, Sauté or French-fried potatoes. Vegetable dishes such as Ratatouille are also good with pork. Roast pork is traditionally served with Roast potatoes, apple or gooseberry sauce, Sage and onion or apple and prune stuffings and redcurrant jelly. Gravy is made in the roasting tin with cooking liquid from vegetables (see Beef).

BRAISING/POT ROASTING	STEWING/CASSEROLING	SERVING SUGGESTIONS
Suitable cuts are shoulder, neck (best end and middle), breast. These joints are better if boned and rolled (ask your butcher to do this). Knuckle of veal can also be braised. Cook all cuts as for Braising/Pot roasting beef above.	Suitable for shoulder, neck, breast, knuckle. Cut into chunks or pieces with or without bone. Stewing veal, sometimes described as 'pie veal', is a mixture of these cuts without bone. Cook as for Stewing Beef above, allowing 1½ to 2 hours cooking time depending on cut of veal. See also Hungarian veal goulash and Osso Bucco.	Serve grilled or fried veal garnished with lemon quarters, parsley sprigs, Maître d'Hôtel butter and tomato wedges. Roast veal is traditionally served with Roast potatoes, bacon rolls and forcemeat stuffing or balls. Gravy is made in the roasting tin with cooking liquid from vegetables (see Beef).

BAKING	BRAISING	SERVING SUGGESTIONS
Suitable cuts: joints of gammon, collar, hock. Soak in cold water to cover overnight. Drain and cook for calculated boiling time. Drain, remove skin and score fat. Brush with glaze of brown sugar, honey, golden syrup or marmalade to taste and stud with cloves if liked. Bake on a rack in a roasting tin in a fairly hot oven for 15 to 20 minutes. See also Glazed baked gammon. Gammon can also be cooked for half the calculated cooking time then drained, wrapped in foil and baked for remaining time. If liked, gammon cooked in this way can be unwrapped, skinned and glazed for last 30 minutes of cooking time, as above.	Suitable cuts: joints of gammon, collar, hock. Soak in cold water to cover overnight. Drain and cook for half calculated cooking time. Drain and put on bed of fried diced root vegetables, add stock and water or wine with seasonings to taste. Cover with a lid and braise for remaining cooking time – glazing joint before end of cooking time if liked.	Grilled bacon rolls are traditionally used to garnish poultry and game. Grilled or fried gammon steaks, chops and baked joints can be served with fried eggs, pineapple or apple rings. Garnish with watercress, tomato halves and French-fried potatoes. Boiled and baked joints are sliced and served hot with Parsley sauce. They can also be sliced cold and served with salads, pickles, etc., or in sandwiches.

Offal – Preparation and Cooking Methods

PREPARATION	GRILLING

Brains (Calf's, Lamb's, Pig's)

Wash thoroughly under cold running water. Cover with cold water and leave to soak for at least 1 hour. Drain. Blanch in boiling water for 5 minutes and drain. Remove membrane and skin. Put in pan with water to cover and seasonings to taste (salt, peppercorns, bay leaf, onion, carrot, etc.). Bring to boil, then lower heat, cover with a lid and simmer gently for 15 to 20 minutes. Drain and refresh.

Heart (Ox, Calf's, Lamb's)

Wash thoroughly under cold running water. Cut out tubes, gristle, etc. Wash again and pat dry with absorbent kitchen paper.
Ox heart can be tough and is therefore usually sliced thinly before cooking.

Kidney (Ox, Calf's, Lamb's, Pig's)

Remove any fat surrounding kidney. Snip thin skin with scissors or point of sharp knife. Pull off and discard. Cut kidneys in half, cut out central white core and ducts. Wash kidneys under cold running water and pat dry on absorbent kitchen paper. Large ox kidneys tend to be tough and are therefore usually sliced or chopped before cooking.

Grill prepared calf's, lamb's, pig's kidneys. Brush with melted butter or oil and season to taste. Cook under preheated hot grill for a few minutes on each side, turning once during cooking time. Serve immediately. For easy grilling, kidneys can be threaded on oiled skewers. Grilled kidneys are a traditional ingredient of mixed grill.

Liver (Ox, Calf's, Lamb's, Pig's, Chicken)

Wash under cold running water. Pat dry with absorbent kitchen paper. Remove any membrane or gristle. Ox liver is strong in flavour and should be soaked in milk or water or a mixture of both for at least 1 hour. Drain, rinse and pat dry before cooking.

Only suitable for sliced calf's or lamb's liver.
Brush with melted butter or oil and season to taste. Cook under preheated grill until juices run faintly pink, turning once during cooking time. Do not overcook as this will toughen liver. Serve immediately.

Oxtail

Ask the butcher to joint the oxtail. Wash thoroughly under cold running water. Pat dry with absorbent kitchen paper. Cut or chop into 5 cm./2 in. pieces before cooking, and remove excess fat.

Sausages (Beef, Pork)

Cook under preheated moderate grill for 10 to 20 minutes until well browned on all sides, turning frequently during cooking time. Do not prick sausages as this will cause them to burst.

Sweetbreads (Calf's, Lamb's)

Wash thoroughly under cold running water. Cover with cold water and leave to soak for at least 2 hours. Drain. Blanch in boiling water for 5 minutes, drain and refresh. Remove ducts and skin, then slice or leave whole for further cooking.

Tongue (Ox, Calf's, Lamb's)

Salted tongues must be soaked before cooking. Cover with cold water, soak overnight, then drain. Soak fresh tongues for approx. 2 hours. Blanch tongues in boiling water for 5 minutes and drain. Simmer with seasonings as for Pressed tongue, allowing half the cooking time stated for unsalted (fresh) tongue. Serve hot with Parsley sauce or pressed cold and sliced.

Tripe (Ox)

Sold 'dressed' – i.e. cleaned and parboiled. Check with butcher for cooking times.

Prepared brains can be sliced and fried in hot butter or oil or equal quantities of both. Can also be coated in egg and breadcrumbs and shallow-fried or deep-fried in batter.
See also Brains with black butter.

Prepared brains can be simmered in a creamy sauce.

Sliced or whole heart is coated in seasoned flour and fried until browned on all sides before cooking in casserole.

Casserole with onions and other vegetables, stock and seasonings to taste in low oven for at least 3 hours or until heart is tender.
Calf's and lamb's hearts are left whole, filled with herb stuffing (Sage and Onion is traditional), sewn up, browned and cooked in casserole as for ox heart. Allow 1½ to 2 hours cooking time or until tender.

Prepared and seasoned calf's, lamb's or pig's kidneys can be fried in hot butter or oil or equal quantities of both. Fry for about 10 minutes, shaking the pan occasionally. Serve immediately.
See also Devilled kidneys and Kidney toasties.

Sliced or chopped ox kidney is usually casseroled with meat and vegetables as for ox heart above, allowing 1½ to 2 hours cooking time depending on other ingredients. Kidneys are also used in dishes such as Steak and Kidney Pudding and in stuffings for meat and poultry.

Only suitable for sliced calf's or lamb's or chicken liver.
Coat in seasoned flour and fry in hot butter or oil or equal quantities of both. Fry until juices run faintly pink, as for grilled liver.
See also Spiced liver and Liver with orange.

Suitable cooking method for sliced or chopped ox and pig's liver. Casserole as for ox heart above, allowing 1 to 1½ hours cooking time depending on other ingredients. Ox and pig's liver is also used in pâtés and terrines.
See Farmhouse pâté.
Chicken livers are used in pâtés. See Quick chicken liver pâté.

Oxtail pieces are fried in hot dripping, lard or oil before braising. They can be coated with seasoned flour beforehand, if liked.

See Braised oxtail and Oxtail soup.

Cook in hot fat (dripping or lard) as for grilled sausages.

Coat prepared sweetbreads in seasoned flour and egg and breadcrumbs and fry in hot butter or oil or equal quantities of both until golden brown on all sides, shaking pan occasionally during cooking time.
Prepared sweetbreads are also fried before braising.

Prepared sweetbreads are simmered in a creamy sauce, often with wine. See Sweetbreads with mushrooms and cream.

Prepared lamb's tongues are usually casseroled with vegetables, stock and seasonings to taste. Cook in moderate oven for 1 hour or until tender. Serve hot.

Beef

Carbonnade of beef

Cooking meat in wine or beer, as in this beef stew, adds a succulent flavour.

METRIC
Vegetable oil for frying
¾–1 kg. chuck steak,
*   trimmed of fat and cut into*
*   large chunks*
Flour for coating
Salt and freshly ground
*   black pepper*
1 large onion, peeled and
*   finely chopped*
4 celery stalks, scrubbed and
*   chopped*
2 large carrots, peeled and
*   sliced*
300 ml. Mackeson or sweet
*   stout*
1 × 5 ml. spoon vinegar
1 bouquet garni
Freshly chopped parsley to
*   finish*

IMPERIAL
Vegetable oil for frying
1½–2 lb. chuck steak,
*   trimmed of fat and cut into*
*   large chunks*
Flour for coating
Salt and freshly ground
*   black pepper*
1 large onion, peeled and
*   finely chopped*
4 celery stalks, scrubbed and
*   chopped*
2 large carrots, peeled and
*   sliced*
½ pint Mackeson or sweet
*   stout*
1 teaspoon vinegar
1 bouquet garni
Freshly chopped parsley to
*   finish*

Heat 2 spoons of oil in a flameproof casserole. Coat the steak in flour seasoned with salt and pepper and put in the casserole. Brown quickly on all sides over high heat. Remove the meat from the casserole with a slotted spoon and set aside. Add the vegetables to the casserole and cook for 5 minutes or until lightly coloured. Return the meat to the casserole, stir in the Mackeson or sweet stout, vinegar and bouquet garni. Cover the casserole and transfer to a warm oven (160°C/325°F or Gas Mark 3). Cook for 2 to 2½ hours or until the meat is tender. Stir a little water into the casserole if it becomes dry during the cooking time.

Discard the bouquet garni and adjust the seasoning. Sprinkle with chopped parsley and serve with creamed potatoes and a seasonal green vegetable.

Boeuf bourguignon

Boeuf bourguignon is a delicious combination of tender beef, mushrooms and baby onions in a rich red wine sauce.

METRIC
Beef dripping or lard for frying
¾–1 kg. chuck steak, trimmed of fat and cut into large chunks
100 g. unsmoked streaky bacon, rinds removed and diced
1 × 15 ml. spoon flour
Salt and freshly ground black pepper
300 ml. red wine (Burgundy)
1 bouquet garni

To finish:
1 × 15 ml. spoon butter
¼ kg. small pickling onions, peeled
¼ kg. button mushrooms, cleaned
1 wineglass red wine
1 × 5 ml. spoon brown sugar

IMPERIAL
Beef dripping or lard for frying
1½–2 lb. chuck steak, trimmed of fat and cut into large chunks
4 oz. unsmoked streaky bacon, rinds removed and diced
1 tablespoon flour
Salt and freshly ground black pepper
½ pint red wine (Burgundy)
1 bouquet garni

To finish:
1 tablespoon butter
½ lb. small pickling onions, peeled
½ lb. button mushrooms, cleaned
1 wineglass red wine
1 teaspoon brown sugar

Melt a knob of dripping or lard in a flameproof casserole. Put in the beef and brown quickly on all sides over high heat. Remove from the casserole with a slotted spoon and set aside.

Add the diced bacon to the casserole and fry for 2 to 3 minutes or until crisp. Stir in the flour, add salt and pepper to taste and return the meat to the casserole.

Heat the wine in a small pan. Set it alight and pour over the meat in the casserole. Add the bouquet garni, cover the casserole and transfer to a warm oven (160°C/325°F or Gas Mark 3). Cook for 2 hours. Stir a little water into the casserole if it becomes dry during the cooking time.

Melt the butter in a small pan. Add the onions and mushrooms and fry gently for 2 to 3 minutes. Pour over the wine, stir in the sugar and bring just to the boil. Stir into the casserole and continue cooking for 30 minutes or until the meat and onions are tender. Discard the bouquet garni and adjust the seasoning. Serve with Gratin Dauphinois and a green salad.

Carbonnade of beef; Boeuf bourguignon

Boeuf en daube

This is an excellent method of cooking brisket or topside of beef. Long, slow braising in a wine-based sauce ensures that the meat becomes both tender and succulent.

METRIC	IMPERIAL
Beef dripping or lard for frying	Beef dripping or lard for frying
1–1 ¼ kg. piece of brisket or topside of beef, trimmed of fat	2–2 ½ lb. piece of brisket or topside of beef, trimmed of fat
Salt and freshly ground black pepper	Salt and freshly ground black pepper
1 large onion, peeled and finely chopped	1 large onion, peeled and finely chopped
1 garlic clove, crushed	1 garlic clove, crushed
1 × 396 g. can tomatoes	1 × 14 oz. can tomatoes
100 g. green or black olives, stoned	4 oz. green or black olives, stoned
150 ml. dry white wine	¼ pint dry white wine
1 × 5 ml. spoon freshly chopped thyme or 1 × 2.5 ml. spoon dried thyme	1 teaspoon freshly chopped thyme or ½ teaspoon dried thyme

Boeuf en daube

Melt a knob of dripping or lard in a flameproof casserole. Season the beef well with salt and pepper and put in the casserole. Brown quickly on all sides over high heat. Remove the meat from the casserole and set aside.

Add the onion and garlic to the casserole. Lower the heat and fry gently for 2 to 3 minutes or until golden. Return the meat to the casserole and add the tomatoes, olives, white wine and thyme. Cover the casserole and transfer to a moderate oven (180°C/350°F or Gas Mark 4). Cook for 2 to 2½ hours or until the meat is very tender. Stir a little water into the casserole if it becomes dry during cooking.

Transfer the meat to a hot serving platter and carve into slices. Adjust the seasoning of the sauce and serve separately in a gravy boat. Serve with creamed potatoes and buttered courgettes or French beans.

Tournedos en croûte

Tournedos en croûte

A version of beef Wellington, these are individual steaks coated in pâté and cooked 'en croûte' (in pastry cases). They are splendid for a dinner party as they are very simple and quick to make, yet very special.

METRIC	IMPERIAL
Butter for frying	Butter for frying
4 fillet steaks (tournedos)	4 fillet steaks (tournedos)
Salt and freshly ground black pepper	Salt and freshly ground black pepper
100 g. liver pâté	4 oz. liver pâté
2 × 15 ml. spoons brandy or dry sherry	2 tablespoons brandy or dry sherry
1 × 212 g. packet frozen puff pastry, thawed	1 × 7½ oz. packet frozen puff pastry, thawed
1 egg, beaten to glaze	1 egg, beaten to glaze

Melt a knob of butter in a large frying pan and heat until foaming. Add the steaks to the pan and sauté for about 1 minute on each side. Remove from the pan, season to taste and set aside to cool.

Soften the liver pâté with the brandy or sherry and spread over the steaks.

Roll out the dough into four squares large enough to encase the steaks. Wrap the squares around the steaks, sealing the edges with a little water. Use the pastry trimmings to decorate the tops of the parcels with leaves, flowers, etc. Brush with beaten egg.

Place on a baking sheet and put into a fairly hot oven (200°C/400°F or Gas Mark 6). Bake for 15 to 20 minutes or until the pastry is golden. Serve immediately with a green salad or a vegetable dish such as ratatouille.

Steak and kidney pudding

Traditional British fare, steak and kidney encased in a suet crust pastry is perfect for a family supper meal on a cold winter's night. Correctly, the pudding basin should be served with a white napkin wrapped around it to keep it hot.

METRIC
For the pastry:
225 g. self-raising flour
1 × 5 ml. spoon salt
100 g. shredded beef suet
Scant 150 ml. water

For the filling:
*½ kg. shin of beef or chuck
steak, trimmed of fat and
cut into small cubes*
*100 g. ox kidney, cleaned
and chopped*
Flour for coating
*Salt and freshly ground
black pepper*
*1 × 5 ml. spoon dried mixed
herbs*
*2 × 5 ml. spoons
Worcestershire sauce*
*2 × 15 ml. spoons sherry
(optional)*

IMPERIAL
For the pastry:
½ lb. self-raising flour
1 teaspoon salt
4 oz. shredded beef suet
Scant ¼ pint water

For the filling:
*1 lb. shin of beef or chuck
steak, trimmed of fat and
cut into small cubes*
*4 oz. ox kidney, cleaned and
chopped*
Flour for coating
*Salt and freshly ground
black pepper*
*1 teaspoon dried mixed
herbs*
*2 teaspoons Worcestershire
sauce*
*2 tablespoons sherry
(optional)*

To make the pastry: sift the flour and salt into a mixing bowl. Stir in the shredded suet. Mix in the water gradually to form a smooth elastic dough that leaves the sides of the mixing bowl.

Turn out onto a floured board and knead lightly. Roll into the shape of a round large enough to line the inside of a 900 ml./1½ pint pudding basin. Cut out one-quarter of the round for the lid and reserve.

Grease the inside of the basin and fit in the pastry lining, joining the edges in the basin with water. To make the filling, coat the steak and kidney in flour, well seasoned with salt and pepper. Mix in the herbs and Worcestershire sauce.

Put the filling in the basin and pour in enough water to come halfway up the sides, adding the sherry if using. Shape the reserved quarter of pastry into a lid and place on top of the basin, tucking the edges in and sealing with a little water. Cover the top of pudding with greased greaseproof paper or foil, pleated in the centre to allow for expansion, and tie a string handle around the rim.

Place the basin in the top of a steamer or double boiler, or in a large pan of gently bubbling water, and steam for at least 3 hours, topping up the water level from time to time during cooking. Remove the basin carefully from the pan. Remove the greaseproof or foil and serve the pudding straight from the basin with boiled mashed potatoes and peas.

Steak and kidney pudding

Sag gosht

Sag gosht

This dry beef and spinach curry is fairly mild, though spicy. Most authentic Indian curries are mild; it is in the blend of spices that the true flavour is achieved. Hot curries are made simply by increasing the amount of chillies or chilli powder used.

METRIC	IMPERIAL
Butter and vegetable oil for frying	*Butter and vegetable oil for frying*
2 medium-sized onions, peeled and finely chopped	*2 medium-sized onions, peeled and finely chopped*
1 garlic clove, crushed with 1 × 5 ml. spoon salt	*1 garlic clove, crushed with 1 teaspoon salt*
1 small piece fresh root ginger, very finely chopped, or 1 × 5 ml. spoon ground ginger	*1 small piece fresh root ginger, very finely chopped, or 1 teaspoon ground ginger*
1 × 5 ml. spoon turmeric	*1 teaspoon turmeric*
1 × 2.5 ml. spoon chilli powder	*½ teaspoon chilli powder*
1 × 15 ml. spoon ground coriander seed	*1 tablespoon ground coriander seed*
1 × 5 ml. spoon ground mustard seeds	*1 teaspoon ground mustard seeds*
¾–1 kg. chuck steak, trimmed of fat and diced	*1½–2 lb. chuck steak, trimmed of fat and diced*
1 × 226 g. packet frozen whole leaf spinach, thawed and dried by heating gently in a saucepan over low heat	*1 × 8 oz. packet frozen whole leaf spinach, thawed and dried by heating gently in a saucepan over low heat*
2 × 141 g. cartons natural unsweetened yogurt	*2 × 5 oz. cartons natural unsweetened yogurt*

Heat a knob of butter and a spoon of oil together in a flameproof casserole. Add the onions, garlic and spices and fry gently for 5 minutes. Add the meat and fry, stirring, until brown on all sides. Add the spinach, then gradually stir in one carton of the yogurt.

Cover the casserole and transfer to a warm oven (160°C/325°F or Gas Mark 3). Cook for 2 to 2½ hours or until the meat is tender. If the curry becomes too dry during the cooking time, add a little water. Stir in the remaining yogurt just before serving. Serve with plain boiled rice, mango chutney and parathas.

Beef Stroganoff

This is a very rich dish, and quite expensive, but perfectly delicious. Rump steak can be substituted for the fillet.

METRIC	IMPERIAL
Butter for frying	*Butter for frying*
1 medium-sized onion, finely chopped	*1 medium-sized onion, finely chopped*
¼ kg. button mushrooms, cleaned and sliced	*½ lb. button mushrooms, cleaned and sliced*
¾ kg. fillet steak, cut into thin strips	*1½ lb. fillet steak, cut into thin strips*
Salt and freshly ground black pepper	*Salt and freshly ground black pepper*
1 × 5 ml. spoon Dijon-style mustard	*1 teaspoon Dijon-style mustard*

To finish:

2 × 15 ml. spoons brandy	*2 tablespoons brandy*
1 × 141 g. carton soured cream	*1 × 5 oz. carton soured cream*
Freshly chopped parsley	*Freshly chopped parsley*

Melt a knob of butter in a large frying pan. Add the onion and fry for 5 minutes or until golden. Add the mushrooms and fry for a further 2 minutes.

Add the steak to the pan, season well with salt and pepper and stir in the mustard. Sauté briskly for 5 minutes or until the juices run pink.

Stir in the brandy and soured cream and heat through gently. Do not allow to boil or the cream will curdle. Adjust seasoning, transfer to a hot serving platter and sprinkle with parsley. Serve immediately with buttered noodles and a green salad.

Beef stroganoff

Lamb

Navarin de mouton

Long, slow cooking ensures that the stewing lamb or chump chops become very tender in this lamb stew.

METRIC
Dripping or lard for frying
1 large onion, peeled and chopped
1 garlic clove, crushed with 1 × 2.5 ml. spoon salt
1–1¼ kg. stewing lamb or 4 chump chops, trimmed of fat
Flour for coating
Freshly ground black pepper
1 × 396 g. can tomatoes
1 × 15 ml. spoon tomato purée
2 large carrots, peeled and sliced
2 turnips or approx. ¼ kg. swede, peeled and chopped
1 bouquet garni
1 × 5 ml. spoon sugar
Freshly chopped parsley to finish

IMPERIAL
Dripping or lard for frying
1 large onion, peeled and chopped
1 garlic clove, crushed with ½ teaspoon salt
2–2½ lb. stewing lamb or 4 chump chops, trimmed of fat
Flour for coating
Freshly ground black pepper
1 × 14 oz. can tomatoes
1 tablespoon tomato purée
2 large carrots, peeled and sliced
2 turnips or approx. ½ lb. swede, peeled and chopped
1 bouquet garni
1 teaspoon sugar
Freshly chopped parsley to finish

Melt a knob of dripping or lard in a flameproof casserole. Add the onion and garlic and fry gently for 5 minutes or until golden.

Coat the lamb in flour seasoned with black pepper. Add to the casserole and brown quickly on all sides. Stir in the tomatoes and tomato purée, then add the remaining ingredients except the parsley. Bring just to the boil, then cover with a lid and transfer to a warm oven (160°C/325°F or Gas Mark 3). Cook for 1½ to 2 hours depending on the cut of lamb used (stewing lamb will take longer) or until the meat is tender and almost falling off the bones. Taste for seasoning, discard the bouquet garni and sprinkle with chopped parsley before serving. Serve with creamed or jacket baked potatoes with soured cream and snipped chives.

Navarin de mouton

Shish kebab

Shish kebab

Kebabs are very popular in the Middle East and this is a Greek recipe using lamb marinated in yogurt. The best way to cook kebabs is on a charcoal barbecue, but an ordinary grill can be used satisfactorily.

METRIC
¾–1 kg. lean lamb (from the fillet end of the leg), cut into small cubes
1 × 141 g. carton natural unsweetened yogurt
Juice of 1 lemon
1 × 15 ml. spoon olive oil
Salt and freshly ground black pepper
4 sprigs of rosemary or marjoram
4 lemon wedges

For the salad:
1 lettuce, shredded

IMPERIAL
1½–2 lb. lean lamb (from the fillet end of the leg), cut into small cubes
1 × 5 oz. carton natural unsweetened yogurt
Juice of 1 lemon
1 tablespoon olive oil
Salt and freshly ground black pepper
4 sprigs of rosemary or marjoram
4 lemon wedges

For the salad:
1 lettuce, shredded

¼ small white cabbage, shredded
½ small onion, peeled and sliced
12 black olives, stoned
6 × 15 ml. spoons olive oil
2 × 15 ml. spoons lemon juice

¼ small white cabbage, shredded
½ small onion, peeled and sliced
12 black olives, stoned
6 tablespoons olive oil
2 tablespoons lemon juice

Put the lamb in a large mixing bowl. Add the yogurt, lemon juice and olive oil and season well. Stir to mix, then chill in the refrigerator for several hours, preferably overnight. Stir from time to time to ensure the lamb is evenly coated in the marinade.

Thread the lamb onto four greased skewers. Prepare the charcoal barbecue and, when hot, lay the rosemary or marjoram sprigs on the grid. (If using a cooker grill, lay the herbs on the grill pan.) Barbecue or grill the kebabs, according to taste, turning and basting occasionally with any marinade left in the mixing bowl.

Combine the salad ingredients in a mixing bowl and season well to taste. Arrange on a serving platter. Place the hot cooked kebabs over the bed of salad and serve immediately with lemon wedges.

Stuffed breast of lamb

Breast of lamb tends to be one of the fattier joints, so be careful to choose the leanest available. Most butchers will bone the breast for you to save you time, usually at no extra cost.

METRIC	IMPERIAL
1 kg. boned breast of lamb	2½ lb. boned breast of lamb
Salt and freshly ground black pepper	Salt and freshly ground black pepper

For the stuffing:

1 × 50 g. can anchovy fillets, drained and soaked in milk for 30 minutes	1 × 2 oz. can anchovy fillets, drained and soaked in milk for 30 minutes
75 g. fresh white breadcrumbs	3 oz. fresh white breadcrumbs
1 small onion, peeled and finely chopped	1 small onion, peeled and finely chopped
100 g. mushrooms, cleaned and finely chopped	4 oz. mushrooms, cleaned and finely chopped
1 × 15 ml. spoon freshly chopped parsley	1 tablespoon freshly chopped parsley
½ egg, beaten	½ egg, beaten

Lay the breast of lamb flat on a board and trim off any excess fat. Sprinkle the meat liberally with salt and pepper.

To prepare the stuffing, drain the anchovies and chop finely. Add to the remaining stuffing ingredients in a mixing bowl, using the egg to bind the mixture. Season to taste. Spread the stuffing along the breast. Roll up carefully, tie with string and secure with skewers if necessary.

Put on a rack in a roasting pan, sprinkle with a little salt and pepper and roast in a fairly hot oven (190°C/375°F or Gas Mark 5) for 1½ to 2 hours or until the meat is tender when pierced with a skewer and the outside skin is crisp.

Transfer to a hot serving platter, remove the strings, and skewers (if used), and carve into slices. Serve with roast potatoes, herbed carrots and thick homemade gravy.

Stuffed breast of lamb

Lancashire hotpot

Lancashire hotpot

Traditional recipes for Lancashire hotpot included oysters and sometimes mushrooms, but that was in the days when these two ingredients were commonplace and therefore relatively cheap. Today, this dish makes a simple family meal with lamb chops and potatoes as the main ingredients.

METRIC	IMPERIAL
1 kg. potatoes, peeled and sliced into rings	2 lb. potatoes, peeled and sliced into rings
Salt and freshly ground black pepper	Salt and freshly ground black pepper
Beef dripping or lard for frying	Beef dripping or lard for frying
1 kg. middle neck lamb chops	2 lb. middle neck lamb chops
2 lamb's kidneys, cleaned and chopped	2 lamb's kidneys, cleaned and chopped
1 large onion, peeled and finely chopped	1 large onion, peeled and finely chopped
1 × 2.5 ml. spoon dried thyme	½ teaspoon dried thyme
600 ml. hot beef stock	1 pint hot beef stock

Put half the potato rings in a layer on the bottom of a deep ovenproof casserole. Season well with salt and pepper.

Melt a knob of dripping or lard in a frying pan. Add the chops and kidneys and brown quickly on all sides. Remove from the pan with a slotted spoon. Lay the chops and kidneys on top of the potatoes, add the onion and sprinkle with the thyme. Pour in the hot stock. Put the remaining potatoes in a layer on top. Season again, cover with a lid and place in a moderate oven (180°C/350°F or Gas Mark 4). Cook for 2 hours, then remove the lid and return to the oven to brown the top layer of potatoes for 15 to 20 minutes. Serve immediately, straight from the casserole, with a seasonal green vegetable or buttered carrots.

Noisettes of lamb with Pernod

English lamb, simmered gently in a sauce of courgettes and tomatoes with a hint of Pernod, makes a superbly-flavoured summer meal. Serve with boiled rice and a tossed green salad.

METRIC	IMPERIAL
Butter for frying	Butter for frying
1 medium-sized onion, peeled and finely chopped	1 medium-sized onion, peeled and finely chopped
1 garlic clove, crushed with 1 × 2.5 ml. spoon salt	1 garlic clove, crushed with ½ teaspoon salt
4–6 noisettes of lamb, or loin or chump chops	4–6 noisettes of lamb, or loin or chump chops
Flour for coating	Flour for coating
2 × 15 ml. spoons tomato purée	2 tablespoons tomato purée
4 × 15 ml. spoons Pernod	4 tablespoons Pernod
4 tomatoes, skinned, seeded and chopped	4 tomatoes, skinned, seeded and chopped
¼ kg. courgettes, sliced	½ lb. courgettes, sliced
1 × 5 ml. spoon freshly chopped rosemary or 1 × 2.5 ml. spoon dried rosemary	1 teaspoon freshly chopped rosemary or ½ teaspoon dried rosemary
Freshly ground black pepper	Freshly ground black pepper

Melt a knob of butter in a large frying pan. Add the onion and garlic and fry until golden. Coat the lamb lightly in flour, add to the pan and brown quickly on both sides. Stir in the tomato purée and Pernod, then add the tomatoes, courgettes and enough water to cover the meat. Sprinkle in the rosemary, and pepper to taste. Bring to the boil, stirring constantly, then lower the heat, cover and simmer gently for about 45 minutes or until the lamb and courgettes are tender, stirring occasionally and turning the meat once during the cooking time. If the sauce becomes dry during the cooking, add a little more water.

Taste for seasoning, transfer to a hot serving platter and serve immediately.

French roast leg of lamb

Lamb roasted in the French way should be tender, pink and juicy, served with a flavoursome gravy made with the pan juices.

METRIC	IMPERIAL
1½–2 kg. leg of lamb	3–4 lb. leg of lamb
1 garlic clove, cut into slivers (optional)	1 garlic clove, cut into slivers (optional)
25 g. dripping or lard, melted	1 oz. dripping or lard, melted
Salt and freshly ground black pepper	Salt and freshly ground black pepper
1 carrot, peeled and sliced	1 carrot, peeled and sliced
1 onion, peeled and quartered	1 onion, peeled and quartered
300–400 ml. beef stock	½–¾ pint beef stock
1 × 15 ml. spoon flour (optional)	1 tablespoon flour (optional)
Watercress to garnish	Watercress to garnish

Make a few incisions in the lamb and insert the garlic slivers if using. Brush the joint with the dripping or lard and sprinkle liberally with salt and pepper.

Put the joint on a rack in a roasting pan and roast on the top shelf of a very hot oven (230°C/450°F or Gas Mark 8) for 15 to 20 minutes to brown the meat, basting occasionally.

Add the carrot and onion to the pan, under the rack, and transfer to the middle shelf of the oven. Lower the heat to moderate (180°C/350°F or Gas Mark 4) and continue roasting for about 1 – 1½ hours or until the juices run rosy pink when the meat is pierced with a skewer.

Remove the meat from the pan and place on a hot serving platter to 'rest' before carving. Drain off the excess fat from the pan and mash the vegetables with a fork. Pour in the beef stock to taste and bring to the boil over high heat, stirring constantly to mix all the meat juices into the gravy. If a thicker gravy is liked, the optional 1 × 15 ml. spoon/1 tablespoon flour can be stirred into the pan and browned before the stock is added. Season the gravy to taste. Carve the lamb into slices, garnish the platter with watercress sprigs and serve the gravy separately in a gravy boat. **Serves 4 to 6.**

Crown roast of lamb

This is an impressive-looking dish for a dinner party. Any stuffing, such as the one suggested here, can be used for the centre or it can be filled with vegetables after roasting. Most butchers will prepare a crown roast and also supply the cutlet frills for the ends of the chops.

METRIC	IMPERIAL
Butter for frying	Butter for frying
1 small onion, peeled and finely chopped	1 small onion, peeled and finely chopped
2 celery stalks, scrubbed and finely chopped	2 celery stalks, scrubbed and finely chopped
175 g. fresh white breadcrumbs	6 oz. fresh white breadcrumbs
2 × 15 ml. spoons freshly chopped mint	2 tablespoons freshly chopped mint
Juice of ½ lemon	Juice of ½ lemon
Salt and freshly ground black pepper	Salt and freshly ground black pepper
1 egg, beaten	1 egg, beaten
1 crown roast of lamb (2 best ends of neck with 4–6 chops each)	1 crown roast of lamb (2 best ends of neck with 4–6 chops each)

Melt a knob of butter in a small pan. Add the onion and celery and fry gently for 5 minutes or until golden. Transfer to a mixing bowl and stir in the breadcrumbs, mint, lemon juice and seasoning, using the egg to bind the mixture.

Weigh the crown roast to calculate the cooking time and put it in a roasting pan. Put the stuffing into the centre of the crown roast. Wrap the ends of the bones with foil and cover the stuffing. Roast in a moderate oven (180°C/350°F or Gas Mark 4) allowing 25 minutes to the ½ kg./1 lb. and 25 minutes over, or until the meat at the base of the chops is tender when pierced with a skewer.

When cooked, remove from the roasting pan, discard the foil and decorate the chop ends with cutlet frills. Transfer to a hot serving platter and serve immediately with spring vegetables such as baby carrots, minted peas and parsleyed new potatoes. **Serves 4 to 6.**

Noisettes of lamb with pernod; Crown roast of lamb; French roast leg of lamb

Shoulder of lamb à la Turque

Shoulder of lamb à la Turque

This economical dish is both tasty and substantial. Serve with roast potatoes and a seasonal green vegetable.

METRIC
1½ kg. shoulder of lamb, boned
1 garlic clove, cut into slivers (optional)
25 g. dripping or lard, melted
Salt and freshly ground black pepper
300 ml. lamb stock, made from the shoulder bones, or beef stock
1 ×15 ml. spoon flour (optional)

For the stuffing:
Butter for frying
1 small onion, peeled and finely chopped
75 g. lamb's liver, chopped
50 g. raisins
75 g. long-grain rice, cooked
1 × 5 ml. spoon freshly chopped rosemary or 1 × 2.5 ml. spoon dried rosemary
½ egg, beaten

IMPERIAL
3 lb. shoulder of lamb, boned
1 garlic clove, cut into slivers (optional)
1 oz. dripping or lard, melted
Salt and freshly ground black pepper
½ pint lamb stock, made from the shoulder bones, or beef stock
1 tablespoon flour (optional)

For the stuffing:
Butter for frying
1 small onion, peeled and finely chopped
3 oz. lamb's liver, chopped
2 oz. raisins
3 oz. long-grain rice, cooked
1 teaspoon freshly chopped rosemary or ½ teaspoon dried rosemary
½ egg, beaten

To garnish:
8 prunes, soaked overnight, drained and stoned
8 × 5 ml. spoons chutney or sweet pickle

To garnish:
8 prunes, soaked overnight, drained and stoned
8 teaspoons chutney or sweet pickle

To prepare the stuffing, melt a knob of butter in a small pan. Add the onion and fry for 5 minutes or until golden. Add the chopped liver and fry briskly until the juices run pink. Remove from the heat and stir in the remaining stuffing ingredients, binding with the egg. Season to taste.

Put the lamb on a board and push the stuffing into the cavity. Roll up the meat and tie securely with string, using skewers if necessary. If using garlic, make incisions in the meat with a sharp knife and insert the garlic slivers. Brush the joint with dripping or lard and sprinkle liberally with salt and pepper.

Put the joint on a rack in a roasting pan and roast on the top shelf of a very hot oven (230°C/450°F or Gas Mark 8) for 15 to 20 minutes to brown the meat, basting occasionally. Transfer the tin to the middle shelf of the oven and lower the heat to moderate (180°C/350°F or Gas Mark 4). Roast for 1 to 1½ hours or until the juices run rosy pink when the meat is pierced with a skewer.

Remove the meat from the pan and place it on a hot serving platter to 'rest'. Drain off the excess fat from the roasting pan. Pour in the lamb or beef stock and bring to the boil over high heat, stirring constantly. If a thicker gravy is liked, 1 × 15 ml. spoon/1 tablespoon flour can be stirred into the pan and browned before the stock is added. Season to taste.

Carve the lamb into slices and arrange in the centre of the serving platter. Garnish the edge of the platter with the prunes stuffed with chutney or pickle. Serve the gravy separately in a gravy boat. **Serves 4 to 6.**

Pork

Hot spiced pork

An unusual dish to cook on a charcoal barbecue, this marinated pork can also be cooked under the grill, though of course the flavour will not be quite so good. Dishes of natural unsweetened yogurt or Cucumber Raita will be welcome to accompany the pork as it is rather hot!

METRIC	IMPERIAL
4 large pork spare rib chops, trimmed or 2 whole pork fillets (about 1 kg.), trimmed and cut in half	4 large pork spare rib chops, trimmed, or 2 whole pork fillets (about 2 lb.), trimmed and cut in half
For the marinade:	**For the marinade:**
2 × 15 ml. spoons vegetable oil	2 tablespoons vegetable oil
1 garlic clove, crushed with 1 × 5 ml. spoon salt	1 garlic clove, crushed with 1 teaspoon salt
1–2 × 15 ml. spoons chilli sauce, according to taste	1–2 tablespoons chilli sauce, according to taste
2 × 15 ml. spoons soya sauce	2 tablespoons soya sauce
1 × 15 ml. spoon Worcestershire sauce	1 tablespoon Worcestershire sauce
1 × 15 ml. spoon soft brown sugar	1 tablespoon soft brown sugar
1 × 15 ml. spoon tomato purée	1 tablespoon tomato purée
1 × 15 ml. spoon wine vinegar	1 tablespoon wine vinegar
1 × 5 ml. spoon ground ginger	1 teaspoon ground ginger
Freshly ground black pepper	Freshly ground black pepper

Hot spiced pork; Pork and apple hotpot

To prepare the marinade: put all the ingredients in a mixing bowl with pepper to taste and stir well.

Put the pork in the marinade and leave for at least 2 hours, preferably overnight. Stir the mixture from time to time to ensure the marinade coats the pork.

When the barbecue charcoal or grill is hot, remove the pork from the marinade. If using pork fillet it can be cut into cubes and threaded onto four greased skewers. Lay chops or halved fillets on the barbecue or grill rack. Cook according to taste, turning the pork and basting with the marinade from time to time until all the marinade is used up. Serve immediately with baked jacket potatoes and ratatouille or buttered courgettes.

Pork and apple hotpot

Substantial and nourishing, Pork and apple hotpot would make a good family supper dish. Serve it straight from the casserole with a seasonal green vegetable.

METRIC	IMPERIAL
¾ kg. lean pork, cut into cubes	1½ lb. lean pork, cut into cubes
1 × 5 ml. spoon dry English mustard	1 teaspoon dry English mustard
1 × 5 ml. spoon freshly chopped sage or 1 × 2.5 ml. spoon dried sage	1 teaspoon freshly chopped sage or ½ teaspoon dried sage
Salt and freshly ground black pepper	Salt and freshly ground black pepper
1 large onion, peeled and finely chopped	1 large onion, peeled and finely chopped
2 large cooking apples, peeled, cored and sliced, and soaked in water mixed with juice of ½ lemon	2 large cooking apples, peeled, cored and sliced, and soaked in water mixed with juice of ½ lemon
4 × 15 ml. spoons cider or water	4 tablespoons cider or water
4 large potatoes, boiled and mashed with 25 g. butter, 2 × 15 ml. spoons milk and 1 beaten egg	4 large potatoes, boiled and mashed with 1 oz. butter, 2 tablespoons milk and 1 beaten egg
25 g. butter	1 oz. butter

Put the pork in a large casserole and mix in the mustard, sage, and salt and pepper to taste. Add the onion and drained apple slices and stir well to mix.

Pour over the cider or water, cover the casserole and bake in a moderate oven (180°C/350°F or Gas Mark 4) for 1½ to 2 hours, depending on the cut of pork, or until the meat is very tender.

Twenty minutes before the end of cooking time, remove the lid, taste for seasoning and spread the mashed potatoes over the top of the casserole. Dot with butter, return to the oven and cook until golden.

Sweet and sour spare ribs

An adaptation of a Chinese recipe, Sweet and sour spare ribs is an unusual, spicy way to serve pork. If available, use the American cut of spare rib. Every scrap of meat should be nibbled off the bones which can be dipped in the sauce and picked up in the fingers.

METRIC
Approx. 2 kg. American pork spare ribs or 4 English pork spare rib chops
Salt
2 × 15 ml. spoons vegetable oil

IMPERIAL
Approx. 4 lb. American pork spare ribs or 4 English pork spare rib chops
Salt
2 tablespoons vegetable oil

For the sauce:
Vegetable oil for frying
1 large onion, peeled and finely chopped
1 garlic clove, crushed with 1 × 2.5 ml. spoon salt
1 × 15 ml. spoon tomato purée
2 × 15 ml. spoons soya sauce
1 × 15 ml. spoon soft brown sugar
1 × 15 ml. spoon clear honey
Freshly ground black pepper
300 ml. chicken stock
Juice of ½ lemon

For the sauce:
Vegetable oil for frying
1 large onion, peeled and finely chopped
1 garlic clove, crushed with ½ teaspoon salt
1 tablespoon tomato purée
2 tablespoons soya sauce
1 tablespoon soft brown sugar
1 tablespoon clear honey
Freshly ground black pepper
½ pint chicken stock
Juice of ½ lemon

To finish:
100 g. mixed dried fruit (prunes, apricots, apples), soaked overnight and drained

To finish:
4 oz. mixed dried fruit (prunes, apricots, apples), soaked overnight and drained

Sprinkle the pork with salt to taste and place in a roasting pan. Pour over the oil and roast in a fairly hot oven (190°C/375°F or Gas Mark 5) for 30 minutes. Remove from the oven and, if using American spare ribs, cut into individual ribs with a very sharp knife. Cut English spare rib chops into bite-sized pieces.

To prepare the sauce, heat a spoon of oil in a small pan. Add the onion and garlic and fry gently for 5 minutes or until golden. Remove from the heat. Stir in the remaining sauce ingredients, adding pepper to taste. Mix well.

Return the meat to the roasting pan, pour over the sauce and continue to roast, covered, for a further 1 to 1½ hours, or until the meat is tender. Twenty minutes before the end of cooking time, remove the lid and add the mixed fruit. When the meat is tender, taste for seasoning. Transfer to a hot serving platter and serve immediately with plain boiled rice.

Pork with orange

This is best served with plain boiled rice or creamed potatoes to offset the richness of the sauce. A green salad tossed in vinaigrette dressing or a green vegetable could complete the accompaniments.

METRIC
4 lean pork chops
Butter for frying
1 large onion, peeled and finely chopped
50 g. flour
1 chicken stock cube, crumbled
350 ml. fresh or diluted frozen orange juice mixed with 350 ml. water
Salt and freshly ground black pepper
1 × 2.5 ml. spoon ground mixed spice
Dash of Tabasco sauce

IMPERIAL
4 lean pork chops
Butter for frying
1 large onion, peeled and finely chopped
2 oz. flour
1 chicken stock cube, crumbled
12 fl. oz. fresh or diluted frozen orange juice mixed with 12 fl. oz. water
Salt and freshly ground black pepper
½ teaspoon ground mixed spice
Dash of Tabasco sauce

To garnish:
1 dessert apple, peeled, cored and sliced into rings
1 large orange, peeled, pith and pips removed and sliced into rings
Watercress sprigs

To garnish:
1 dessert apple, peeled, cored and sliced into rings
1 large orange, peeled, pith and pips removed and sliced into rings
Watercress sprigs

Trim any excess fat off the pork. Melt a knob of butter in a deep flameproof casserole and add the pork. Brown quickly on both sides, then remove from the casserole. Add the onion and reduce the heat. Cook the onion gently for 5 minutes or until it is golden. Stir in the flour and stock cube and cook gently for 1 minute, stirring constantly.

Remove the pot from the heat and gradually stir in the orange juice mixture. Return to the heat and bring to the boil, stirring. Add salt and pepper to taste with the spice and Tabasco sauce and return the pork to the casserole. Spoon the sauce over so the pork is completely covered.

Cook, uncovered, in a moderate oven (180°C/350°F or Gas Mark 4) for about 1 hour or until the pork is tender and the sauce has reduced. If the sauce becomes too thick before the meat is cooked, stir in more diluted orange juice or water.

Fifteen minutes before the end of cooking time, add the apple and orange rings to the casserole and spoon the sauce over them.

Transfer the pork and fruit rings to a hot serving platter. Stir the sauce well, adjust seasoning, and pour over the pork. Garnish with sprigs of watercress.

Sweet and sour spare ribs; Pork with orange

83

Pork Alsacienne

Any good medium or dry white wine will be suitable for this pork dish.

METRIC	IMPERIAL
approx. 1-1¼ kg. piece boneless pork (loin, shoulder, leg)	approx. 2-2½ lb. piece boneless pork (loin, shoulder, leg)
2 × 15 ml. spoons lard	2 tablespoons lard
Salt	Salt
1 small white cabbage (approx. ½ kg.), shredded	1 small white cabbage (approx. 1 lb.), shredded
Butter for frying	Butter for frying
1 small onion, peeled and finely chopped	1 small onion, peeled and finely chopped
2 cooking apples, peeled, cored and sliced, and soaked in water to cover with juice of ½ lemon	2 cooking apples, peeled, cored and sliced, and soaked in water to cover with juice of ½ lemon
300 ml. white wine	½ pint white wine
1 × 5 ml. spoon caraway seeds	1 teaspoon caraway seeds
Freshly ground black pepper	Freshly ground black pepper
Freshly chopped parsley to finish	Freshly chopped parsley to finish

Score the fat on the pork. Put in a roasting pan, rub with the lard and sprinkle with salt. Roast in a fairly hot oven (200°C/400°F or Gas Mark 6) for 1 hour.

Meanwhile, parboil the cabbage for 5 minutes in boiling salted water to cover. Drain and refresh under cold running water. Melt a knob of butter in a pan. Add the onion and fry gently for 5 minutes or until golden. Add the parboiled cabbage, drained apples, wine, caraway seeds and salt and pepper to taste. Bring to the boil, stirring constantly, then take off the heat.

Drain the excess fat from the roasting pan. Add the cabbage and apple mixture, cover the pan and continue roasting for a further 1 hour or until the pork is tender, stirring the cabbage mixture from time to time.

Transfer the pork to a hot serving platter and carve into slices. Arrange the cabbage mixture around the edges of the platter. Sprinkle with parsley and serve immediately with buttered boiled potatoes.

Pork fillet with prunes

A sumptuous dish of tender nuggets of pork cooked in white wine with cream and prunes for a garnish, this may be served with a simple green salad and chilled white wine.

METRIC	IMPERIAL
Butter for frying	Butter for frying
1 small onion, peeled and finely chopped	1 small onion, peeled and finely chopped
2 whole pork fillets (about 1 kg.), trimmed of fat and cut into cubes	2 whole pork fillets (about 2 lb.), trimmed of fat and cut into cubes
1 × 15 ml. spoon flour	1 tablespoon flour

Pork alsacienne; Pork fillet with prunes;
Roast loin of pork with garlic

Salt and freshly ground
black pepper
12 prunes, stoned and
soaked overnight in
300 ml. dry white wine
1 × 15 ml. spoon redcurrant
jelly
150–300 ml. fresh double
cream

Salt and freshly ground
black pepper
12 prunes, stoned and
soaked overnight in ½
pint dry white wine
1 tablespoon redcurrant jelly
¼–½ pint fresh double
cream

Melt a knob of butter in a shallow flameproof casserole. Add the onion and fry gently for 5 minutes or until golden. Add the pork, increase the heat and sauté briskly, stirring constantly, until the pork is browned on all sides. Stir in the flour and salt and pepper to taste, then add the prunes and the wine. Bring just to the boil, then cover the casserole. Simmer gently on top of the stove or bake in a moderate oven (180°C/350°F or Gas Mark 4) for ¾ hour to 1 hour or until the pork is tender.

Stir in the redcurrant jelly and gradually add the cream on top of the stove; the amount of cream needed will vary according to the pan juices –the finished sauce should be thick and glossy. Do not allow the sauce to boil or the cream will curdle. Adjust seasoning and serve immediately.

Roast loin of pork with garlic

This is the traditional French method of roasting a joint of pork and although there is no crispy crackling as with an English pork roast, the meat is juicier and more succulent. If pork crackling is liked, the rind and some of the fat can be removed before the loin is cooked, sprinkled with salt and cooked in a separate roasting tin with a little dripping or lard.

METRIC	IMPERIAL
1 loin of pork (about 1½ kg.), rind removed and boned	*1 loin of pork (about 3 lb.), rind removed and boned*
Salt and freshly ground black pepper	*Salt and freshly ground black pepper*
1 × 5 ml. spoon freshly chopped sage or 1 × 2.5 ml. spoon dried sage	*1 teaspoon freshly chopped sage or ½ teaspoon dried sage*
Pinch of ground allspice	*Pinch of ground allspice*
1 garlic clove, slivered	*1 garlic clove, slivered*
150 ml. dry white wine or water	*¼ pint dry white wine or water*

Put the pork in a large bowl or dish and rub the salt, pepper, sage and allspice into the joint. Leave in a cool place for several hours or overnight if possible.

Place the garlic slivers at regular intervals along the inside of the joint. Roll up and tie securely with string. Put in a roasting pan and pour in the wine or water. Cover with a lid or foil and roast in a cool oven (150°C/300°F or Gas Mark 2) for 2 to 2½ hours or until the meat is tender and the juices are no longer pink when pierced with a skewer. If the joint becomes dry during cooking, add a little water to the roasting pan.

Before serving, remove the string and carve the joint into slices. Arrange on a hot serving platter. Serve with gravy made in the roasting pan with the cooking juices, and vegetables as for an English roast.

Glazed baked gammon

Glazed baked gammon

A dish to serve hot or cold, a glazed gammon joint always looks attractive on the table. For extra effect, garnish the serving platter with drained canned pineapple slices fried in butter and soft brown sugar.

METRIC	IMPERIAL
1 gammon joint (about 1½ kg.), soaked in cold water overnight	*1 gammon joint (about 3 lb.), soaked in cold water overnight*
6 peppercorns	*6 peppercorns*
6 juniper berries (optional)	*6 juniper berries (optional)*
1 bay leaf	*1 bay leaf*
1 onion stuck with a few cloves	*1 onion stuck with a few cloves*
2 × 15 ml. spoons honey	*2 tablespoons honey*
12 cloves (approx.)	*12 cloves (approx.)*
Watercress to garnish	*Watercress to garnish*

Drain the gammon and place in a large saucepan with the peppercorns, juniper berries (if using), bay leaf and onion. Cover with cold water and bring to the boil, skimming the scum with a slotted spoon. Lower the heat and simmer gently for about 1½ hours (allowing 25 to 30 minutes per pound) or until tender.

Remove from the pan and allow to cool slightly. Cut off the rind and some of the fat. Score the remaining fat in a diamond pattern with a sharp knife, then brush with the honey and stud the diamond shapes with cloves.

Place on a rack in a roasting pan and bake in a fairly hot oven (200°C/400°F or Gas Mark 6) for 15 to 20 minutes or until glazed and crisp. Transfer to a hot serving platter, carve into slices and garnish with watercress sprigs. Serve with parsleyed new potatoes and a seasonal green vegetable such as spinach.

Veal

Wiener schnitzel

Wiener schnitzel

Veal escalopes marinated in lemon juice and coated in egg and breadcrumbs are a great Austrian speciality and they are very quick and easy to prepare. Get the butcher to beat the escalopes well to make them almost paper thin. Serve with a mixed salad tossed in French dressing.

METRIC	IMPERIAL
4 veal escalopes (about 100 g. each), beaten	4 veal escalopes (about 4 oz. each), beaten
Juice of 2 lemons	Juice of 2 lemons
Salt and freshly ground black pepper	Salt and freshly ground black pepper
1 large egg, beaten	1 large egg, beaten
100 g. dried breadcrumbs	4 oz. dried breadcrumbs
Butter for frying	Butter for frying
2 lemons, quartered, to finish	2 lemons, quartered, to finish

Sprinkle the escalopes with the lemon juice and salt and pepper to taste, and leave to marinate for about 1 hour. Dip the escalopes in the egg, then in the breadcrumbs, ensuring that they are evenly coated. Chill in the refrigerator for 10 minutes. Melt a knob of butter in a large frying pan and, when foaming, add two of the escalopes. Fry over high heat for about 2 to 3 minutes on each side, or until tender and golden-brown.

Drain on absorbent kitchen paper, then transfer to hot serving platter. Keep hot while you cook the remaining escalopes in the same way. Serve immediately with lemon quarters.

Veal escalopes with cream sauce

These are delicious served with a seasonal green vegetable such as buttered courgettes or broccoli. Fresh tarragon has a far better flavour than dried tarragon in this recipe, so be sure to use it, if available.

METRIC	IMPERIAL
4 veal escalopes (about 100 g. each), beaten	4 veal escalopes (about 4 oz. each), beaten
1 × 15 ml. spoon freshly chopped tarragon or 1 × 5 ml. spoon dried tarragon	1 tablespoon freshly chopped tarragon or 1 teaspoon dried tarragon
Salt and freshly ground black pepper	Salt and freshly ground black pepper
Olive oil and butter for frying	Olive oil and butter for frying
Juice of ½ lemon	Juice of ½ lemon
175 g. button mushrooms, cleaned and sliced	6 oz. button mushrooms, cleaned and sliced
150 ml. fresh single cream	¼ pint fresh single cream

Sprinkle the escalopes with the tarragon and salt and pepper to taste. Heat a spoon of oil and knob of butter in a large frying pan and, when foaming, add two of the escalopes and half the lemon juice. Fry over high heat for 2 to 3 minutes on each side or until tender. Remove from the pan and set aside. Heat a little more oil and butter in the pan. Add the remaining escalopes and fry as before. When they are tender, remove from the pan and add to the other escalopes. Add the mushrooms to the pan and fry for 1 minute. Stir in the cream and return the escalopes to the pan. Reheat gently for 1 to 2 minutes. Do not let the sauce boil or it will curdle. Adjust seasoning and transfer to a hot serving platter. Serve immediately.

Veal escalopes with cream sauce

Hungarian veal goulash

Veal is the traditional meat used for goulash, although beef is sometimes substituted. It is a good idea to cook this dish a day ahead of time: when reheated, the flavours of the rich sauce will penetrate the meat and enhance the flavour of the dish.

METRIC
Dripping or lard for frying
1 large onion, peeled and finely chopped
1 garlic clove, crushed with 1 × 2.5 ml. spoon salt
1 kg. pie veal, trimmed of fat and cut into cubes
1 × 2.5 ml. spoon caraway seeds
2 × 15 ml. spoons sweet paprika
1 × 5 ml. spoon dried mixed herbs
Freshly ground black pepper
1 red pepper, cored, seeded and sliced into rings
1 green pepper, cored, seeded and sliced into rings

IMPERIAL
Dripping or lard for frying
1 large onion, peeled and finely chopped
1 garlic clove, crushed with ½ teaspoon salt
2 lb. pie veal, trimmed of fat and cut into cubes
½ teaspoon caraway seeds
2 tablespoons sweet paprika
1 teaspoon dried mixed herbs
Freshly ground black pepper
1 red pepper, cored, seeded and sliced into rings
1 green pepper, cored, seeded and sliced into rings
1 × 14 oz. can tomatoes
¼ pint chicken stock

1 × 396 g. can tomatoes
150 ml. chicken stock
¼ kg. button mushrooms, cleaned and sliced
1 × 141 g. carton soured cream

½ lb. button mushrooms, cleaned and sliced
1 × 5 oz. carton soured cream

Melt the dripping or lard in a flameproof casserole. Add the onion and garlic and fry gently for 5 minutes or until golden. Add the veal to the casserole and fry briskly until browned on all sides. Stir in the caraway seeds, paprika, mixed herbs, and black pepper to taste. Continue cooking for 1 to 2 minutes, stirring constantly. Add the peppers, tomatoes and stock, cover and transfer to a cool oven (150°C/300°F or Gas Mark 2). Cook for about 2 hours or until the veal is quite tender, adding the mushrooms 30 minutes before the end of cooking time.

Before serving, adjust seasoning. Transfer to a hot serving dish and spoon the soured cream on top. Serve with plain boiled potatoes or buttered noodles and a green salad tossed in a sharp vinaigrette dressing.

Hungarian veal goulash

Veal olives

Although they take time to prepare, Veal olives are well worth the extra effort – they make a very attractive main course for a dinner party. If the escalopes seem large, cut each one in two and serve two per person.

METRIC
4 veal escalopes (approx. 100 g. each), beaten
Flour for coating
Butter for frying
150 ml. chicken stock
150 ml. dry white wine
1 bouquet garni
Salt and freshly ground black pepper
4 × 15 ml. spoons fresh single cream to finish

IMPERIAL
4 veal escalopes (approx. 4 oz. each), beaten
Flour for coating
Butter for frying
¼ pint chicken stock
¼ pint dry white wine
1 bouquet garni
Salt and freshly ground black pepper
4 tablespoons fresh single cream to finish

For the stuffing:
Butter for frying
1 small onion, peeled and finely chopped
100 g. button mushrooms, cleaned and finely chopped
75 g. fresh white breadcrumbs

For the stuffing:
Butter for frying
1 small onion, peeled and finely chopped
4 oz. button mushrooms, cleaned and finely chopped
3 oz. fresh white breadcrumbs

2 × 15 ml. spoons freshly chopped parsley
Finely grated rind and juice of 1 lemon

2 tablespoons freshly chopped parsley
Finely grated rind and juice of 1 lemon

To prepare the stuffing, melt a knob of butter in a small frying pan. Add the onion and fry until golden. Add the mushrooms and continue cooking for a further 2 minutes. Remove the pan from the heat and stir in the remaining stuffing ingredients and salt and freshly ground black pepper to taste, pressing well together with a wooden spoon to combine.

Lay the escalopes flat on a board or working surface and divide the stuffing equally among them. Roll up the escalopes and tie with string. Roll in flour until evenly coated.

Melt a knob of butter in a flameproof casserole. Put in the escalopes and brown quickly on all sides, over high heat. Pour in the chicken stock and white wine and bring to the boil, stirring constantly. Lower the heat, put in the bouquet garni and season to taste. Cover and simmer gently for 45 minutes to 1 hour or until the escalopes feel tender when pierced with a skewer.

Before serving, remove the bouquet garni. Take off the heat and stir in the fresh cream. Adjust seasoning and serve immediately.

Veal olives

Osso buco

A classic Italian dish, Osso buco is delicious yet economical. If available, knuckle of veal is the best cut to use – the marrow jelly from the bones adds richness and flavour to the sauce and can be scooped out and eaten.

METRIC	IMPERIAL
Olive oil for frying	*Olive oil for frying*
1 large onion, peeled and finely chopped	*1 large onion, peeled and finely chopped*
1 garlic clove, crushed with 1 × 2.5 ml. spoon salt	*1 garlic clove, crushed with ½ teaspoon salt*
About 1 kg. shin or knuckle of veal, cut into pieces	*About 2 lb. shin or knuckle of veal, cut into pieces*
2 × 15 ml. spoons flour	*2 tablespoons flour*
Freshly ground black pepper	*Freshly ground black pepper*
1 × 396 g. can tomatoes	*1 × 14 oz. can tomatoes*
300 ml. dry white wine	*½ pint dry white wine*
300 ml. chicken stock	*½ pint chicken stock*
2 × 15 ml. spoons tomato purée	*2 tablespoons tomato purée*

To finish:
2 × 15 ml. spoons freshly chopped parsley
1 garlic clove, finely chopped
Finely grated rind and juice of ½ lemon

To finish:
2 tablespoons freshly chopped parsley
1 garlic clove, finely chopped
Finely grated rind and juice of ½ lemon

Heat 2 spoons of oil in a large flameproof casserole. Add the onion and garlic and fry gently for 5 minutes or until golden. Add the veal and brown quickly on all sides. Sprinkle in the flour and pepper to taste, then gradually stir in the remaining ingredients. Bring just to the boil. Lower the heat, cover and simmer gently for 1½ to 2 hours or until the veal is tender and the sauce is thick. Adjust the seasoning.

To serve, mix together the parsley, garlic, lemon rind and juice and cover the top of the casserole with this mixture. Serve immediately with plain boiled rice or buttered noodles and a green salad.

Veal cordon bleu

Escalopes of veal with slices of ham topped with Gruyère cheese and coated in egg and breadcrumbs is quite a tricky dish to prepare. Try to make the ham and cheese slices as near to the size of the escalopes as possible, and press them well together before coating in the egg and breadcrumb mixture.

METRIC	IMPERIAL
4 veal escalopes (approx. 100 g. each), beaten	*4 veal escalopes (approx. 4 oz. each), beaten*
Salt and freshly ground black pepper	*Salt and freshly ground black pepper*
4 slices Gruyère cheese	*4 slices Gruyère cheese*
4 slices cooked ham	*4 slices cooked ham*
1 egg, beaten	*1 egg, beaten*
100 g. dried breadcrumbs	*4 oz. dried breadcrumbs*
Vegetable oil and butter for frying	*Vegetable oil and butter for frying*

To finish:
4 lemon wedges
Parsley sprigs

To finish:
4 lemon wedges
Parsley sprigs

Season the veal well with salt and pepper. Lay a slice of cheese on top of each slice of veal, and then a slice of ham, pressing down well.

Brush with beaten egg, then coat with the breadcrumbs, ensuring that the escalopes are thoroughly coated. Chill in the refrigerator for 10 minutes.

Heat a spoon of oil and knob of butter in a large frying pan. Add two escalopes and cook for 10 to 15 minutes or until golden-brown, turning once during the cooking time. Drain on absorbent kitchen paper and keep hot while cooking the remaining escalopes in more oil and butter.

Arrange the escalopes on a hot serving platter. Garnish with lemon wedges and parsley sprigs and serve.

Osso buco; Veal Orloff; Veal cordon bleu

Veal Orloff

This is a much simplified version of a classic French recipe for roasted veal; it is a rich and impressive dish. Serve with plain vegetables such as boiled rice or creamed potatoes and chopped spinach.

METRIC	IMPERIAL
1¼–1½ kg. piece boneless veal (leg or loin)	*2½–3 lb. piece boneless veal (leg or loin)*
Vegetable oil for frying	*Vegetable oil for frying*
Salt and freshly ground black pepper	*Salt and freshly ground black pepper*
2 large onions, peeled	*2 large onions, peeled*
2 carrots, peeled and sliced	*2 carrots, peeled and sliced*
1 bouquet garni	*1 bouquet garni*
Butter for frying	*Butter for frying*
175 g. mushrooms, cleaned and chopped	*6 oz. mushrooms, cleaned and chopped*

For the cheese sauce:	For the cheese sauce:
25 g. butter	*1 oz. butter*
40 g. flour	*1½ oz. flour*
150 ml. hot milk	*¼ pint hot milk*
Pinch of grated nutmeg	*Pinch of grated nutmeg*
75 g. Cheddar cheese, grated	*3 oz. Cheddar cheese, grated*

If the butcher has not done so, tie the veal with string to ensure that it keeps its shape during cooking. Heat 2 spoons of oil in a flameproof casserole. Add the veal and brown quickly on all sides over high heat. Season to taste with salt and pepper and lower the heat. Cut one onion into quarters and add to the casserole with the carrots, bouquet garni and enough water to cover the bottom of the pot. Cover with a lid and transfer to a fairly hot oven (200°C/400°F or Gas Mark 6). Braise for 30 minutes, then lower heat to moderate (180°C/350°F or Gas Mark 4) and continue braising for 1½ hours or until the juices of the meat run clear when the meat is pierced with a skewer.

Take the meat from the casserole and keep hot. (The pan juices and vegetables can be used to make a gravy to serve with the meat if liked.)

Meanwhile, melt a knob of butter in a small pan. Chop the remaining onion very finely and add to the pan. Fry for 5 minutes or until golden. Add the mushrooms and cook for 2 to 3 minutes more. Season to taste, set aside and keep warm.

To prepare cheese sauce, melt the butter in a pan. Stir in the flour and cook for 1 to 2 minutes, stirring constantly. Remove the pan from the heat and gradually add the milk, stirring vigorously. When all the milk is incorporated, return the pan to the heat and bring slowly to the boil, stirring constantly. Lower the heat. Season to taste and add the nutmeg and 50 g./2 oz. of the grated cheese. Cook for a further 2 minutes or until the cheese melts into the sauce.

Carve the veal into four to six slices, untying strings as necessary. Divide the mushroom mixture equally between the slices and reshape the veal on a hot heatproof serving platter. Pour over the hot cheese sauce and sprinkle with the remaining 25 g./1 oz. grated cheese.

Put the platter in a fairly hot oven (200°C/400°F or Gas Mark 6) for 15 to 20 minutes. Serve immediately.

Serves 4 to 6.

Offal

Liver with orange

This is a good way to make something special out of liver. Oranges give both a piquant flavour to the dish and an attractive finish for serving.

METRIC	IMPERIAL
Cooking oil and butter for frying	Cooking oil and butter for frying
1 large onion, peeled and finely chopped	1 large onion, peeled and finely chopped
1 garlic clove, crushed with 1 × 2.5 ml. spoon salt	1 garlic clove, crushed with ½ teaspoon salt
½ kg. lamb's liver, sliced	1 lb. lamb's liver, sliced
Flour for coating	Flour for coating
Freshly ground black pepper	Freshly ground black pepper
400 ml. chicken stock	¾ pint chicken stock
2 × 5 ml. spoons dark soft brown sugar	2 teaspoons dark soft brown sugar

To finish:	To finish:
2 oranges, peeled, pips removed and sliced into rings	2 oranges, peeled, pips removed and sliced into rings
2 × 15 ml. spoons snipped chives	2 tablespoons snipped chives

Heat a spoon of oil and knob of butter in a large frying pan. Add the onion and garlic and fry gently for 5 minutes or until golden. Coat the liver in flour seasoned with black pepper to taste and add to the pan. Brown gently on all sides, then gradually stir in the chicken stock. Add the sugar and bring just to the boil, stirring constantly. Lower the heat and simmer gently for 10 to 15 minutes or until the juices from the liver run faintly pink when the liver is pricked with a fork.

Add the orange rings a few minutes before serving. Heat them through and adjust the sauce for seasoning. Transfer to a hot serving platter, arranging the oranges on the top. Sprinkle with snipped chives and serve immediately.

Sweetbreads with mushrooms and cream

Despite long preparation, this dish is well worth the time and effort. Serve with light vegetables such as creamed or boiled new potatoes and French or runner beans.

METRIC	IMPERIAL
Cooking oil and butter for frying	Cooking oil and butter for frying
12 pickling onions, peeled	12 pickling onions, peeled
½ kg. calf's or lamb's sweetbreads, prepared	1 lb. calf's or lamb's sweetbreads, prepared
1 × 15 ml. spoon flour	1 tablespoon flour
Salt and freshly ground black pepper	Salt and freshly ground black pepper
2 × 15 ml. spoons brandy (optional)	2 tablespoons brandy (optional)
300 ml. dry white wine or dry white wine and chicken stock, mixed	½ pint dry white wine or dry white wine and chicken stock, mixed
1 bouquet garni	1 bouquet garni
175 g. button mushrooms, cleaned and sliced	6 oz. button mushrooms, cleaned and sliced
150 ml. fresh double cream	¼ pint fresh double cream
Freshly chopped parsley to finish	Freshly chopped parsley to finish

Heat a spoon of oil and knob of butter in a frying pan. Add the onions and fry gently until golden. Add the sweetbreads and fry until golden-brown, stirring constantly. Stir in the flour and sprinkle with the seasoning. If using brandy, pour in and set it alight.

Add the wine or wine and stock, stirring well. Bring slowly to the boil, then lower the heat. Add the bouquet garni, cover the pan and simmer gently for 45 minutes or until the sweetbreads are tender. Add the mushrooms 5 minutes before the end of cooking time and discard the bouquet garni.

Stir in the double cream. Be careful not to let the sauce boil or the cream will curdle. Adjust seasoning. Transfer to a hot serving platter, sprinkle with a little parsley and serve immediately.

Braised oxtail

A hearty winter's meal, Braised oxtail takes a long time to cook, so be sure to prepare well in advance. As oxtail is rather fatty it is a good idea to cook this dish the day before; when completely cold, skim off the surplus fat, then reheat and add the beurre manié for serving.

METRIC	IMPERIAL
25 g. dripping or lard	*1 oz. dripping or lard*
2 large onions, peeled and sliced	*2 large onions, peeled and sliced*
1 oxtail, chopped into pieces	*1 oxtail, chopped into pieces*
2 large carrots, peeled and chopped	*2 large carrots, peeled and chopped*
1 head of celery, scrubbed and chopped	*1 head of celery, scrubbed and chopped*
1 turnip or swede, peeled and chopped	*1 turnip or swede, peeled and chopped*
Salt	*Salt*

Liver with orange; Sweetbreads with mushrooms and cream; Braised oxtail

6 black peppercorns, crushed	*6 black peppercorns, crushed*
1 bay leaf	*1 bay leaf*
150 ml. red wine or port (optional)	*¼ pint red wine or port (optional)*
Beurre manié, made with 50 g. butter mixed with 25 g. flour	*Beurre manié, made with 2 oz. butter mixed with 1 oz. flour*
Freshly chopped parsley to finish	*Freshly chopped parsley to finish*

Melt the dripping or lard in a large saucepan. Add the onions and cook for 5 minutes or until golden. Put in the oxtail and brown quickly on all sides over high heat. Add the remaining vegetables and seasonings and cover with water. Stir in the red wine or port, if using. Bring slowly to the boil, stirring constantly, then skim off any scum with a slotted spoon. Lower the heat, cover the pan and simmer gently for 3 to 4 hours or until the oxtail is tender and the meat falling off the bones, adding more water if the liquid level becomes low.

Discard the bay leaf. Add the beurre manié, in small pieces, and simmer, stirring constantly, until the sauce has thickened. Adjust seasoning, stir in plenty of parsley and serve with boiled or creamed potatoes.

Chinese Liver

A simple way of giving liver an exotic flavour. Chicken livers may be substituted for the lamb's liver if preferred.

METRIC	IMPERIAL
For the marinade:	**For the marinade:**
2 × 15 ml. spoons soya sauce	2 tablespoons soya sauce
1 × 15 ml. spoon honey	1 tablespoon honey
1 × 15 ml. spoon soft brown sugar	1 tablespoon soft brown sugar
2 × 15 ml. spoons wine vinegar	2 tablespoons wine vinegar
1 small piece of fresh root ginger, very finely chopped	1 small piece of fresh root ginger, very finely chopped
1 garlic clove, crushed	1 garlic clove, crushed
Salt and freshly ground black pepper	Salt and freshly ground black pepper
450 g. lamb's liver, sliced into very thin strips	1 lb. lamb's liver, sliced into very thin strips
1 × 15 ml. spoon cornflour	1 tablespoon cornflour
150 ml. chicken or beef stock	¼ pint chicken or beef stock
2 × 15 ml. spoons vegetable oil	2 tablespoons vegetable oil
4 spring onions, finely chopped	4 spring onions, finely chopped
To garnish:	**To garnish:**
Few spring onion flowers	Few spring onion flowers

Mix together the ingredients for the marinade and pour over the liver in a bowl. Leave to marinate for at least 2 hours, stirring occasionally.

Chinese liver; Devilled kidneys; Pressed tongue

Drain the liver and mix the cornflour and stock into the marinade. Heat the oil in a large frying pan, add the chopped spring onions and fry until golden. Remove from the pan with a slotted spoon and set aside.

Add the liver to the pan and fry briskly until lightly coloured and just cooked through. Pour in the marinade with the fried onions and cook until thick, stirring constantly. Taste and adjust seasoning, then serve immediately on a bed of buttered noodles or fried bean sprouts. Garnish the platter with spring onion flowers.

Devilled kidneys

A good dish for family suppers or even informal entertaining, this recipe for Devilled kidneys makes a delicious combination of quite simple ingredients, and is very quick to prepare. Serve in a ring of plain boiled rice with a separate vegetable dish of French Beans with Bacon.

METRIC	IMPERIAL
Cooking oil and butter for frying	Cooking oil and butter for frying
1 medium-sized onion, peeled and finely chopped	1 medium-sized onion, peeled and finely chopped
100 g. unsmoked streaky bacon, rinds removed and finely chopped	4 oz. unsmoked streaky bacon, rinds removed and finely chopped
8 lambs' kidneys, cleaned and chopped	8 lambs' kidneys, cleaned and chopped
1 × 226 g. can tomatoes	1 × 8 oz. can tomatoes
Salt	Salt
1 × 5 ml. spoon dried oregano	1 teaspoon dried oregano
	½ teaspoon cayenne pepper

1 × 2.5 ml. spoon cayenne pepper
1 × 5 ml. spoon Worcestershire sauce
Dash of Tabasco sauce
4 × 15 ml. spoons medium sherry
Freshly chopped parsley to finish

1 teaspoon Worcestershire sauce
Dash of Tabasco sauce
4 tablespoons medium sherry
Freshly chopped parsley to finish

Heat a spoon of oil and knob of butter in a large frying pan. Add the onion and bacon and fry gently until golden. Add the kidneys and brown quickly on all sides.

Stir in the tomatoes, salt to taste, oregano, cayenne, Worcestershire, Tabasco and sherry. Bring to the boil, then lower the heat and simmer gently for 10 minutes or until the kidneys are cooked through and the sauce has reduced slightly. Taste for seasoning.

Arrange boiled rice in a ring around the edge of a hot serving platter and spoon the kidneys and sauce in the middle. Sprinkle with plenty of parsley and serve immediately.

Pressed tongue

The flavour of tongue pressed at home is far better than the sliced tongue available commercially. It is possible to buy tongue presses in some good kitchen shops and if it will be used regularly it is well worth the expense of buying one. If a tongue press is not to be used, a small cake tin makes a good substitute – it should be just too small for the tongue to fit so that it has to be squeezed into the tin. This helps the pressing.

METRIC
1 prepared unsalted ox tongue, (about 2½–3 kg.)
1 bouquet garni
1 × 5 ml. spoon salt
6 black peppercorns
6 juniper berries (optional)
1 onion, peeled and stuck with a few cloves
1 carrot, peeled and sliced

IMPERIAL
1 prepared unsalted ox tongue (about 5–6 lb.)
1 bouquet garni
1 teaspoon salt
6 black peppercorns
6 juniper berries (optional)
1 onion, peeled and stuck with a few cloves
1 carrot, peeled and sliced

To finish:
1 lemon, sliced thinly, pips removed
1 bunch of watercress

To finish:
1 lemon, sliced thinly, pips removed
1 bunch of watercress

Put the tongue in a large saucepan. Cover with water and add the remaining ingredients, except the lemon and watercress. Bring to the boil, skimming off any scum with a slotted spoon. Lower the heat, cover the pan and simmer gently for 4 to 5 hours or until the tongue is very tender. (To test if done, pierce the thickest part near the root with a skewer.) Remove from the heat and leave to cool in the cooking liquid.

When quite cold, drain the tongue, discarding the cooking liquid. Remove the skin, gristle and any bones. Roll up from the thinnest end and push into the tongue press. Tighten according to instructions. If using a cake tin, push into the tin and place a plate on top with heavy weights on. Leave in a cool place overnight.

For serving, turn the tongue out of the press or tin and arrange on a serving platter with lemon slices and watercress sprigs.   **Serves 6 to 8.**

Poultry and game

Poultry, in the form of chicken, duck and turkey, has become a very popular meat, both for everyday meals and for special occasions. Oven-ready chilled and frozen birds are available all year round and, together with the availability of jointed poultry, either chilled fresh or frozen, has contributed to this popularity. Fresh poultry is still considered to have better flavour and texture.

When buying fresh poultry, look for plump birds and fresh-looking skin. The breast bone should be pliable. Remove the giblets from the inside of the bird and keep in the refrigerator until cooking time. Fresh poultry should not be kept for any length of time, however – one to two days at the most.

Frozen poultry should be completely thawed before cooking. Leave in polythene wrapping and thaw on a plate or dish in the refrigerator. Where thawing times are given on wrappings of frozen poultry these should always be followed. Do not try to speed up the thawing process by placing birds in hot water.

Fresh and frozen poultry can be prepared in numerous ways, and the basic and more advanced cooking methods for chicken, duck and turkey are included here.

Quantities and roasting times for turkey

2¼–4½ kg./5–10 lb. turkey: is sufficient to serve 6–10 people. Cook by slow roasting method in a warm oven (160°C/325°F or Gas Mark 3) for 3–3¾ hours, or by quick roasting method in a very hot oven (230°C/450°F or Gas Mark 8) for 2¼–2¾ hours.

4½–5½ kg./10–12 lb. turkey: is sufficient to serve 10–12 people. Cook by slow roasting method (temperatures above) for 3¾–4 hours, or by quick roasting method for 2¾–3 hours.

5½–6½ kg./12–14 lb. turkey: is sufficient to serve about 15 people. Cook by slow roasting method (temperatures above) for 4–4½ hours, or by quick roasting method for 3 hours.

6½–8½ kg./14–18 lb. turkey: is sufficient to serve 15–20 people. Cook by slow roasting method (temperatures above) for 4½–4¾ hours, or by quick roasting method for 3–3½ hours.

If roasting by the quick method, it is best to wrap the bird in foil, unwrapping it 30 minutes before the end of cooking time and basting to allow the breast skin to brown.

To test if turkey is done, pierce the thickest part of the thigh with a skewer – if the juices run clear the turkey is ready to serve.

For roasting times for other poultry, see individual recipes.

Unless otherwise stated, quantities of stuffings are sufficient to stuff a joint, chicken or duck for four persons. When stuffing a turkey, double or treble the quantities, depending on the size of the bird. Stuff just before roasting.

Parsley and thyme stuffing

Used for the body of roast turkey, Parsley and thyme is a versatile stuffing as it goes well with chicken and most meats. It can also be made into stuffing balls (see Forcemeat stuffing) and roasted around the bird or joint.

METRIC	IMPERIAL
100 g. fresh white breadcrumbs	*4 oz. fresh white breadcrumbs*
25 g. shredded beef suet	*1 oz. shredded beef suet*
2 × 15 ml. spoons freshly chopped parsley	*2 tablespoons freshly chopped parsley*
1 × 15 ml. spoon freshly chopped thyme or 1 × 5 ml. spoon dried thyme	*1 tablespoon freshly chopped thyme or 1 teaspoon dried thyme*
1 egg, beaten	*1 egg, beaten*
Salt and freshly ground black pepper	*Salt and freshly ground black pepper*
A little milk (if necessary)	*A little milk (if necessary)*

Put all the ingredients together in a mixing bowl and stir well to combine thoroughly, with salt and pepper to taste. If the mixture seems too stiff, soften with a little milk.

Chestnut and sausagemeat stuffing

One of the most delicious and moist stuffings, Chestnut and sausagemeat is perfect with roast turkey. This is sufficient quantity to stuff the body of a 7 kg./14 lb. turkey.

METRIC	IMPERIAL
Butter for frying	*Butter for frying*
1 large onion, peeled and finely chopped	*1 large onion, peeled and finely chopped*
2 large cooking apples, peeled, cored and chopped	*2 large cooking apples, peeled, cored and chopped*
¼ kg. pork sausagemeat	*8 oz. pork sausagemeat*
100 g. fresh white breadcrumbs	*4 oz. fresh white breadcrumbs*
1 × 440 g. can unsweetened chestnut purée	*1 × 15½ oz. can unsweetened chestnut purée*
Salt and freshly ground black pepper	*Salt and freshly ground black pepper*

Melt a knob of butter in a pan. Add the onion and fry until golden. Transfer to a mixing bowl. Add the remaining ingredients, and salt and pepper to taste. Stir well to combine thoroughly.

Celery, apricot and walnut stuffing

This is a tasty stuffing, ideal for roast duck. It can also be served with roast pork or goose.

METRIC	IMPERIAL
Butter for frying	*Butter for frying*
3 celery stalks, scrubbed and chopped	*3 celery stalks, scrubbed and chopped*
100 g. long-grain rice, cooked and drained	*4 oz. long-grain rice, cooked and drained*
100 g. dried apricots, soaked overnight, drained and chopped	*4 oz. dried apricots, soaked overnight, drained and chopped*
50 g. walnuts, finely chopped	*2 oz. walnuts, finely chopped*
1 egg, beaten	*1 egg, beaten*
Salt and freshly ground black pepper	*Salt and freshly ground black pepper*

Melt a knob of butter in a pan. Add the celery and fry until softened. Transfer to a mixing bowl and stir in remaining ingredients with salt and pepper to taste. Stir well to combine thoroughly.

Bread sauce

This is the traditional accompaniment to roast chicken, turkey or pheasant. If a stronger flavour of onion is preferred, leave the quartered onion in the sauce until serving time.

METRIC	IMPERIAL
1 small onion, peeled and quartered	*1 small onion, peeled and quartered*
400 ml. milk	*¾ pint milk*
4 black peppercorns	*4 black peppercorns*
1 bay leaf	*1 bay leaf*
2 cloves	*2 cloves*
100 g. fresh white breadcrumbs	*4 oz. fresh white breadcrumbs*
25 g. butter	*1 oz. butter*
Salt	*Salt*

Put the onion, milk and seasonings in a saucepan and bring to the boil. Remove the pan from the heat, cover tightly and leave to infuse for 15 to 20 minutes. Strain and return to the rinsed-out pan with the breadcrumbs, butter, and salt to taste. Simmer gently to reheat, stirring occasionally. Taste for seasoning before serving.

Circassian chicken; Coq au vin

Chicken

Coq au vin

A time-honoured favourite, this chicken casserole with red wine and mushrooms may be served with Gratin Dauphinois and a tossed green salad. The flavour is especially good if the chicken is cooked the day before eating, the beurre manié and mushrooms being added after reheating.

METRIC	IMPERIAL
Butter and cooking oil for frying	*Butter and cooking oil for frying*
12 small pickling onions, peeled	*12 small pickling onions, peeled*
1 garlic clove, crushed (optional)	*1 garlic clove, crushed (optional)*
100 g. unsmoked streaky bacon, rinds removed and diced	*4 oz. unsmoked streaky bacon, rinds removed and diced*
4 chicken portions, skinned	*4 chicken portions, skinned*
2 × 15 ml. spoons brandy (optional)	*2 tablespoons brandy (optional)*
300 ml. red wine (Burgundy-type)	*½ pint red wine (Burgundy-type)*
150 ml. chicken stock	*¼ pint chicken stock*
1 bouquet garni	*1 bouquet garni*
Salt and freshly ground black pepper	*Salt and freshly ground black pepper*

To finish:
Beurre manié made with 25 g. butter mixed with 2 × 15 ml. spoons flour
Knob of butter
¼ kg. button mushrooms, cleaned and sliced

To finish:
Beurre manié made with 1 oz. butter mixed with 2 tablespoons flour
Knob of butter
½ lb. button mushrooms, cleaned and sliced

Heat a knob of butter and spoon of oil in a large flameproof casserole. Add the onions, garlic (if using), and bacon. Fry until golden-brown, then remove from the casserole with a slotted spoon and set aside. Add the chicken portions and fry gently until golden on all sides. Pour over the brandy (if using) and set alight.

Return the onions, garlic (if used), and bacon to the casserole. Pour in the wine and half the stock and add the bouquet garni and seasoning. Stir well and bring to the boil. Lower the heat, cover and transfer to a moderate oven (180°C/350°F or Gas Mark 4). Cook for 1 to 1½ hours or until the chicken is tender and the juices run clear when it is pierced with a skewer. Add more stock if the casserole becomes too dry during the cooking.

Return the casserole to the top of the stove and discard the bouquet garni. Add the beurre manié in small pieces, stirring constantly, and simmer until the sauce thickens.

Melt the knob of butter in a small pan and, when foaming, add the mushrooms. Sauté for 1 minute over high heat, then remove with a slotted spoon and pile on top of casserole. Adjust seasoning and serve immediately.

Circassian chicken

Spicy and oriental, Circassian chicken is a good dish to cook in a chicken brick. Remember to start the marinade the day before the dish is required as the flavours need a long while to penetrate the meat. Serve with plain boiled rice.

METRIC	IMPERIAL
1 3/4–2 kg. roasting chicken, skinned, giblets removed	3 1/2–4 lb. roasting chicken, skinned, giblets removed
3 × 141 g. cartons natural unsweetened yogurt	3 × 5 oz. cartons natural unsweetened yogurt
1 garlic clove, crushed with 1 × 2.5 ml. spoon salt	1 garlic clove, crushed with 1/2 teaspoon salt
2 pieces fresh root ginger, finely chopped, or 1 × 5 ml. spoon ground ginger	2 pieces fresh root ginger, finely chopped, or 1 teaspoon ground ginger
2 dried chillis, crushed, or 1 × 2.5 ml. spoon chilli powder	2 dried chillis, crushed, or 1/2 teaspoon chilli powder
1 × 2.5 ml. spoon ground turmeric	1/2 teaspoon ground turmeric
1 × 2.5 ml. spoon ground mixed spice	1/2 teaspoon ground mixed spice
2 × 15 ml. spoons freshly chopped mint	2 tablespoons freshly chopped mint
1 × 15 ml. spoon ground cumin seeds	1 tablespoon ground cumin seeds
1 × 5 ml. spoon salt	1 teaspoon salt
2 × 5 ml. spoons sugar	2 teaspoons sugar
1 bunch of watercress to garnish	1 bunch of watercress to garnish

Wash the chicken and dry thoroughly with a clean tea-towel or kitchen paper. Score the chicken flesh with a very sharp knife and put in a large mixing bowl. Mix the remaining ingredients together, using only two cartons of yogurt, and pour over the chicken. Leave to marinate for 8 hours or overnight in the refrigerator, spooning the marinade over the chicken from time to time.

Transfer to a chicken brick lined with oiled greaseproof paper, pouring the marinade over the bird. Close the brick and place in a cold oven. Turn the oven to hot (220°C/425°F or Gas Mark 7) and roast for 1 1/2 hours, without opening the oven.

Transfer the chicken to a hot serving platter. Scrape the juices from the brick and pour into a sauceboat to serve separately; stir in the remaining yogurt.

Garnish the serving platter with sprigs of watercress and serve immediately.

NOTE: if a chicken brick is not available, the chicken can be roasted in a covered casserole dish in a fairly hot oven (190°C/375°F or Gas Mark 5) for 1 1/2 to 2 hours or until the chicken is tender and the juices run clear when it is pierced with a skewer. Baste occasionally with the marinade during the cooking time.

Oven-baked chicken

Oven-baked chicken

Quick and simple to prepare, this is an ideal dish for the family as everyone will love its crisp, crunchy topping. Serve with a mixed salad or a vegetable dish such as Ratatouille.

METRIC	IMPERIAL
50 g. butter	2 oz. butter
4 chicken portions, skinned	4 chicken portions, skinned
1 × 70 g. packet plain crisps, crushed	1 × 2 1/2 oz. packet plain crisps, crushed
100 g. grated cheese, preferably Parmesan or Cheddar	4 oz. grated cheese, preferably Parmesan or Cheddar
1 × 15 ml. spoon freshly chopped parsley	1 tablespoon freshly chopped parsley
1 × 1.25 ml. spoon garlic powder	1/4 teaspoon garlic powder
1 × 5 ml. spoon freshly chopped tarragon or 1 × 2.5 ml. spoon dried tarragon	1 teaspoon freshly chopped tarragon or 1/2 teaspoon dried tarragon
Salt and freshly ground black pepper	Salt and freshly ground black pepper

Melt the butter and brush half over the chicken. Mix the crisps together with the remaining ingredients and season to taste. Press this mixture around the chicken portions and put in an ovenproof casserole. Sprinkle over the remaining melted butter.

Bake in a moderate oven (180°C/350°F or Gas Mark 4) for 45 minutes to 1 hour or until the chicken is tender and the juices run clear when it is pierced with a skewer. Serve from the casserole dish.

Poulet bonne femme

This simple French country recipe is suitable for either a whole chicken or chicken portions. For a special occasion, a dry white wine can be substituted for the chicken stock, or half wine, half stock could be used. Serve with boiled new potatoes and Petits Pois à la Française.

METRIC	IMPERIAL
Butter for frying	*Butter for frying*
100 g. unsmoked streaky bacon, rinds removed and diced	*4 oz. unsmoked streaky bacon, rinds removed and diced*
12 small pickling onions, peeled	*12 small pickling onions, peeled*
1 ¾–2 kg. chicken, with the giblets, or 4 chicken portions	*3 ½–4 lb. chicken, with the giblets, or 4 chicken portions*
Flour for coating	*Flour for coating*
Salt and freshly ground black pepper	*Salt and freshly ground black pepper*
600 ml. chicken stock (made from the giblets if using whole chicken)	*1 pint chicken stock (made from the giblets if using whole chicken)*
1 bouquet garni	*1 bouquet garni*
3–4 carrots, peeled and thinly sliced	*3–4 carrots, peeled and thinly sliced*
175 g. mushrooms, cleaned and sliced (optional)	*6 oz. mushrooms, cleaned and sliced (optional)*
Freshly chopped parsley to finish	*Freshly chopped parsley to finish*

Melt a knob of butter in a large flameproof casserole. Add the bacon and onions and fry until golden. Remove from the casserole with a slotted spoon and set aside.

Wash the chicken and dry thoroughly with a clean tea-towel or kitchen paper. Coat the chicken in flour seasoned with salt and pepper to taste, then put in the casserole and brown quickly on all sides. Return the bacon and onions to the casserole, pour in the stock and stir to blend. Bring slowly to the boil, stirring constantly, then lower the heat and put in the bouquet garni and carrots. Cover the casserole and simmer gently on top of the stove for about 1½ hours if using a whole chicken, or 30 to 40 minutes if using portions. If using mushrooms, add these 10 minutes before the end of cooking time.

Discard the bouquet garni and adjust the sauce for seasoning. The whole chicken should be removed from the casserole, cut into serving portions and arranged on a hot serving platter. The sauce can either be poured over the chicken and the whole dish sprinkled with parsley, or the chicken can be sprinkled with parsley and the sauce served separately. Chicken portions can be served straight from the casserole.

Chicken Maryland

A popular American dish, Chicken Maryland is a colourful and tasty way of serving chicken. The full traditional recipe includes a garnish of Sweetcorn fritters, fried bananas and bacon rolls, but it is not necessary to serve all three. A mixed salad makes a good accompaniment.

METRIC	IMPERIAL
4 chicken portions, skinned	*4 chicken portions, skinned*
Flour for coating	*Flour for coating*
Salt and freshly ground	*Salt and freshly ground*
* black pepper*	* black pepper*
1–2 eggs, beaten	*1–2 eggs, beaten*
100 g. dried breadcrumbs	*4 oz. dried breadcrumbs*
Butter and cooking oil for	*Butter and cooking oil for*
* frying*	* frying*

For the garnish:

4 bananas	*4 bananas*
Juice of ½ lemon	*Juice of ½ lemon*
Flour for coating	*Flour for coating*
4 back or streaky bacon	*4 back or streaky bacon*
* rashers, rinds removed*	* rashers, rinds removed*
1 bunch of watercress	*1 bunch of watercress*

Coat the chicken portions in flour seasoned with salt and pepper, then dip in the beaten egg. Cover with the breadcrumbs, making sure the chicken is thoroughly coated.

Melt a knob of butter and 2 spoons of oil in a large frying pan. Put in the chicken portions and fry gently until golden-brown on all sides. Transfer to a casserole dish, cover and bake in a moderate oven (180°C/350°F or Gas Mark 4) for about 45 minutes or until the chicken is tender when pierced with a skewer.

Meanwhile prepare the garnish. Peel the bananas, sprinkle with lemon juice and coat in flour. Add to the frying pan, with more butter if necessary, and fry on both sides until golden-brown. Keep warm.

To make the bacon rolls, stretch the bacon rashers with the blade of a sharp knife, then roll up and pierce onto a skewer. Cook under a preheated hot grill until crisp and golden-brown, turning occasionally.

Transfer the chicken to a hot serving platter and garnish with Sweetcorn fritters, fried bananas and bacon rolls. Decorate the platter with sprigs of watercress and serve immediately.

Paprika chicken

This is the way the Hungarians like to cook their chicken – in a rich, pungent purée that gives the meat a delicious flavour.

METRIC	IMPERIAL
Butter for frying	*Butter for frying*
½ kg. onions, peeled and	*1 lb. onions, peeled and*
* finely chopped*	* finely chopped*
1 garlic clove, crushed	*1 garlic clove, crushed*
4 chicken portions, skinned	*4 chicken portions, skinned*
1 × 15 ml. spoon sweet	*1 tablespoon sweet paprika*
* paprika*	*Salt and freshly ground*
Salt and freshly ground	* black pepper*
* black pepper*	*Approx. ¼ pint chicken*
Approx. 150 ml. chicken	* stock*
* stock*	*1 × 5 oz. carton soured*
1 × 141 g. carton soured	* cream*
* cream*	*Snipped chives to finish*
Snipped chives to finish	

Melt a knob of butter in a large flameproof casserole dish. Add the onions and garlic, cover and fry on a very low heat for 45 minutes or until golden and soft – almost a purée.

Add the chicken. Increase the heat slightly and sprinkle in the paprika, and salt and pepper to taste. Spoon the onion over the chicken. Continue to cook gently, covered, for a further 45 minutes or until the chicken is tender and the juices run clear when it is pierced with a skewer. Add a little stock from time to time if the casserole becomes too dry. Traditionally this dish does not have a sauce – the onion purée should just coat the chicken portions – so do not add too much liquid.

When cooked, adjust seasoning and transfer to a hot serving platter. Spoon over the soured cream. Sprinkle with a few snipped chives and serve immediately with plain boiled rice or baked jacket potatoes.

Chicken Maryland; Poulet bonne femme; Paprika chicken

Chicken Kiev

It is now possible to buy ready-prepared chicken breasts which make this classic chicken dish easy and more economical to prepare. Serve 1 to 2 breasts per person depending on their size. As it is a fairly involved recipe, it is perhaps better reserved for special occasions, served with a tossed green or mixed salad and potato croquettes or French fries.

METRIC	IMPERIAL
100 g. butter, softened	*4 oz. butter, softened*
Finely grated rind and juice of ½ lemon	*Finely grated rind and juice of ½ lemon*
1 × 15 ml. spoon freshly chopped parsley	*1 tablespoon freshly chopped parsley*
1 × 15 ml. spoon finely snipped chives	*1 tablespoon finely snipped chives*
1 garlic clove, crushed (optional)	*1 garlic clove, crushed (optional)*
Freshly ground black pepper	*Freshly ground black pepper*
4–8 chicken breasts, boned, skinned and beaten thin	*4–8 chicken breasts, boned, skinned and beaten thin*
Flour for coating	*Flour for coating*
Salt	*Salt*
1–2 eggs, beaten	*1–2 eggs, beaten*
100–175 g. dried bread-crumbs	*4–6 oz. dried breadcrumbs*
Oil for deep-fat frying	*Oil for deep-fat frying*
Lemon twists to garnish	*Lemon twists to garnish*

Put the butter in a mixing bowl and beat in the lemon rind and juice, parsley, chives, garlic (if using), and pepper to taste. Beat vigorously until well blended, then divide into four or eight portions, depending on the number of chicken breasts to be stuffed and wrap in greaseproof paper or foil. Chill until firm in the freezing compartment of the refrigerator.

Lay the breasts flat on a board. Place a portion of stuffing on each breast and roll up, making sure that the stuffing is completely enclosed. Coat with flour seasoned with salt and pepper, then dip in the beaten egg. Cover with the bread-crumbs, making sure that the chicken is thoroughly coated. Chill in the refrigerator for at least 1 hour before frying.

Heat the oil gently in a deep-fat fryer until it is hot enough to turn a stale bread cube golden in 30 seconds (190°C/375°F on a deep-frying thermometer). Fry the chicken portions two at a time for 8 to 10 minutes or until crisp and golden-brown. Drain on absorbent kitchen paper and keep warm until all the breasts are fried. Arrange on a hot serving platter with the lemon twists and serve immediately.

Chicken dhansak

A Persian curry made with lentils and spices, dhansak can be prepared with most meats, but is particularly good with chicken. Traditionally served with saffron rice, the chicken meat should be taken off the bone after cooking, mixed with the spices and reheated before serving.

Chicken dhansak; Chicken Kiev

METRIC	IMPERIAL
4 chicken portions, skinned	4 chicken portions, skinned
175 g. brown lentils, washed, soaked overnight and drained	6 oz. brown lentils, washed, soaked overnight and drained
2 medium-sized onions, peeled and chopped	2 medium-sized onions, peeled and chopped
1 × 396 g. can tomatoes	1 × 14 oz. can tomatoes
2 medium-sized potatoes, peeled and sliced	2 medium-sized potatoes, peeled and sliced
1 × 2.5 ml. spoon chilli powder	½ teaspoon chilli powder
1 × 5 ml. spoon ground turmeric	1 teaspoon ground turmeric
1 × 15 ml. spoon ground coriander	1 tablespoon ground coriander
1 × 5 ml. spoon ground cumin seeds	1 teaspoon ground cumin seeds
150–300 ml. chicken stock	¼–½ pint chicken stock
Salt	Salt
Juice of 1 lemon	Juice of 1 lemon
25 g. butter	1 oz. butter

Put the chicken, lentils, vegetables, spices and 150 ml./¼ pint of the stock in a pan. Add salt to taste and bring slowly to the boil. Lower the heat, cover the pan and simmer gently for 45 minutes or until the chicken, vegetables and lentils are cooked and all the liquid has been absorbed.

When cooked, remove the chicken from the pan and allow to cool slightly. Take the meat off the bone and cut into bite-sized pieces. Purée the lentils and vegetables in an electric blender or Mouli-légumes. Return to the rinsed-out pan with the chicken, lemon juice and butter and heat through gently, adding more hot stock if the sauce is too thick (it should just coat the chicken pieces). Adjust seasoning. Transfer to a hot serving dish and arrange saffron rice around the edge of the dish. Serve with mango chutney and yogurt.

Duck

Duck with orange

Orange is the favourite accompaniment to roast duck, because its tangy sharp flavour contrasts well with the richness of duck meat. This recipe combines the two in a simple casserole. Serve it with boiled rice and a salad of sliced beetroot tossed in vinaigrette dressing and snipped chives.

METRIC	IMPERIAL
Butter for frying	Butter for frying
1 medium-sized onion, peeled and finely chopped	1 medium-sized onion, peeled and finely chopped
1 duck (2–2½ kg.), jointed, skinned and fat removed, with the giblets	1 duck (4–5 lb.), jointed, skinned and fat removed, with the giblets
Flour for coating	Flour for coating
Salt and freshly ground black pepper	Salt and freshly ground black pepper
1 × 5 ml. spoon ground mixed spice	1 teaspoon ground mixed spice
150 ml. duck stock (made with the giblets)	¼ pint duck stock (made with the giblets)
300 ml. diluted frozen orange juice	½ pint diluted frozen orange juice
Beurre manié made with 25 g. butter mixed with 25 g. flour	Beurre manié made with 1 oz. butter mixed with 1 oz. flour
2 oranges, peeled, pith and pips removed, and sliced into rings	2 oranges, peeled, pith and pips removed, and sliced into rings
2 × 5 ml. spoons soft brown sugar	2 teaspoons soft brown sugar

Melt a knob of butter in a large flameproof casserole dish. Add the onion and fry gently until golden. Coat the duck joints in flour seasoned with salt and pepper to taste and mixed spice, and add to the casserole. Brown on both sides, then stir in the stock and orange juice. Bring slowly to the boil, stirring.

Cover the casserole and transfer to a moderate oven (180°C/350°F or Gas Mark 4). Bake for 1 hour or until the duck is tender when pierced with a skewer. Adjust seasoning. Spoon off any fat from the surface of the liquid.

Five minutes before the end of the cooking time, stir the beurre manié into the liquid in small pieces. Bring to the boil, stirring constantly until the sauce thickens. Melt another knob of butter in a small frying pan. Put in the orange slices and sprinkle with the sugar. Sauté over high heat until the oranges are caramelised, then transfer to the casserole and place on top of the duck. Serve immediately.

Duck with orange

Braised duck in red wine

Braised duck makes an ideal dinner party dish as it can be made in advance and reheated before serving. Plain boiled rice and buttered Brussels sprouts would make good accompaniments.

METRIC	IMPERIAL
Butter for frying	Butter for frying
12 small pickling onions, peeled	12 small pickling onions, peeled
Few celery stalks, scrubbed and finely chopped	Few celery stalks, scrubbed and finely chopped
4 duck portions, skinned	4 duck portions, skinned
300 ml. red wine (Burgundy-type)	½ pint red wine (Burgundy-type)
1 bouquet garni	1 bouquet garni
2 × 5 ml. spoons sugar	2 teaspoons sugar
Salt and freshly ground black pepper	Salt and freshly ground black pepper
Beurre manié made with 25 g. butter mixed with 2 × 15 ml. spoons flour	Beurre manié made with 1 oz. butter mixed with 2 tablespoons flour

To finish:

175 g. button mushrooms, cleaned and sliced	6 oz. button mushrooms, cleaned and sliced
2 × 15 ml. spoons brandy	2 tablespoons brandy

Melt a knob of butter in a large flameproof casserole. Add the onions and celery and fry gently until golden. Remove from the casserole with a slotted spoon and set aside.

Put the duck portions in the casserole and brown on both sides. Return the onions and celery to the casserole. Pour in the red wine and add the bouquet garni, sugar, and salt and pepper to taste. Bring just to the boil, stirring constantly, then cover and transfer to a moderate oven (180°C/350°F or Gas Mark 4). Cook for 1 hour or until the duck is tender when pierced with a skewer.

Return the casserole to the top of the stove and discard the bouquet garni. Add the beurre manié in small pieces, stirring constantly, and simmer until the sauce thickens.

Melt a spoon of butter in a small pan and, when foaming, add the mushrooms. Sauté for 1 minute over high heat, then pour over the brandy and set alight. When the flames die down, spoon on top of the casserole and serve.

Roast duck with apricot stuffing

An excellent weekend lunch dish, this duck is roasted with honey to make the skin sweet and crisp. The stuffing of apricots, rice and nuts helps to make the dish into a substantial meal for four persons. Serve with roast potatoes, a seasonal green vegetable and creamed carrots. Use the duck giblets for stock to make gravy in the roasting tin.

METRIC	IMPERIAL
1 duck (2–2½ kg.)	1 duck (4–5 lb.)
25 g. butter, melted	1 oz. butter, melted
Salt and freshly ground black pepper	Salt and freshly ground black pepper
2 × 15 ml. spoons warmed honey	2 tablespoons warmed honey

Braised duck in red wine

For the stuffing:

100 g. long-grain rice, cooked and drained	4 oz. long-grain rice, cooked and drained
100 g. dried apricots, soaked overnight, drained and chopped	4 oz. dried apricots, soaked overnight, drained and chopped
50 g. chopped almonds or hazelnuts	2 oz. chopped almonds or hazelnuts
50 g. currants or raisins	2 oz. currants or raisins
3 × 15 ml. spoons freshly chopped parsley	3 tablespoons freshly chopped parsley
1 egg, beaten	1 egg, beaten

To garnish:

8 canned apricot halves, drained	8 canned apricot halves, drained
Knob of butter	Knob of butter

Wash the duck and dry thoroughly with a tea-towel or absorbent kitchen paper.

To prepare the stuffing, put all the ingredients in a mixing bowl and season to taste, binding the mixture with the beaten egg.

Place the duck on a board and fill the cavity with the stuffing, reserving 8 × 5 ml. spoons/8 teaspoons for the garnish. Tie or sew with trussing string, securing with skewers if necessary. Brush with the butter, sprinkle liberally with salt and pepper and coat with the honey. Prick all over with a fork and place on a rack in a roasting tin. Roast in a fairly hot oven (200°C/400°F or Gas Mark 6) for 1½ to 2 hours or until the duck is tender when pierced with a skewer, turning occasionally.

Fifteen minutes before the end of cooking time, put 1 × 5 ml./1 teaspoon of the reserved stuffing into each apricot half. Dot each with a little butter and put in a greased dish or on a baking sheet. Put in the oven to heat through.

Remove the duck from the rack and discard the trussing string, and skewers if used. Transfer to a hot serving platter and garnish with the stuffed apricot halves.

Turkey

French roast turkey

French cooks do not 'dry roast' their poultry as is most often the custom here. Instead the bird is covered and roasted with stock in the roasting tin, which keeps the flesh moist. Turkey is the ideal bird for this method of cooking as turkey meat, especially on the larger frozen birds, does tend to dry out quickly. The traditional French stuffing for turkey is Chestnut and sausagemeat, but any favourite stuffing can be used with equally good results.

METRIC	IMPERIAL
1 turkey	*1 turkey*
100–175 g. butter, melted	*4–6 oz. butter, melted*
Salt and freshly ground black pepper	*Salt and freshly ground black pepper*
900 ml. turkey stock (made with the giblets)	*1½ pints turkey stock (made with the giblets)*
1 × 15 ml. spoon flour	*1 tablespoon flour*
1 wineglass red wine or port	*1 wineglass red wine or port*

Wash the turkey and dry thoroughly with a clean tea-towel or kitchen paper. Put the prepared stuffing into the turkey cavities, both neck and body, and tie or sew with trussing string, securing with skewers if necessary. Brush the bird liberally with half the butter and sprinkle with plenty of salt and black pepper. Put the bird on a rack in a roasting tin. Brush the remaining butter onto greaseproof paper or foil and use to cover the bird. The amount of butter used will vary depending on the size of the turkey.

Pour 600 ml./1 pint of the stock into the roasting tin under the rack and roast the turkey in a warm oven (160°C/325°F or Gas Mark 3) for the required cooking time (see table), basting the bird occasionally with the stock and adding more stock if necessary. Remove the greaseproof paper or foil for the last 15 minutes to brown the skin. To test if the bird is cooked, pierce the thigh with a skewer; if the juices run clear it is ready to serve.

Remove from the oven and transfer to a hot serving platter, discarding the greaseproof paper or foil, trussing string and skewers (if used). Remove any surplus fat from the roasting tin, leaving the stock and sediment. Pour the hot stock and any remaining cold stock into a jug and set aside. Put the roasting tin on top of the stove and stir in the flour. Cook for 1 to 2 minutes, stirring constantly, then gradually add the stock and red wine or port. Bring to the boil, stirring, then lower the heat and simmer gently for a further 1 to 2 minutes. Adjust seasoning. Serve separately in a gravy boat.

Roast duck with apricot stuffing

French roast turkey

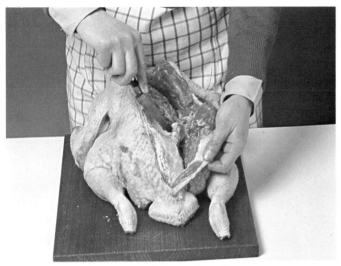

1. *Cut down the centre of the underside*

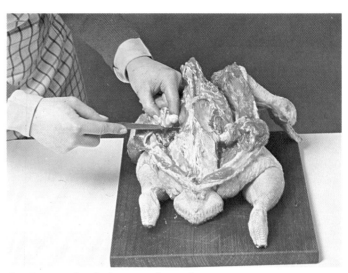

2. *Scrape the flesh away from the carcass*

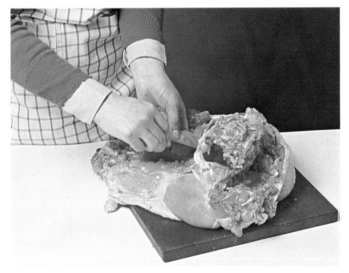

5. *Scrape the flesh away from the rib cage*

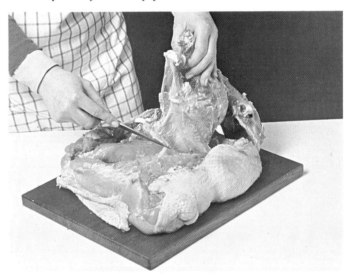

6. *Lift out the carcass frame carefully*

Boned and rolled turkey with lemon stuffing

Boning a turkey is the same as boning a chicken, only on a slightly larger scale. It may seem difficult at first, but it becomes easier after the initial attempt. It is certainly worth the time and effort because the bird is so much easier to carve – a boon particularly on Christmas Day when there are so many other things to do at the last minute.

METRIC	IMPERIAL
1 turkey (approx. 5 kg.)	*1 turkey (approx. 10 lb.)*
Salt and freshly ground black pepper	*Salt and freshly ground black pepper*
100 g. butter, melted	*4 oz. butter, melted*

For the stuffing:

½ kg. pork sausagemeat	*1 lb. pork sausagemeat*
½ kg. lean veal, minced finely	*1 lb. lean veal, minced finely*
100 g. fresh white breadcrumbs	*4 oz. fresh white breadcrumbs*
Finely grated rind and juice of 2 medium lemons	*Finely grated rind and juice of 2 medium lemons*
25 g. parsley, finely chopped	*1 oz. parsley, finely chopped*
2 × 5 ml. spoons dried thyme or mixed herbs	*2 teaspoons dried thyme or mixed herbs*
1 egg, beaten	*1 egg, beaten*
¼ kg. cooked ham, thickly sliced	*½ lb. cooked ham, thickly sliced*

TO BONE AND STUFF A TURKEY

Wash the turkey and dry thoroughly with a clean tea-towel or kitchen paper. Put the turkey on a board or working surface, breast side down. With a sharp knife cut down the centre of the underside, working from the neck to the tail end. Scrape the flesh away from one side of the carcass, always keeping the blade of the knife facing the bones as opposed to the flesh. Scrape down to the ball joint of leg. Repeat this process with the other side of carcass.

To bone the legs, remove the scaly tip of the leg. Cut the sinew that joins the leg to the carcass and, holding the leg bone, scrape the flesh away until the bone is free. Take out and discard the bones. Repeat with the other leg.

To bone the wings, cut them through where the wing joins the body and scrape flesh away from bones as for the legs, discarding bones.

With legs and wings free, continue now to scrape the flesh away from the rib cage, working on both sides until the

106

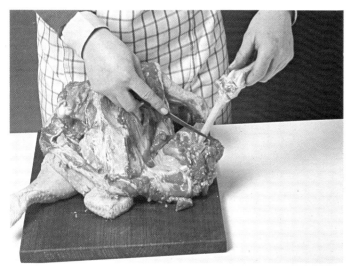

3. Scrape down to the ball joint of the leg

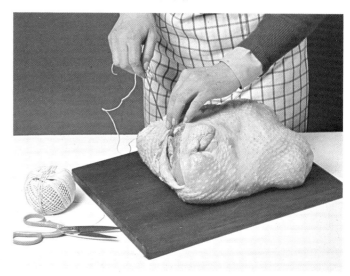

4. Free the bone and remove it

7. Place the ham slices on the stuffing

8. Roll up and sew with trussing string

breastbone is reached. Carefully cut along the breastbone, from neck to tail end, and lift out the carcass frame from the bird, being sure not to slit the thin flesh or skin over the breastbone. Lay the boned out turkey flat on a board, skin side down, and sprinkle with salt and pepper.

To prepare the stuffing, mix all the ingredients, except the ham, together in a large mixing bowl. Season to taste and bind with the beaten egg. Spread half of the prepared stuffing on the turkey. Place the ham slices neatly on top of this and top with the remaining stuffing. Roll up, tucking legs and wings inside, and sew the bird with trussing string.

Brush all over with the butter and place breast side uppermost on a rack in a roasting tin. Sprinkle liberally with salt and pepper. Cover with well-buttered greaseproof paper or foil and roast in a moderate oven (180°C/350°F or Gas Mark 4) for 3 to 3½ hours or until the juices of the turkey run clear when it is pierced with a skewer. Baste and turn occasionally during the cooking. Remove the greaseproof paper or foil for the last 15 minutes to brown the outside.

When the turkey is cooked, remove from the rack and discard the trussing string. Transfer to a hot serving platter and carve into neat slices to show the stuffing layers. Serve with roast potatoes and Brussels sprouts with chestnuts.

Serves 8 to 10.

Turkey croquettes

A good recipe for using leftover turkey or the filleted turkey meat now widely available, Turkey croquettes make a super snack lunch or supper served with a mixed salad, Coleslaw, or cranberry sauce.

METRIC
Approx. 350 g. cooked turkey meat, finely chopped
100 g. mushrooms, cleaned and finely chopped
150 ml. thick white sauce, made with 25 g. butter, 2 × 15 ml. spoons flour, 150 ml. milk and pinch of grated nutmeg
Salt and freshly ground black pepper
1 × 15 ml. spoon freshly chopped parsley
1 × 2.5 ml. spoon cayenne pepper
Flour for coating
1 egg, beaten
175 g. dried breadcrumbs
Oil for deep-fat frying

To garnish:
Parsley sprigs
Lemon wedges

IMPERIAL
Approx. 12 oz. cooked turkey meat, finely chopped
4 oz. mushrooms, cleaned and finely chopped
¼ pint thick white sauce, made with 1 oz. butter, 2 tablespoons flour, ¼ pint milk and pinch of grated nutmeg
Salt and freshly ground black pepper
1 tablespoon freshly chopped parsley
½ teaspoon cayenne pepper
Flour for coating
1 egg, beaten
6 oz. dried breadcrumbs
Oil for deep-fat frying

To garnish:
Parsley sprigs
Lemon wedges

Turkey croquettes; Turkey escalopes (below)

Put the turkey, mushrooms and sauce in a large mixing bowl and mix together with salt and pepper to taste, parsley and cayenne. Shape into balls or flat cakes with floured hands and coat in flour. Dip in the beaten egg, ensuring that they are evenly coated, then coat in dried breadcrumbs. Chill in the refrigerator for at least 1 hour before frying.

Heat the oil gently in a deep-fat fryer until it is hot enough to turn a stale bread cube golden in 30 seconds (190°C/375°F on a deep-frying thermometer). Fry the croquettes, a few at a time, for 10 minutes or until crisp and golden. Drain on absorbent kitchen paper and keep warm until all the croquettes are fried. Arrange on a hot serving platter, garnish with parsley sprigs and lemon wedges and serve.

Makes approx. 8 croquettes.

Turkey escalopes

This is a simple, quick dish to make using either leftover slices of roast turkey breast or the ready-trimmed turkey escalopes now available. Serve on a bed of fried rice.

METRIC	IMPERIAL
Butter for frying	*Butter for frying*
8 thick slices of roast turkey breast or 4 fresh turkey escalopes, beaten	*8 thick slices of roast turkey breast or 4 fresh turkey escalopes, beaten*
¼ kg. button mushrooms, cleaned and sliced	*½ lb. button mushrooms, cleaned and sliced*
4 × 15 ml. spoons cranberry sauce	*4 tablespoons cranberry sauce*
A little chicken stock	*A little chicken stock*
Salt and freshly ground black pepper	*Salt and freshly ground black pepper*

Melt a knob of butter in a large frying pan. Add the turkey and fry gently for a few minutes on both sides. If using fresh turkey escalopes they will take about 5 minutes on each side before they are tender, depending on thickness.

Add the mushrooms to the pan and fry for 1 to 2 minutes, then stir in the cranberry sauce and a few spoonfuls of chicken stock to make a thin sauce. Season to taste with salt and pepper and transfer to a hot serving platter.

Curried turkey meatballs

By the end of the Christmas season everyone has had their fill of roast turkey. Currying the leftover meat disguises the fact that it's turkey again and at the same time provides a tasty and nourishing family meal.

METRIC	IMPERIAL
½ kg. cooked turkey meat, minced	*1 lb. cooked turkey meat, minced*
2 small onions, peeled and finely chopped	*2 small onions, peeled and finely chopped*
¼ kg. freshly cooked or leftover mashed potato	*½ lb. freshly cooked or leftover mashed potato*
1 garlic clove, crushed with 1 × 2.5 ml. spoon salt	*1 garlic clove, crushed with ½ teaspoon salt*
2 × 5 ml. spoons garam masala	*2 teaspoons garam masala*
1 egg, beaten	*1 egg, beaten*
Flour for coating	*Flour for coating*

Vegetable or corn oil for frying	*Vegetable or corn oil for frying*
1 × 5 ml. spoon ground ginger	*1 teaspoon ground ginger*
1 × 5 ml. spoon ground coriander	*1 teaspoon ground coriander*
1 × 5 ml. spoon ground cumin seeds	*1 teaspoon ground cumin seeds*
1 × 5 ml. spoon ground turmeric	*1 teaspoon ground turmeric*
Salt and freshly ground black pepper	*Salt and freshly ground black pepper*
1 × 396 g. can tomatoes, sieved	*1 × 14 oz. can tomatoes, sieved*

Put the turkey in a mixing bowl with half of the onions, the potato, garlic and garam masala. Mix well together and bind with the beaten egg. Shape into 24 balls with floured hands. Roll in flour to coat evenly. Chill in the refrigerator for at least 15 minutes.

Heat 2 to 3 spoons of oil in a large flameproof casserole dish. Add the meatballs, a few at a time, and brown all over, adding more oil if necessary. Remove from the casserole with a slotted spoon and set aside. When all the meatballs are browned, add another 2 spoons of oil and the remaining onion to the casserole with the spices, and salt and pepper to taste. Stir well and fry for a few minutes. Make the sieved tomatoes up to 600 ml./1 pint with water. Stir into the onion mixture and bring to the boil, then lower the heat. Return the meatballs to the casserole, cover and simmer gently for 20 minutes.

Adjust seasoning. Transfer to a hot serving dish and serve with rice and natural yogurt. **Makes approx. 24 meatballs.**

Curried turkey meatballs

Traditional English roast turkey

No Christmas seems quite complete without traditional roast turkey and all its trimmings. Stuff the turkey with Veal forcemeat in the neck end, Chestnut and sausagemeat or Parsley and thyme in the body. Crisp roasted stuffing balls make an attractive accompaniment with cranberry and bread sauces and giblet gravy served separately.

METRIC	IMPERIAL
1 turkey (about 5–6 kg.)	*1 turkey (about 10–12 lb.)*
Veal forcemeat and	*Veal forcemeat and*
Chestnut and	*Chestnut and*
sausagemeat or Parsley	*sausagemeat or Parsley*
and thyme stuffing	*and thyme stuffing*
50 g. dripping or butter,	*2 oz. dripping or butter,*
melted	*melted*
Salt and freshly ground	*Salt and freshly ground*
black pepper	*black pepper*

For the gravy:

Giblets from the turkey	*Giblets from the turkey*
1 carrot, peeled and sliced	*1 carrot, peeled and sliced*
1 onion slice	*1 onion slice*
1 bay leaf	*1 bay leaf*
2 × 15 ml. spoons flour	*2 tablespoons flour*
Hot stuffing balls to garnish	*Hot stuffing balls to garnish*

Wash the turkey and dry thoroughly with a clean tea-towel or kitchen paper.

Traditional English roast turkey

Spoon the prepared stuffings into the bird – Veal forcemeat into neck end, Chestnut and sausagemeat or Parsley and thyme in the body cavity. Sew both openings with trussing string, securing with skewers if necessary.

Brush the turkey liberally with the dripping or butter and sprinkle with salt and pepper. Cover with greased greaseproof paper or foil and place on a rack in a roasting tin. Roast the turkey in a warm oven (160°C/325°F or Gas Mark 3) for the required cooking time (see table), basting and turning occasionally. Remove the greaseproof paper or foil for the last 15 minutes to brown the skin. To test if the bird is cooked, pierce the thigh with a skewer; if the juices run clear it is ready to serve.

To prepare the giblet gravy, put the giblets (gizzard, heart and liver) in a saucepan and cover with water. Add the carrot, onion, bay leaf, and salt and pepper to taste. Bring to the boil, then lower the heat and simmer gently for about 1 hour. Strain into a measuring jug and make up to 600 ml./1 pint with water from cooked vegetables.

Remove the turkey from the oven and transfer to a hot serving platter. Discard the paper or foil, trussing string, and skewers (if used). Arrange hot stuffing balls around the bird. Keep hot. Drain off surplus fat from the roasting tin, leaving the sediment. Place the tin on top of the stove and stir in the flour. Cook for 1 to 2 minutes, stirring constantly, then gradually add the giblet stock, stirring constantly.

Bring to the boil, stirring, then lower the heat and simmer gently for a further 1 to 2 minutes. Adjust seasoning. Serve separately in a gravy boat with the turkey.

Game

Roast pheasant

Be sure to take advantage of pheasant when it is in season – there is nothing quite like its flavour, and simple roasting is one of the best methods of cooking. Traditionally, it should be served with bread sauce, bacon rolls and sausages.

METRIC	IMPERIAL
1 young pheasant, dressed	*1 young pheasant, dressed*
and cleaned	*and cleaned*
A little vegetable oil or	*A little vegetable oil or*
melted butter	*melted butter*
Salt and freshly ground	*Salt and freshly ground*
black pepper	*black pepper*
4 unsmoked streaky or fat	*4 unsmoked streaky or fat*
bacon rashers	*bacon rashers*
Approx. 600 ml. giblet stock	*Approx. 1 pint giblet stock*

To finish:

4 unsmoked middle cut	*4 unsmoked middle cut*
bacon rashers, rinds	*bacon rashers, rinds*
removed and cut into	*removed and cut into*
three	*three*
8 cocktail sausages	*8 cocktail sausages*
Bread sauce	*Bread sauce*

Wash the pheasant and dry thoroughly with a clean tea-towel or kitchen paper. Brush all over with the oil or butter, then sprinkle liberally with salt and pepper. Stretch the bacon rashers with the blade of a sharp knife and use to cover the pheasant.

Put the pheasant on a rack in a roasting tin and pour 400 ml./¾ pint of the stock into the tin. Roast in a fairly hot oven (200°C/400°F or Gas Mark 6) for about 40 to 45 minutes or until the bird is tender when pierced with a skewer. Baste occasionally during the roasting. Remove the bacon rashers covering the breast for the last 10 minutes to brown the skin.

Twenty minutes before the end of cooking time, roll the bacon pieces up and pierce onto skewers. Place on the rack around the pheasant with the sausages.

When the pheasant is ready, remove from the oven and transfer to a hot serving platter. Take the bacon rolls from the skewers and arrange around the pheasant with the sausages. Keep hot while quickly making gravy in the roasting tin (see recipe for French roast turkey), adding more stock if the gravy is too thick. Serve the gravy separately in a gravy boat. **Serves 3 to 4; if appetites are large, roast 2 pheasants.**

Jugged hare

This is a simple, country version of the classic jugged hare. If the hare is hung and drawn at home, the blood may be collected and used in the gravy to thicken it and give it colour and goodness. You can also ask the butcher to keep the blood for you. Be careful to keep the blood fresh by storing it in the refrigerator as it is collected – it does not keep well. Serve with deep-fried Veal forcemeat balls, redcurrant or blackcurrant jelly, and Jacket baked potatoes.

METRIC	IMPERIAL
Beef dripping for frying	*Beef dripping for frying*
1 hare, jointed	*1 hare, jointed*
Flour for coating	*Flour for coating*
Salt and freshly ground black pepper	*Salt and freshly ground black pepper*
Dry cider or water to cover	*Dry cider or water to cover*
Blood from hare (if available)	*Blood from hare (if available)*
2 medium-sized onions, peeled and stuck with a few cloves	*2 medium-sized onions, peeled and stuck with a few cloves*
1 bouquet garni	*1 bouquet garni*

Melt a knob of dripping in a large flameproof casserole. Coat the hare joints in flour seasoned with salt and pepper and fry in the dripping until browned on all sides. Stir in cider or water to cover, or a mixture of both. If using the blood, add it now. Bring to the boil, then put in the onions and bouquet garni. Cover, transfer to a warm oven (160°C/325°F or Gas Mark 3) and cook for 3 to 4 hours or until the hare is tender when pierced with a skewer. The cooking time will vary depending on the age of the hare.

Remove the joints and onions from the casserole. Discard the bouquet garni. Take the meat off the bones, discard the cloves from the onions and break the onions into slices. Return the hare and onions to the casserole to heat through. Adjust seasoning and serve straight from the casserole.

Roast pheasant

Jugged hare

Gamekeeper's casserole

Any kind of game can be used for this casserole, though rabbit is probably the most economical, and foreign imported rabbit is available all year round. Serve with creamed or Jacket baked potatoes and butter.

METRIC	IMPERIAL
Cooking oil for frying	Cooking oil for frying
1 onion, peeled and finely chopped	1 onion, peeled and finely chopped
100 g. unsmoked streaky bacon, rinds removed and diced	4 oz. unsmoked streaky bacon, rinds removed and diced
Approx. 1 kg. rabbit, jointed	Approx. 2 lb. rabbit, jointed
Flour for coating	Flour for coating
Salt and freshly ground black pepper	Salt and freshly ground black pepper
1 × 15 ml. spoon tomato purée	1 tablespoon tomato purée
400 ml. dry cider	¾ pint dry cider
1 bouquet garni or 1 × 5 ml. spoon dried mixed herbs	1 bouquet garni or 1 teaspoon dried mixed herbs
3 medium-sized carrots, peeled and thinly sliced	3 medium-sized carrots, peeled and thinly sliced

Heat 2 to 3 spoons of oil in a flameproof casserole dish. Add the onion and bacon, and fry until golden-brown. Coat the rabbit in flour seasoned with plenty of salt and pepper and add to the casserole. Brown on all sides. Stir in the tomato purée and cider and bring slowly to the boil, stirring constantly. Add the bouquet garni or mixed herbs and the carrots.

Cover the casserole and cook in a moderate oven (180°C/350°F or Gas Mark 4) for 1 to 1½ hours or until the rabbit is tender when pierced with a skewer. Discard the bouquet garni (if used), adjust seasoning and serve straight from the casserole dish.

Partridge-in-a-pear-tree

This is an unusual dish, combining the richness of partridge with the sweet juiciness of pears in a delicious wine sauce. If partridge is not available, you can substitute grouse.

METRIC	IMPERIAL
Butter for frying	Butter for frying
2–4 partridges, according to size, jointed if large, and skinned	2–4 partridges, according to size, jointed if large, and skinned
1 × 15 ml. spoon redcurrant jelly	1 tablespoon redcurrant jelly
150 ml. chicken stock	¼ pint chicken stock
150 ml. red wine (Burgundy-type)	¼ pint red wine (Burgundy-type)
Salt and freshly ground black pepper	Salt and freshly ground black pepper
4 small Conference pears, peeled and quartered	4 small Conference pears, peeled and quartered
Beurre manié made with 2 × 15 ml. spoons butter, mixed with 1 × 15 ml. spoon flour	Beurre manié made with 2 tablespoons butter, mixed with 1 tablespoon flour
4 × 15 ml. spoons fresh double cream	4 tablespoons fresh double cream
1 bunch of watercress to garnish	1 bunch of watercress to garnish

Gamekeeper's casserole; Partridge-in-a-pear-tree; Game pie

Melt a knob of butter in a large flameproof casserole. Add the partridges and brown on all sides. Stir in the redcurrant jelly, stock, wine and salt and pepper to taste. Bring to the boil, then lower the heat. Add the pears to the casserole dish. Cover and simmer gently for 40 minutes, or until the partridges are tender when pierced with a skewer, and the pears are nicely coloured.

Remove the pears and partridges from the casserole and keep hot on a serving platter. Add the beurre manié in small pieces to the cooking liquid, stirring constantly, and simmer gently until the sauce thickens. Adjust the sauce for seasoning. Stir in the cream and heat gently. Do not allow to boil or the cream will curdle. Pour some of the sauce over the partridges and put the rest in a sauceboat. Garnish with sprigs of watercress and serve immediately.

Game pie

Game pies, like pork pies, are often encased in a hot-water crust pastry, but this simple recipe uses frozen puff pastry. Serve hot with seasonal green vegetables, or sliced cold with redcurrant jelly.

METRIC	IMPERIAL
½ kg. boneless stewing venison, cut into small cubes	1 lb. boneless stewing venison, cut into small cubes
Flour for coating	Flour for coating
1 × 2.5 ml. spoon ground cinnamon	½ teaspoon ground cinnamon
Salt and freshly ground black pepper	Salt and freshly ground black pepper
1 wineglass red wine or port	1 wineglass red wine or port
350 g. pork sausagemeat	12 oz. pork sausagemeat
¼ kg. cooked ham, cut into small cubes	½ lb. cooked ham, cut into small cubes
1 × 212 g. packet frozen puff pastry, thawed	1 × 7½ oz. packet frozen puff pastry, thawed
1 egg, beaten to glaze	1 egg, beaten to glaze
Approx. 150 ml. jellied beef stock, warmed	Approx. ¼ pint jellied beef stock, warmed

Coat the venison cubes in flour seasoned with cinnamon and plenty of salt and pepper and put in a casserole dish. Stir in the red wine or port, cover and cook in a moderate oven (180°C/350°F or Gas Mark 4) for 1½ to 2 hours or until the venison is tender.

Put half the sausagemeat in a 900 ml./1½ pint pie dish. Mix the ham into the venison mixture, and put this on top of the sausagemeat. Finish with a layer of sausagemeat.

Roll out the dough to fit the top of the pie dish, cutting a strip to go round the lip of the dish. Wet the lip and press the dough strip around it. Wet the strip and put the dough lid on top, pressing down well to seal and making a hole in the middle to fit a pastry funnel. Decorate the top of the pie with the dough trimmings. Brush with beaten egg.

Bake in a fairly hot oven (200°C/400°F or Gas Mark 6) for about 30 minutes or until the pastry is golden-brown. Gradually pour in the stock through a funnel, being careful that it does not overflow. Serve immediately or leave until cold before slicing.

113

Vegetables and salads

There is one golden rule for vegetables – always buy and use fresh. When buying any vegetable, choose the freshest looking ones, preferably those in season for that time of year (imported out-of-season vegetables are often tasteless and therefore not worth the extra expense). If not using on the day of purchase, store vegetables in a rack in a cool larder, or in the vegetable compartment of the refrigerator.

To preserve the vitamin and mineral content and texture of fresh vegetables, cook them only for the time stated in the recipe: it is better to undercook rather than to overcook. In addition to this, all vegetables should be served as soon as possible after cooking – keeping cooked vegetables spoils their texture and flavour.

Vegetables are among the most versatile of all our foods and yet they are the most often neglected and spoilt. Use the chart in this Chapter for basic simple cooking methods of vegetables; the recipes that follow are more unusual. Some accompany main course dishes, others can make meals in themselves.

	PREPARATION	BOILING
Artichoke (Globe)	Remove any tough or damaged leaves from outside. Cut off stalk. Wash well. If braising, slice into quarters lengthways and discard chokes (the hairy centres).	Put in large pan boiling salted water and simmer for 25 to 40 minutes or until leaf pulls out easily. Drain and refresh. Discard a few centre leaves until chokes are reached. Discard chokes to expose the hearts.
Asparagus	Cut off hard ends, keeping bundles tied. Make sticks same length. Untie and scrape well from tip to end under cold running water.	Re-tie in small bundles and place in plenty of boiling salted water, standing asparagus upright with tips just above water level. Simmer gently 10 to 15 minutes or until tender. Drain.
Aubergine	Wipe clean, top and tail. *Dégorge*: slice thinly, sprinkle cut surfaces with salt and leave for 30 minutes. Drain and rinse.	
Beans – Broad	Remove from pods and wash under cold running water. Very young broad beans need not be shelled: simply top and tail.	Simmer gently in salted water or chicken stock for 15 to 20 minutes or until tender. Drain.
Beans – French	Wash under cold running water. Top and tail. If mature, string and slice into 2.5 cm./1 in. lengths.	Boil in a little salted water for 10 to 15 minutes or longer if mature. Drain.
Beans – Haricot	Wash under cold running water. Soak in water to cover for 8 to 12 hours before cooking. Drain and rinse.	Simmer in salted water to cover for ¾ to 1 hour or until tender. Drain.
Beetroot	Wash carefully under cold running water; do not break skin. Leave 2.5 cm./1 in. stalk and root.	Simmer in water to cover for 1 to 2 hours or until skin rubs off.
Broccoli	Wash under cold running water; cut off stalk ends. Divide into flowerets if liked.	Cook in boiling salted water for 10 to 15 minutes or until tender. Drain.

FRYING	BAKING/ROASTING	SERVING SUGGESTIONS
Parboil hearts (see Boiling) for 10 minutes, drain and refresh. Fry in butter with freshly chopped herbs until tender.	Parboil for 10 minutes, drain and refresh. Cook in casserole with root vegetables, wine, stock and seasonings in moderate oven for 1 to 1½ hours or until tender.	Cold – with Vinaigrette dressing Hot – with melted butter or Hollandaise sauce – stuffed
		Cold – with Vinaigrette dressing Hot – with butter – with Cheese or Hollandaise sauce – also in soups
Dégorge and fry in oil and butter until golden-brown. Can also be deep-fried in batter or coated in egg and breadcrumbs and deep- or shallow-fried.	Can be baked in casserole with tomatoes and onions, etc., for 30 minutes after having been dégorged and fried. Halved aubergines can be stuffed and baked for approx. 30 minutes.	See Ratatouille and Moussaka
		Cold – in salads Hot – with melted butter and freshly chopped herbs –with White or Parsley sauce, or cream
		Cold – in salads Hot – toss in butter and herbs. – See also French beans with bacon
	See Spanish baked beans.	Cold – in salads with French or Vinaigrette dressing Hot – purée with seasoning and tomato sauce – also in soups, stews
	Wrap whole prepared beetroots in buttered foil and bake in moderate oven for ¾ hour or until tender and skins rub off.	Cold – sliced in salads with Vinaigrette dressing – with onions/oranges Hot – with soured cream and chives
		Hot – toss in melted butter or cheese sauce – use in soufflés or cook in a mould as for Brussels sprouts

115

	PREPARATION	BOILING
Brussels Sprouts	Discard outer damaged leaves and trim stalk. Wash under cold running water. Cut a cross in base of stalk.	Cook in boiling salted water for 8 to 10 minutes or until tender. Drain.
Cabbage Green/White/ Red/Spring	Cut into quarters; discard hard centre stalk. Wash under cold running water and leave in quarters, separate leaves or shred.	Cook in boiling salted water for 10 to 12 minutes; shredded cabbage for 5 minutes; Spring cabbage for 7 to 10 minutes. Drain.
Carrots	Top and tail and scrape. Wash under cold running water. Slice or quarter old carrots; leave young ones whole.	Cook in boiling salted water or stock for 15 to 20 minutes, depending on age. Drain or, if using stock, cook until evaporated.
Cauliflower	Leave whole or cut into flowerets and remove coarse stalks. Wash under cold running water.	Cook in boiling salted water for 10 to 15 minutes or until tender. Drain.
Celeriac	Peel; wash under cold running water. Cut into chunks for cooking. Grate for salads, sprinkle with lemon juice to prevent discolouration.	Cook in boiling salted water for 15 to 20 minutes or until tender. Drain.
Celery	Discard outer damaged stalks and cut off leaves and root ends. Divide into individual stalks and scrub well with vegetable brush under cold running water. Halve stalks crossways.	Cook in boiling salted water for 15 to 20 minutes or until tender. Drain.
Chicory	Discard outer damaged leaves. Separate into leaves or slice and wash under cold running water.	
Courgettes	Wipe clean; top and tail. Slice crossways, lengthways into strips, or in half lengthways if stuffing.	
Cucumber	Wash; peel (optional). If stuffing, halve lengthways and scoop out seeds with a teaspoon. If to fry, halve lengthways, scoop out seeds and cut into small strips.	
Fennel	Wash under cold running water. Trim and slice lengthways into quarters or slice thinly crossways.	
Leeks	Trim tops and roots, split lengthways and wash well under cold running water. Can be left whole, sliced into quarters lengthways or sliced crossways into rings.	Cook in boiling salted water for 10 to 20 minutes if whole, 10 if sliced. Drain.
Mushrooms	Wipe clean (do not wash or peel unless very dirty). Trim stalks, leave whole or slice.	Cover with milk, add salt and pepper to taste and bay leaf or grated nutmeg. Simmer 5 minutes. Drain.
Onions Common or Spanish	Top, tail and peel. Rinse under cold running water. Leave whole, quarter, slice or chop according to recipe. Breathe through mouth when slicing or chopping onions to prevent tears.	Cook whole in a little boiling salted water for 20 to 30 minutes or until tender but still in shape. Remove from pan with slotted spoon and drain.
Spring Onion	Should be trimmed of most of green tops and roots. Wash under cold running water.	

FRYING	BAKING/ROASTING	SERVING SUGGESTIONS
	See Brussels sprouts in a mould.	Hot – Toss in melted butter, freshly ground black pepper and nutmeg or with whole cooked chestnuts
See Chinese Style cabbage.	Shred and casserole with onions, apples, dried fruit, stock and/or wine. Cover and cook in moderate oven 1 hour or until tender.	Cold – raw white cabbage in Coleslaw and other salads Hot – toss in melted butter, freshly ground black pepper, nutmeg or caraway seeds
	Can be roasted in meat tin around joint with other vegetables, then pulped down into gravy.	Cold – in Coleslaw and other salads Hot – toss in melted butter and freshly chopped herbs or White sauce – also in soups, stews, etc.
Parboil flowerets for 5 minutes, drain and coat in egg and breadcrumbs. Deep-fry until crisp and golden. Drain on absorbent kitchen paper.		Cold – with Vinaigrette or French dressing Hot – coat with White or Cheese sauce – also in soup
Parboil for 10 minutes. Drain. Fry in butter for a further 10 minutes or until tender. Season to taste with salt and freshly ground black pepper.	Slice and casserole with root vegetables, stock and seasonings. Bake in moderate oven for 45 minutes.	Cold – in salads Hot – coat in White or Cheese sauce – in soups and stews
	Casserole with other vegetables, stock and/or wine and seasonings. Cover and cook in warm oven for 30 to 40 minutes or until tender. See Braised celery.	Cold – grate in salads – with Mayonnaise Hot – coat in white sauce – purée in electric blender – also with potato
	Leave whole, casserole with stock and/or wine. Cover and cook in moderate oven for 1 hour or until tender.	Cold – in salads, particularly with orange or grapefruit Hot – sauté and serve with hot tomato sauce
Fry in oil and butter for 10 to 15 minutes or until tender. Can also be shallow-fried in dried breadcrumbs or deep-fried in batter.	Halve, scoop out flesh and fill with savoury stuffing (cheese, minced beef, tomato, onion, etc.). Bake in moderate oven for 30 to 45 minutes depending on stuffing.	Cold – in salads with Vinaigrette dressing Hot – in numerous different dishes; see Ratatouille and lamb with pernod
Fry in butter and freshly chopped herbs for 5 to 10 minutes.	Can be halved lengthways and stuffed. Bake in fairly hot oven for 30 minutes, depending on stuffing.	Cold – raw in salads – stuff with cream cheese – also in soups (cold and hot)
See Fennel à la Grecque.		Cold – raw in salads with Vinaigrette dressing or Mayonnaise
	Cover and cook whole leeks in stock, wine or water and seasonings in moderate oven for ¾ to 1 hour or until tender.	Cold – raw in salads with dressing Hot – with White or Cheese sauce – good in casseroles, stews and soups, particularly with potato
Fry in butter for 1 to 2 minutes (longer if large), stirring constantly; season to taste. Add cream, if liked. Whole button mushrooms can be deep-fried in batter. See also Mushroom and potato sauté.		Cold – raw in salads; see Mushrooms à la Grècque Hot – use in numerous ways, in casseroles, stews, pies, etc. – also in soups
Fry in equal quantities of butter and oil for 5 minutes or until soft and golden. Cook longer time for browned onions. Can also be deep-fried.	Parboil for 10 minutes, drain and bake whole (unpeeled and stuffed) in moderate oven for 40 minutes. Can be roasted in meat tin around joint with other vegetables. May be pulped down into gravy.	Cold – in salads Hot – in stews, casseroles, ragoûts, pies, quiches, soups, etc.
See Petits Pois à la Française.		Cold – in salads and as a garnish

	PREPARATION	BOILING
Parsnips	Top, tail and peel. Wash under cold running water. Cut in thick slices or chunks; remove hard centre core if using old parsnips.	Cook in boiling salted water for 30 to 35 minutes or until tender, depending on age. Drain.
Peas	Shell (mange-tout are left whole but topped, tailed and stringed if necessary) and wash in colander under cold running water.	Cook in boiling salted water to cover with a pinch of sugar and sprig of mint. Simmer for 10 to 15 minutes or until tender, depending on age. Drain. See also Petits Pois à la Française.
Peppers (Capsicum)	To peel: grill, turning until charred, then rub off skin with a tea towel. Core and seed. Wash under cold running water to remove all seeds. Leave whole and blanch (bring to boil from cold then drain and refresh) if stuffing. Slice for salads and other dishes.	Blanch to remove any bitter or strong flavour.
Potatoes	Scrub new potatoes with vegetable brush. Old potatoes may be peeled or, if for baking, scrubbed under cold running water. Slice or cut according to recipe or method using.	Boil new potatoes in their skins in salted water for 15 to 20 minutes or until tender. Drain. Skins may be peeled off, if liked. Old potatoes should be halved and boiled in salted water for 15 to 20 minutes or until tender. Drain.
Pumpkin	Cut in quarters, peel off skin and discard seeds. Slice thickly.	Boil in plenty of salted water for 30 minutes or until tender. Drain.
Spinach	Wash thoroughly under cold running water. Discard discoloured leaves and large coarse stalks.	Put in large saucepan with salt to taste. Heat gently until juices flow from spinach. Cover pan and cook gently for 5 to 10 minutes or until tender. Drain well.
Swede	Peel and slice into thick chunks. Wash under cold running water.	Cook in boiling salted water for 20 to 30 minutes or until tender. Drain.
Sweetcorn	Corn-on-the-Cob: discard husks and silk, trim ends.	Cook in boiling water for 7 to 10 minutes. Drain.
Tomato	To skin: put tomatoes in bowl, cover with boiling water and leave to stand for 30 seconds. Drain and rinse under cold running water. Peel off skin. To seed: cut tomatoes in half and scrape out seeds with a teaspoon.	Cook in plenty of boiling salted water for approx. 5 to 15 minutes or until tender when pierced with a skewer. Drain.
Turnip	Peel and wash under cold running water. Leave whole if young and small, slice into thick chunks if mature.	Cook in boiling salted water for 20 to 30 minutes or until tender. Drain. See also Sweet-glazed turnips.

FRYING	BAKING/ROASTING	SERVING SUGGESTIONS
See Parsnip chips. Can also be boiled and fried in butter with freshly chopped herbs and onions.	Bake boiled parsnips with butter, sugar and a little stock or water in fairly hot oven until glazed. Can be roasted in the meat tin around joint with other vegetables, then pulped down into gravy.	Hot – purée in electric blender, also with potato. – add to casseroles, stews – also curried parsnip or soup
		Cold – in salads Hot – toss in melted butter, freshly chopped mint and black pepper – also in soups
See Italian-style peppers.	Can be filled with numerous stuffings – rice, cheese, meat, breadcrumbs – and baked in the oven.	Cold – in salads Hot – in stews, Hungarian-style goulash, Ratatouille, etc.
French fries: cut peeled potatoes into chip shapes, soak in cold water, then dry thoroughly. Deep-fry in hot oil for approx. 5 minutes. Drain on absorbent kitchen paper. Just before serving, return to hot oil and deep-fry for 1 to 2 minutes or until crisp and golden. Drain. Sauté: parboil potatoes in skins for 10 minutes. Drain, leave to cool, then peel and slice into rounds. Sauté in equal quantities of hot oil and butter for 10 to 15 minutes or until crisp and golden, turning occasionally. Drain.	Jacket baked potatoes: prick and put on shelf of fairly hot oven. Bake for approx. 1 hour or until tender. Split and serve with butter, soured cream and snipped chives. See also Jacket Baked Potatoes for different fillings. See also Gratin Dauphinois. Roast potatoes: Parboil peeled and halved potatoes for 10 minutes. Drain. Place in meat tin around joint with hot dripping or fat. Roast in fairly hot oven for approx. 1½ hours until crisp and golden-brown, turning occasionally.	Cold – see Potato salad Hot – creamed (mash or purée cooked old potatoes in electric blender, mix with butter, top of the milk and beaten egg; season to taste) – toss new potatoes in melted butter, freshly chopped mint, season to taste
Fry boiled pumpkin slices in butter and oil until browned.	Can be roasted in meat tin around joint with other vegetables. May be pulped down into gravy.	Cold – in pumpkin pie Hot – purée in electric blender or mash with butter, top of the milk and seasoning to taste – also in soup
		Hot – chop or purée in electric blender; combine with butter, cream, nutmeg and seasoning to taste – also in soufflés, pancakes, quiches, soups and with cheese – with eggs – see Oeufs Florentine – in curries – see Sag gosht
	Can be roasted in meat tin around joint with other vegetables. May be pulped down into gravy.	Hot – toss in melted butter with seasoning to taste – mash or purée in electric blender with seasonings to taste – also in casseroles, stews and soups
		Hot – serve as starter with butter, salt and freshly ground black pepper to taste – use frozen or canned sweetcorn kernels in salads, rice-based dishes, soups, chowders – see also Sweetcorn fritters
Halve or slice thinly and fry until soft in hot dripping, oil or butter. Drain on absorbent kitchen paper. Good cooking method for soft over-ripe tomatoes.	Cut tomatoes in half and place, cut sides uppermost, in buttered baking tin or dish. Dot each tomato half with butter and sprinkle with salt, pepper and sugar to taste. Bake in moderate oven for 15 to 20 minutes or until soft, but still in shape. Can also be baked whole or in casserole with cheese and cream. See Tomato and Gruyère casserole.	Cold – stuffed as starter – in salads, skinned, seeded and sliced or chopped Hot – see Ratatouille and Italian-style peppers – large continental tomatoes can be stuffed (minced beef, rice, cheese, bacon, herbs, etc.) and baked
	Can be roasted in meat tin around joint with other vegetables. May be pulped down into gravy.	Hot – as for Swede above – can also be boiled and served whole or in chunks coated in well-seasoned white sauce

Aubergine and tomato casserole

This vegetable dish is a delicious creamy blend of aubergines, tomatoes and yogurt, with a crisp topping of grated Parmesan cheese. It makes an ideal accompaniment to grilled or roast lamb, or shish kebab.

METRIC	IMPERIAL
Butter and vegetable or cooking oil for frying	Butter and vegetable or cooking oil for frying
2 large aubergines (approx. ¾ kg.), sliced and dégorgé	2 large aubergines (approx. 1½ lb.), sliced and dégorgé
1 large onion, peeled and thinly sliced	1 large onion, peeled and thinly sliced
1 garlic clove, crushed (optional)	1 garlic clove, crushed (optional)
1 × 396 g. can tomatoes, sieved	1 × 14 oz. can tomatoes, sieved
1 × 15 ml. spoon tomato purée	1 tablespoon tomato purée
1 × 5 ml. spoon freshly chopped oregano or basil or 1 × 2.5 ml. spoon dried oregano or basil	1 teaspoon freshly chopped oregano or basil or ½ teaspoon dried oregano or basil
1 × 2.5 ml. spoon sugar	½ teaspoon sugar
Salt and freshly ground black pepper	Salt and freshly ground black pepper
1 × 141 g. carton natural unsweetened yogurt	1 × 5 oz. carton natural unsweetened yogurt
25 g. Parmesan cheese, grated	1 oz. Parmesan cheese, grated
25 g. fresh white breadcrumbs	1 oz. fresh white breadcrumbs

Heat a knob of butter and a spoon of oil in a large frying pan. When foaming, add enough aubergine slices to cover the bottom of the pan. Fry until browned on both sides, then remove from the pan with a slotted spoon and drain on absorbent kitchen paper. Fry the remaining aubergine slices in this way, adding more oil and butter when necessary.

Fry the onion and garlic (if using) until golden in the same pan. Stir in the sieved tomatoes, tomato purée, oregano or basil, sugar, and salt and pepper to taste. Bring to the boil, then lower the heat and simmer for 5 minutes to reduce the sauce slightly.

Divide the aubergines into three equal portions and put one portion in the bottom of a shallow ovenproof dish. Divide the tomato sauce into two and put one half on top of the aubergine layer. Spoon half of the yogurt on top of the tomato sauce. Repeat these three layers once more, then finish with the remaining portion of aubergines. Sprinkle the top with the grated Parmesan and breadcrumbs. Bake in a moderate oven (180°C/350°F or Gas Mark 4) for 30 minutes or until the topping is golden brown and bubbling.

French beans with bacon

Dwarf French beans are delicious freshly picked from the garden, but by the end of the season everyone has probably had their fill of them. Try this unusual way to serve beans and give the family a real treat. The recipe can be made equally well with frozen or runner beans.

METRIC	IMPERIAL
½ kg. fresh French beans, trimmed, or 1 × 283 g. packet frozen whole green beans, thawed	1 lb. fresh French beans, trimmed, or 1 × 10 oz. packet frozen whole green beans, thawed
Salt	Salt
Butter for frying	Butter for frying
1 bunch of spring onions, topped, tailed and chopped, or ½ small onion, peeled and chopped	1 bunch of spring onions, topped, tailed and chopped, or ½ small onion, peeled and chopped
100 g. streaky bacon, rind removed and chopped	4 oz. streaky bacon, rind removed and chopped
Freshly ground black pepper	Freshly ground black pepper

To finish:	**To finish:**
4 × 15 ml. spoons fresh single cream	4 tablespoons fresh single cream
1 × 15 ml. spoon freshly chopped mint or parsley	1 tablespoon freshly chopped mint or parsley

Cook the beans in boiling salted water for 12 to 15 minutes or until just tender. Drain. Cook frozen beans according to the directions on the packet.

Meanwhile, melt a knob of butter in a frying pan. Add the onions and bacon and fry until the onions are golden and the bacon pieces are crisp. Stir in the drained beans and season to taste with salt and pepper. Heat through, stirring constantly. Stir in the cream and chopped mint or parsley and transfer to a hot serving dish. Serve immediately.

Aubergine and tomato casserole

Spanish baked beans

A dish that requires a long cooking time, Spanish baked beans can be left to cook overnight.

METRIC	IMPERIAL
¼ kg. salt belly pork, rind and bone removed and soaked overnight	½ lb. salt belly pork, rind and bone removed and soaked overnight
1 onion, peeled and sliced	1 onion, peeled and sliced
1 garlic clove, crushed	1 garlic clove, crushed
2 × 15 ml. spoons tomato purée	2 tablespoons tomato purée
2 × 15 ml. spoons freshly chopped parsley	2 tablespoons freshly chopped parsley
2 × 5 ml. spoons soft brown sugar	2 teaspoons soft brown sugar
¼ kg. haricot beans, soaked overnight	½ lb. haricot beans, soaked overnight
Freshly ground black pepper	Freshly ground black pepper

Drain the belly pork and rinse under cold running water. Put in the bottom of a deep casserole dish, preferably an earthenware one. Mix together the onion, garlic, tomato purée, parsley and sugar, and put this mixture in a layer on top of the pork. Drain the beans and rinse under cold running water. Add to the casserole. Sprinkle with plenty of pepper and stir in enough water to cover.

Cover the casserole with a lid and bake in a very cool oven (140°C/275°F or Gas Mark 1) for 5 hours or until the beans are tender. Check the water level occasionally, adding a little more water if the casserole becomes too dry. If you want to leave the beans to cook overnight, put into an even cooler oven (100–125°C/225–250°F or Gas Mark ¼–½).

When cooked, remove the belly pork from the casserole and chop into bite-sized pieces. Stir back into the casserole and adjust seasoning before serving.

Beetroot in soured cream

Beetroot in soured cream is popular throughout Eastern Europe. Serve with any grilled or roasted meat.

METRIC	IMPERIAL
Butter for frying	Butter for frying
4 medium-sized beetroot, cooked and sliced	4 medium-sized beetroot, cooked and sliced
1 × 2.5 ml. spoon ground allspice (Jamaican pepper)	½ teaspoon ground allspice (Jamaican pepper)
Salt and freshly ground black pepper	Salt and freshly ground black pepper
1 × 141 g. carton soured cream, at room temperature	1 × 5 oz. carton soured cream, at room temperature
Snipped chives to finish	Snipped chives to finish

Melt a knob of butter in a large heavy-based saucepan. Add the sliced beetroot, sprinkle with the allspice, and salt and pepper to taste, and fry lightly until hot.

Turn off the heat and stir in the soured cream. Transfer to a hot serving dish and sprinkle with snipped chives.

Beetroot in soured cream; Spanish baked beans; French beans with bacon

121

Red cabbage casserole

Red cabbage, casseroled with apples, onion and raisins, makes a perfect accompaniment to roast pork. This recipe makes double the quantity required, and it is excellent reheated on top of the stove with a knob of butter on the following day.

METRIC	IMPERIAL
2 cooking apples, peeled, cored and sliced	2 cooking apples, peeled, cored and sliced
Approx. ¾ kg. red cabbage, washed, trimmed and thinly sliced	Approx 1½ lb. red cabbage, washed, trimmed and thinly sliced
1 large onion, peeled and thinly sliced	1 large onion, peeled and thinly sliced
50 g. raisins	2 oz. raisins
2 × 5 ml. spoons sugar	2 teaspoons sugar
Salt and freshly ground black pepper	Salt and freshly ground black pepper
Approx. 300 ml. dry white wine or chicken stock	Approx. ½ pint dry white wine or chicken stock
25 g. butter	1 oz. butter

Put the apples in an ovenproof casserole dish with the red cabbage, onion, raisins, sugar, and salt and pepper to taste. Pour in the wine or stock, or a mixture of both, and stir well to mix.

Cover the casserole with a lid or buttered greaseproof paper or foil and bake in a moderate oven (180°C/350°F or Gas Mark 4) for 1 hour or until the cabbage is tender.

Remove the casserole dish from oven. Adjust seasoning and stir in the butter until melted. Serve straight from the casserole.

Creamed carrots

New baby carrots are delicious when gently simmered in stock and finished with a luxurious touch of fresh cream. Serve with new season's spring lamb and homemade mint sauce.

METRIC	IMPERIAL
½ kg. young carrots, topped, tailed and scraped	1 lb. young carrots, topped, tailed and scraped
Approx. 300 ml. chicken stock	Approx. ½ pint chicken stock
1 × 5 ml. spoon sugar	1 teaspoon sugar
Salt and freshly ground black pepper	Salt and freshly ground black pepper
150 ml. fresh single cream	¼ pint fresh single cream
1 × 15 ml. spoon freshly chopped parsley	1 tablespoon freshly chopped parsley

Leave the carrots whole if they are very small, otherwise slice them. Put them in a saucepan with enough chicken stock to cover. Add the sugar, and salt and pepper to taste.

Bring slowly to the boil, then lower the heat and simmer gently for about 15 minutes or until the carrots are just tender and the stock has evaporated. Stir in the cream and parsley and heat very gently. Adjust seasoning. Transfer to a hot serving dish and serve immediately.

Red cabbage casserole; Creamed carrots; Brussels sprouts in a mould; Chinese-style cabbage

Brussels sprouts in a mould

This is an unusual way to serve Brussels sprouts. In winter-time it makes a welcome change from the usual vegetable dishes. Serve with roast poultry or beef.

METRIC	IMPERIAL
¾ kg. Brussels sprouts, washed, trimmed and cut	*1½ lb. Brussels sprouts, washed, trimmed and cut*
Salt	*Salt*
¼ kg. mashed potatoes	*½ lb. mashed potatoes*
25 g. butter	*1 oz. butter*
1 egg, beaten	*1 egg, beaten*
2 × 15 ml. spoons fresh single cream or milk	*2 tablespoons fresh single cream or milk*
1 × 1.25 ml. spoon grated nutmeg	*¼ teaspoon grated nutmeg*
Salt and freshly ground black pepper	*Salt and freshly ground black pepper*

Cook the Brussels sprouts in boiling salted water for 10 to 15 minutes or until just tender. Drain and purée in an electric blender or work through a Mouli-légumes.

Put the puréed sprouts in a large mixing bowl. Mix in the mashed potatoes with the remaining ingredients, and salt and pepper to taste. Beat well with a wooden spoon to combine.

Put this mixture in a well-buttered 17.5 cm./7 in. round mould or cake tin. Stand in a roasting tin half-full of hot water and bake in a fairly hot oven (190°C/375°F or Gas Mark 5) for 45 minutes or until a knife inserted into the mould comes out clean. Leave to stand for 5 minutes. Carefully turn out onto a hot serving platter. Serve immediately.

Chinese-style cabbage

The Chinese know how to cook cabbage – it should be tender, yet still crisp. Overcooked, cabbage is unappetising and tasteless.

METRIC	IMPERIAL
Butter for frying	*Butter for frying*
Approx. ½ kg. white or green cabbage, washed, trimmed and thinly sliced	*Approx. 1 lb. white or green cabbage, washed, trimmed and thinly sliced*
Juice of ½ lemon	*Juice of ½ lemon*
Salt and freshly ground black pepper	*Salt and freshly ground black pepper*
Approx. 150 ml. hot chicken stock	*Approx. ¼ pint hot chicken stock*
2 × 15 ml. spoons dry sherry (optional)	*2 tablespoons dry sherry (optional)*

Melt a knob of butter in a large frying pan. Put in the sliced cabbage, sprinkle with lemon juice and plenty of salt and pepper. Fry, stirring constantly, for 1 to 2 minutes, then add just enough hot stock to cover. Simmer gently for a further 8 minutes, stirring occasionally, or until the cabbage is just tender.

Stir in the sherry, if using. Transfer to a hot serving dish and serve immediately.

Fennel à la Grecque

In this country, fennel is usually thought of as a salad vegetable, yet on the Continent, where it is more widely used, it is more often braised or sautéed. This recipe for fennel is delicious with roast lamb or chicken.

METRIC	IMPERIAL
Olive oil for frying	Olive oil for frying
2 heads of fennel, washed, trimmed and sliced lengthways into quarters	2 heads of fennel, washed, trimmed and sliced lengthways into quarters
Juice of 1 lemon	Juice of 1 lemon
1 × 15 ml. spoon freshly chopped marjoram or 1 × 2.5 ml. spoon dried marjoram	1 tablespoon freshly chopped marjoram or ½ teaspoon dried marjoram
1 × 5 ml. spoon ground coriander	1 teaspoon ground coriander
Salt and freshly ground black pepper	Salt and freshly ground black pepper
1 × 15 ml. spoon tomato purée	1 tablespoon tomato purée
¼ kg. tomatoes, skinned, seeded and chopped, or 1 × 226 g. can tomatoes, sieved	½ lb. tomatoes, skinned, seeded and chopped, or 1 × 8 oz. can tomatoes, sieved
1 × 15 ml. spoon freshly chopped parsley to finish	1 tablespoon freshly chopped parsley to finish

Fennel à la grecque

Heat 2 spoons of olive oil in a large saucepan. Put in the fennel and sprinkle with the lemon juice. Sauté until the fennel is lightly coloured. Sprinkle in the marjoram and coriander, with salt and pepper to taste, and sauté for a further 2 minutes, stirring constantly.

Stir in the tomato purée and tomatoes. Bring to the boil, then lower the heat, half cover and simmer gently for 30 minutes or until the fennel is tender, stirring occasionally. If the mixture becomes dry during the cooking time, stir in a little water.

Just before serving, adjust seasoning and stir in the chopped parsley. Transfer to a hot serving dish.

Braised celery

Celery is so often used for salads that it is neglected as a vegetable. This casserole of celery with onion, tomatoes and carrots is especially good with roast lamb.

METRIC	IMPERIAL
Butter and cooking oil for frying	Butter and cooking oil for frying
1 medium-sized onion, peeled and chopped	1 medium-sized onion, peeled and chopped
4 tomatoes, skinned, seeded and chopped	4 tomatoes, skinned, seeded and chopped
2 heads of celery, stalks scrubbed and halved crossways	2 heads of celery, stalks scrubbed and halved crossways
2 carrots, peeled and sliced	2 carrots, peeled and sliced
Approx. 600 ml. chicken stock	Approx. 1 pint chicken stock
1 bouquet garni	1 bouquet garni
Salt and freshly ground black pepper	Salt and freshly ground black pepper

Heat a knob of butter and a spoon of oil in a flameproof casserole. Add the onion and fry until golden. Stir in the tomatoes, celery and carrots. Pour in just enough stock to cover the vegetables, and bring to the boil. Add the bouquet garni, and salt and pepper to taste, and transfer to a warm oven (160°C/325°F or Gas Mark 3). Cook for 30 to 40 minutes or until the celery is just tender when pricked with a fork. Adjust seasoning and discard the bouquet garni, then transfer to a hot serving dish with a little of the cooking liquid. Alternatively, the vegetables can be served straight from the casserole after draining off most of the cooking liquid.

Mushroom and potato sauté

Whole button mushrooms should be used for this recipe as the flat open variety would discolour the creamy sauce. When new potatoes are in season they are by far the best to use; however, in winter time, canned new potatoes make a good substitute.

METRIC	IMPERIAL
Approx. ¾ kg. small new potatoes, scraped or 1 × 539 g. can new potatoes, drained	Approx. 1½ lb. small new potatoes, scraped, or 1 × 1 lb. 3 oz. can new potatoes, drained

Salt
Butter for frying
175 g. button mushrooms,
  cleaned
4 × 15 ml. spoons fresh
  single cream
Salt and freshly ground
  black pepper
1 × 15 ml. spoon freshly
  chopped mint or parsley

Salt
Butter for frying
6 oz. button mushrooms,
  cleaned
4 tablespoons fresh single
  cream
Salt and freshly ground
  black pepper
1 tablespoon freshly
  chopped mint or parsley

Cook fresh potatoes in boiling salted water for about 15 to 20 minutes or until just tender. Drain.

Melt a knob of butter in a large frying pan. Add the mushrooms and sauté, stirring constantly, for 2 minutes. Add the potatoes to the pan (if using canned potatoes they should be added at this stage), and heat through. Turn off the heat and add the cream, salt and pepper to taste, and the chopped mint or parsley. Stir until the potatoes are thoroughly coated in the cream and herbs. Transfer to a hot serving dish and serve immediately.

Ratatouille

Ratatouille is a vegetable stew from the Provence region of Southern France. It makes a colourful and delicious summer vegetable dish when courgettes, tomatoes, aubergines and peppers are relatively cheap. Serve it hot with roast or grilled lamb and pork, or chilled with garlic bread as a starter.

METRIC	IMPERIAL
Olive oil for frying	*Olive oil for frying*
1 large onion, peeled and finely chopped	*1 large onion, peeled and finely chopped*
1 garlic clove, crushed with 1 × 2.5 ml. spoon salt	*1 garlic clove, crushed with ½ teaspoon salt*
½ kg. courgettes, sliced	*1 lb. courgettes, sliced*
½ kg. tomatoes, skinned, seeded and chopped or 1 × 396 g. can tomatoes	*1 lb. tomatoes, skinned, seeded and chopped, or 1 × 14 oz. can tomatoes*
1 large aubergine, sliced and dégorgé	*1 large aubergine, sliced and dégorgé*
1 green pepper, cored, seeded and sliced	*1 green pepper, cored, seeded and sliced*
Freshly ground black pepper	*Freshly ground black pepper*

Heat 2 spoons of oil in a large saucepan. Add the onion and garlic and fry until golden. Add the remaining vegetables, season well with black pepper and stir in enough water to come about half way up the mixture. Bring to the boil, stirring constantly, then lower the heat, cover and simmer gently for at least 30 minutes, stirring occasionally. The vegetables should be broken down and soft, and the juices quite thick. Adjust seasoning and transfer to a hot serving dish, or cool and chill in the refrigerator.   **Serves 4 to 6.**

Ratatouille; Mushroom and potato sauté; Braised celery

Petits pois à la Française

A classic French recipe, Petits pois à la française is best made with tender young garden peas for their sweet flavour. However, frozen petits pois are available all year round and may be used instead.

METRIC	IMPERIAL
½ kg. shelled fresh peas, or frozen petits pois, thawed	1 lb. shelled fresh peas or frozen petits pois, thawed
6 lettuce leaves, washed and shredded	6 lettuce leaves, washed and shredded
8 spring onions, topped, tailed and chopped	8 spring onions, topped, tailed and chopped
1 × 5 ml. spoon sugar	1 teaspoon sugar
Salt and freshly ground black pepper	Salt and freshly ground black pepper

To finish:

25 g. butter	1 oz. butter
1 × 15 ml. spoon freshly chopped mint	1 tablespoon freshly chopped mint

Put the peas, lettuce, spring onions, sugar, and salt and pepper to taste, in a saucepan and just cover the bottom of the pan with water. Bring slowly to the boil, then lower the heat and simmer gently for 20 minutes or until the peas are tender. There should be almost no liquid left in the pan.

Stir in the butter and mint, adjust seasoning and transfer to a hot serving dish.

NOTE: if using frozen petits pois, simmer the lettuce and spring onions in approx. 4 × 15 ml. spoons/4 tablespoons water with the seasonings for 10 minutes. Then add the frozen peas and the butter and cook for a further 3 minutes, or according to packet directions. Sprinkle in the chopped mint before serving.

Parsnip chips

Parsnip chips make a welcome alternative to potato chips, and they have more flavour. Serve them sprinkled with grated Parmesan cheese as an accompaniment to grilled chops or sausages.

METRIC	IMPERIAL
Approx. ½ kg. parsnips, peeled and sliced into chip shapes	Approx. 1 lb. parsnips, peeled and sliced into chip shapes
Salt	Salt
Oil for deep-fat frying	Oil for deep-fat frying
50 g. Parmesan cheese, grated, to finish	2 oz. Parmesan cheese, grated, to finish

Cook the parsnips in boiling salted water for 10 to 15 minutes, or until just tender. Drain and dry thoroughly on a clean tea towel or absorbent kitchen paper.

Gently heat oil in a deep-frying pan until it is hot enough to turn a stale bread cube golden in 30 seconds (190°C/375°F on a deep-frying thermometer). Put in the parsnips, in a frying basket, and fry for 5 minutes or until golden-brown. Lift out and drain on absorbent kitchen paper. Transfer to a hot serving dish, sprinkle with the cheese and serve immediately.

Parsnip chips; Petits pois à la française

Italian-style peppers; Gratin dauphinois

Italian-style peppers

This is a kind of vegetable stew, not unlike Ratatouille but made simply with peppers and tomatoes. It makes a colourful vegetable accompaniment to most grilled or roast meats, particularly if both red and green peppers are used. It can also be served chilled as a starter.

METRIC	IMPERIAL
Butter and olive oil for frying	Butter and olive oil for frying
1 large onion, peeled and finely chopped	1 large onion, peeled and finely chopped
1 garlic clove, crushed with 1 × 2.5 ml. spoon salt	1 garlic clove, crushed with ½ teaspoon salt
½ kg. red and green peppers, cored, seeded and chopped	1 lb. red and green peppers, cored, seeded and chopped
½ kg. tomatoes, skinned, seeded and chopped	1 lb. tomatoes, skinned, seeded and chopped
Freshly ground black pepper	Freshly ground black pepper
1 × 5 ml. spoon sugar	1 teaspoon sugar
1 × 5 ml. spoon freshly chopped basil or 1 × 2.5 ml. spoon dried basil	1 teaspoon freshly chopped basil or ½ teaspoon dried basil

Heat a knob of butter and 2 spoons of oil in a large saucepan. Add the onion and garlic and fry until golden. Add the peppers and tomatoes and stir in plenty of black pepper, the sugar and basil. Fry the mixture over high heat for a few minutes, then cover, lower the heat and simmer very gently, stirring occasionally, for 20 to 30 minutes or until the peppers and tomatoes are almost a purée. If the mixture becomes too dry during the cooking time, add a little water. Adjust seasoning and transfer to a hot serving dish.

Gratin Dauphinois

A superb potato dish that is made with floury winter potatoes, Gratin Dauphinois is a recipe to reserve for special occasions, as it is rather extravagant! For a slightly cheaper version it can be made with milk and Cheddar cheese rather than Gruyère and cream, but the finished result is not quite the same.

METRIC	IMPERIAL
25 g. butter, softened	1 oz. butter, softened
Approx. 1 kg. potatoes, peeled and sliced into thin rings	Approx. 2 lb. potatoes, peeled and sliced into thin rings
1 large onion, peeled and finely chopped	1 large onion, peeled and finely chopped
¼ kg. Gruyère cheese, grated	½ lb. Gruyère cheese, grated
Salt and freshly ground black pepper	Salt and freshly ground black pepper
150 ml. fresh single cream	¼ pint fresh single cream

Brush the base and sides of a flameproof casserole dish with some of the butter. Put a layer of potato slices, overlapping, in the bottom of the casserole. Dot with more butter and sprinkle with some of the onion and cheese, and salt and pepper to taste. Pour over about one-quarter of the cream. Continue with these layers until all the ingredients are used up, finishing with a layer of cheese and pouring the remaining cream over the top.

Cover with a lid or buttered greaseproof paper or foil, and bake in a moderately hot oven (190°C/375°F or Gas Mark 5) for 1 hour or until the potatoes are tender when pierced with a skewer. Transfer the casserole dish to a preheated hot grill and brown for 5 minutes or until the top layer of cheese is bubbling.

Sweetcorn fritters

This is an unusual accompaniment that goes well with most grilled, fried or roast meats. Sweetcorn fritters are particularly good with chicken – the Americans serve them as a traditional garnish to Chicken Maryland.

METRIC	IMPERIAL
100 g. flour	4 oz. flour
1 × 1.25 ml. spoon salt	¼ teaspoon salt
1 egg, beaten	1 egg, beaten
150 ml. milk	¼ pint milk
1 × 326 g. can sweetcorn, drained	1 × 11½ oz. can sweetcorn, drained
Freshly ground black pepper	Freshly ground black pepper
Cooking oil for frying	Cooking oil for frying

Sift the flour and salt into a mixing bowl. Make a well in the centre, put in the beaten egg and gradually beat in half the milk, drawing in the flour from the sides of the bowl.

Beat the mixture vigorously for a few minutes, then pour in the remaining milk and beat to remove any lumps. Mix in the sweetcorn, and black pepper to taste.

Heat 2 spoons of oil in a frying pan. Put in a few spoonfuls of the sweetcorn batter, well-spaced, leaving room for the mixture to spread. Fry for 2 to 3 minutes on each side until risen and golden-brown. Drain on absorbent kitchen paper and keep hot while cooking the remainder, adding and heating additional oil as necessary. Serve immediately.

Makes approx. 12 fritters.

Sweet glazed turnips

Turnips are a rather underrated vegetable, probably because they are often not cooked properly. This is a more unusual way to serve turnips.

METRIC	IMPERIAL
Approx. ¾ kg. turnips, peeled and thickly sliced	Approx. 1½ lb. turnips, peeled and thickly sliced
Salt	Salt
25 g. butter	1 oz. butter
1 × 15 ml. spoon soft brown sugar	1 tablespoon soft brown sugar
8 × 15 ml. spoons chicken stock	8 tablespoons chicken stock
Freshly ground black pepper	Freshly ground black pepper
1 × 15 ml. spoon freshly chopped parsley to finish	1 tablespoon freshly chopped parsley to finish

Put the turnips into boiling salted water and cook for 20 to 30 minutes or until they are almost tender. Drain and refresh under cold running water.

Melt the butter in the rinsed-out pan. Add the sugar and stir gently with a wooden spoon until dissolved, then pour in the stock. Bring to the boil. Add the turnips, lower the heat and simmer gently for 8 to 10 minutes or until the stock is reduced and the turnips are glazed.

Transfer to a hot serving dish. Sprinkle with black pepper and parsley and serve immediately.

Sweet glazed turnips; Sweetcorn fritters; Tomato and Gruyère casserole

Tomato and Gruyère casserole

This is best made during the summer months when tomatoes are both plentiful and flavoursome.

METRIC	IMPERIAL
¾ kg. tomatoes, skinned and sliced	1½ lb. tomatoes, skinned and sliced
150 ml. fresh single cream	¼ pint fresh single cream
100 g. Gruyère cheese, grated	4 oz. Gruyère cheese, grated
25 g. Parmesan cheese, grated	1 oz. Parmesan cheese, grated
Salt and freshly ground black pepper	Salt and freshly ground black pepper
1 × 5 ml. spoon freshly chopped basil or 1 × 2.5 ml. spoon dried basil	1 teaspoon freshly chopped basil or ½ teaspoon dried basil
2 × 5 ml. spoons caster sugar	2 teaspoons caster sugar
25 g. butter	1 oz. butter

Put some of the tomatoes in the bottom of an ovenproof casserole dish. Pour over some of the cream and sprinkle with a little Gruyère and Parmesan. Season to taste with salt and pepper and sprinkle with a little basil and sugar. Continue with these layers until all the ingredients are used up, finishing with a layer of Gruyère and Parmesan.

Dot the top of the dish with pieces of butter and bake in a moderate oven (180°C/350°F or Gas Mark 4) for 20 minutes or until the casserole is bubbling.

Salads

Coleslaw

Coleslaw is a very popular salad to eat with cooked meats and quiches. Try making it at home – it's quick and cheap to make, and a little goes a long way.

METRIC	IMPERIAL
½ large white cabbage (approx. ¼ kg.), shredded finely	½ large white cabbage (approx. ½ lb.), shredded finely
2 large carrots, peeled and shredded	2 large carrots, peeled and shredded
1 medium-sized onion, peeled and chopped	1 medium-sized onion, peeled and chopped
1 green pepper, cored, seeded and sliced (optional)	1 green pepper, cored, seeded and sliced (optional)
150 ml. thick homemade mayonnaise	¼ pint thick homemade mayonnaise
Juice of ½ lemon	Juice of ½ lemon
Salt and freshly ground black pepper	Salt and freshly ground black pepper

Put all the vegetables in a large mixing bowl. Add the mayonnaise and stir to combine. Stir in the lemon juice and plenty of salt and pepper and continue stirring until all the vegetables are evenly coated in the mayonnaise.

Transfer to a serving dish. Cover and chill in the refrigerator until required.

Coleslaw

Salade Niçoise

A classic French salad combining tuna fish and anchovies with crisp lettuce, celery and peppers, Salade Niçoise has an attractive garnish of black olives and hard-boiled eggs.

METRIC	IMPERIAL
1 crisp Cos lettuce, leaves separated and washed	1 crisp Cos lettuce, leaves separated and washed
4 celery stalks, scrubbed and chopped	4 celery stalks, scrubbed and chopped
4 tomatoes, skinned, seeded and chopped	4 tomatoes, skinned, seeded and chopped
1 green pepper, cored, seeded and chopped	1 green pepper, cored, seeded and chopped
1 × 200 g. can tuna fish, drained and flaked	1 × 7 oz. can tuna fish, drained and flaked
1 × 50 g. can anchovies in oil, drained, soaked in milk for 30 minutes and rinsed	1 × 2 oz. can anchovies in oil, drained, soaked in milk for 30 minutes and rinsed
2 hard-boiled eggs, quartered	2 hard-boiled eggs, quartered
50 g. black olives, stoned	2 oz. black olives, stoned
150 ml. French dressing	¼ pint French dressing

Arrange the lettuce leaves to cover the bottom and sides of a large salad bowl. Put the celery, tomatoes and pepper on top of the lettuce in the bottom of the bowl, then add the tuna and anchovies. Garnish the salad with the egg quarters and olives. Sprinkle French dressing over the salad just before serving.

Rice salad

This is a good salad to make in the winter, using frozen French beans. Serve for lunch with cold chicken, turkey or any cold cooked meat.

METRIC	IMPERIAL
¼ kg. long-grain rice, cooked and drained	½ lb. long-grain rice, cooked and drained
1 × 326 g. can sweetcorn, drained	1 × 11½ oz. can sweetcorn, drained
100 g. French beans, cooked and drained	4 oz. French beans, cooked and drained
2 celery stalks, scrubbed and chopped	2 celery stalks, scrubbed and chopped
1 red or green pepper, cored, seeded and chopped	1 red or green pepper, cored, seeded and chopped
4 tomatoes, skinned, seeded and chopped	4 tomatoes, skinned, seeded and chopped
150 ml. Mustard dressing	¼ pint Mustard dressing

Put the rice and sweetcorn in a large serving bowl and stir to mix. Stir in the beans, celery and pepper, adding the tomatoes last. Pour over the prepared dressing and fold in, being careful not to break the vegetables. Cover and chill in the refrigerator until required, stirring before serving.

Tuna and bean salad

An Italian-style starter, Tuna and bean salad is tangy and refreshing. Serve with fresh granary bread and butter.

METRIC	IMPERIAL
175 g. black-eye or haricot beans, soaked overnight and drained	6 oz. black-eye or haricot beans, soaked overnight and drained
Salt	Salt
1 small onion, peeled and finely chopped	1 small onion, peeled and finely chopped
1 × 200 g. can tuna fish, drained and flaked	1 × 7 oz. can tuna fish, drained and flaked
For the dressing:	**For the dressing:**
300 ml. olive or salad oil	½ pint olive or salad oil
150 ml. lemon juice	¼ pint lemon juice
4 × 15 ml. spoons freshly chopped parsley	4 tablespoons freshly chopped parsley
Freshly ground black pepper	Freshly ground black pepper

Cook the beans in boiling salted water for 40 minutes or until tender. Drain and refresh under cold running water. Put in a serving bowl with the onion and flaked tuna and stir carefully to combine.

To prepare the dressing, put the ingredients in a screw-top jar and shake well to mix.

Pour the dressing over the bean mixture and season to taste. Chill in the refrigerator for several hours. Stir well before serving.

Nutty orange salad

Light and refreshing, Nutty orange salad combines chicory, orange and walnuts together in a vinaigrette dressing. It is a good salad to serve with roast pork or game.

METRIC	IMPERIAL
4 heads of chicory, leaves separated and washed	4 heads of chicory, leaves separated and washed
Salt and freshly ground black pepper	Salt and freshly ground black pepper
2 large oranges, peel, pith and pips removed and sliced into rings	2 large oranges, peel, pith and pips removed and sliced into rings
50 g. walnuts, chopped	2 oz. walnuts, chopped
150 ml. Vinaigrette dressing	¼ pint Vinaigrette dressing

Put the chicory in a salad bowl and sprinkle with a little salt and pepper. Add the orange rings and walnuts and mix well together.

Pour in the prepared dressing and toss well before serving.

Rice salad; Tuna and bean salad (top shelf);
Salade Niçoise; Nutty orange salad

Avocado salad

This is a very simple salad that is tangy and refreshing, ideal to serve as a dinner party starter or as an accompaniment to rich meat and game dishes, or pâté.

METRIC	IMPERIAL
1 crisp Cos lettuce, leaves separated and washed	*1 crisp Cos lettuce, leaves separated and washed*
8 × 15 ml. spoons olive oil	*8 tablespoons olive oil*
4 × 15 ml. spoons tarragon vinegar	*4 tablespoons tarragon vinegar*
1 × 5 ml. spoon freshly chopped tarragon or mint	*1 teaspoon freshly chopped tarragon or mint*
1 × 5 ml. spoon caster sugar	*1 teaspoon caster sugar*
Salt and freshly ground black pepper	*Salt and freshly ground black pepper*
2 avocado pears	*2 avocado pears*
1 large grapefruit, peel and pips removed, divided into segments	*1 large grapefruit, peel and pips removed, divided into segments*

Arrange the lettuce leaves to cover the bottom and sides of a shallow salad bowl or dish.

To prepare the dressing, put the oil, vinegar, tarragon or mint, sugar and salt and pepper to taste in a screw-top jar. Shake vigorously until thoroughly mixed.

Peel, halve and stone the avocados and slice the flesh thinly. Put in a mixing bowl with the grapefruit segments and quickly toss in the prepared dressing. Pile in the serving bowl on top of the lettuce and serve immediately.

Cucumber raita

An Indian side dish, Cucumber raita is a delicious accompaniment to any roast or grilled meat, and is particularly good with kebabs and curries. It's the ideal vegetable to serve on hot summer days, as it is cool and refreshing.

METRIC	IMPERIAL
1 large cucumber, peeled, halved, seeded and sliced into small strips	*1 large cucumber, peeled, halved, seeded and sliced into small strips*
1 × 2.5 ml. spoon salt	*½ teaspoon salt*
1 × 5 ml. spoon sugar	*1 teaspoon sugar*
2 × 141 g. cartons natural unsweetened yogurt	*2 × 5 oz. cartons natural unsweetened yogurt*
2 × 15 ml. spoons freshly chopped mint	*2 tablespoons freshly chopped mint*
Freshly ground black pepper	*Freshly ground black pepper*
1 × 15 ml. spoon olive oil	*1 tablespoon olive oil*

Put the cucumber strips in a bowl and sprinkle with the salt and sugar. Stir to mix and leave to drain in a colander or sieve for 30 minutes.

Mix the cucumber and yogurt together with half the mint and plenty of pepper, then pile into a serving dish. Pour the oil evenly over the surface of the raita, then decorate with the remaining mint. Chill in the refrigerator until serving time.

Avocado salad
Cucumber raita

Tomato salad

This is one of the nicest summer salads, yet it is also one of the simplest. Serve with any meat or fish dish or with cheese-based quiches. Tomato salad also makes an excellent starter when served with garlic bread. If fresh basil is not available, use fresh parsley instead.

METRIC	IMPERIAL
350 g. tomatoes, skinned, seeded and sliced	*¾ lb. tomatoes, skinned, seeded and sliced*
1 × 15 ml. spoon grated onion	*1 tablespoon grated onion*

For the dressing:

8 × 15 ml. spoons olive oil	*8 tablespoons olive oil*
3 × 15 ml. spoons lemon juice	*3 tablespoons lemon juice*
1 garlic clove, halved	*1 garlic clove, halved*
1 × 5 ml. spoon freshly chopped basil	*1 teaspoon freshly chopped basil*
1 × 5 ml. spoon caster sugar	*1 teaspoon caster sugar*
1 × 2.5 ml. spoon salt	*½ teaspoon salt*
Freshly ground black pepper	*Freshly ground black pepper*

Arrange the tomatoes in a shallow serving dish and sprinkle with the grated onion.

To prepare the dressing, put all the ingredients, with pepper to taste, in a screw-top jar and shake vigorously until thoroughly mixed. Leave to stand for at least 30 minutes to allow the garlic and basil to flavour the dressing. Remove garlic before using.

Pour the dressing over the tomatoes. Chill in the refrigerator before serving, spooning over the dressing from time to time.

NOTE: the dressing can be kept in the jar for up to 1 week in the refrigerator.

Potato salad

One of the all-time favourites, homemade Potato salad should be made with firm, waxy potatoes. These will not crumble when mixed with the mayonnaise. For a change, try using soured cream instead of mayonnaise, or add 50 g./2 oz. cubed Gruyère or Emmenthal cheese to the salad before coating in the mayonnaise.

METRIC	IMPERIAL
Approx. ¾ kg. new potatoes or 1 × 539 g. can new potatoes, drained	*Approx. 1½ lb. new potatoes or 1 × 1 lb. 3 oz. can new potatoes, drained*
Salt	*Salt*
1 bunch of spring onions, topped, tailed and finely chopped	*1 bunch of spring onions, topped, tailed and finely chopped*
150 ml. thick homemade mayonnaise	*¼ pint thick homemade mayonnaise*
1 × 15 ml. spoon lemon juice	*1 tablespoon lemon juice*
Freshly ground black pepper	*Freshly ground black pepper*
2 × 15 ml. spoons freshly chopped mint or parsley to finish	*2 tablespoons freshly chopped mint or parsley to finish*

Cook the potatoes in their skins in boiling salted water for 15 minutes or until just tender. Remove from the water and allow to cool slightly. Peel off the skin. Cut the cooked or canned potatoes into chunks and place in a mixing bowl with the spring onions. Pour in the mayonnaise and lemon juice and add black pepper to taste. Coat the potato slices carefully in the mayonnaise, folding it in with a large metal spoon. Transfer to a serving bowl and sprinkle with more black pepper and the chopped mint or parsley.

Tomato salad
Potato salad

Blender mayonnaise

It is essential to know how to make mayonnaise properly, as it is used in all kinds of dishes apart from salads; it is used as a base for sauces such as Tartare and Horseradish, for example. For mayonnaise made by hand and for tips on making mayonnaise, see the recipe for Egg mayonnaise in the 'Starters' chapter.

METRIC	IMPERIAL
1 whole egg	1 whole egg
1 × 1.25 ml. spoon dry English mustard	¼ teaspoon dry English mustard
1 × 2.5 ml. spoon salt	½ teaspoon salt
2 × 15 ml. spoons red or white wine or tarragon vinegar or lemon juice	2 tablespoons red or white wine or tarragon vinegar or lemon juice
150 ml. olive, corn or nut oil	¼ pint olive, corn or nut oil

Put the egg, mustard, salt and vinegar or lemon juice into the blender and blend until well mixed. With the blender still on, add the oil slowly through the hole in the lid, drop by drop at first, gradually increasing the addition of the oil until the mayonnaise begins to thicken. At this point the oil can be added in a thin steady stream.

French dressing

No green salad is complete without a good French dressing. The best dressings are made with the best quality oil – it is false economy to use cooking or vegetable oil when making dressings as they will be thin and watery. Add a pinch of sugar for dressing tomatoes or salads that contain tomatoes or cucumber.

METRIC	IMPERIAL
150 ml. olive, corn or nut oil	¼ pint olive, corn or nut oil
3 × 15 ml. spoons red or white wine or tarragon vinegar	3 tablespoons red or white wine or tarragon vinegar
1 garlic clove, crushed with 1 × 2.5 ml. spoon salt	1 garlic clove, crushed with ½ teaspoon salt
Freshly ground black pepper	Freshly ground black pepper
Pinch of sugar (see above)	Pinch of sugar (see above)

Put the oil and vinegar in a bowl and beat with a fork until quite thick. Beat in the garlic and black pepper to taste. Sprinkle with sugar, if using. If the dressing seems too oily, add more salt.

NOTE: if a larger quantity of dressing is required, it is often a good idea to make it in a jar with a screw-top lid; put all the ingredients in the jar, screw the lid on tightly and shake vigorously until thoroughly combined. The jar can then be stored in the refrigerator for up to 1 week. Shake well before use.

Vinaigrette dressing

Add 1 × 15 ml. spoon/1 tablespoon freshly chopped parsley, thyme or basil to French dressing.

Yogurt dressing

This simple dressing can be used instead of mayonnaise for those who prefer a light, refreshing dressing, or for those who are slimming.

METRIC	IMPERIAL
1 × 141 g. carton natural unsweetened yogurt	1 × 5 oz. carton natural unsweetened yogurt
2 × 15 ml. spoons olive, corn or nut oil	2 tablespoons olive, corn or nut oil
2 × 5 ml. spoons lemon juice	2 teaspoons lemon juice
Salt and freshly ground black pepper	Salt and freshly ground black pepper
2 × 15 ml. spoons snipped chives	2 tablespoons snipped chives

Put the yogurt in a mixing bowl and stir in the oil and lemon juice. Season to taste with salt and pepper. Stir in snipped chives and transfer to a serving bowl. Refrigerate until required.

Devilled dressing

This is for those who like a hot, spicy dressing for salads and to serve with hamburgers or cooked meats. It is best to make this dressing in an electric blender so that it will be smooth.

METRIC	IMPERIAL
½ small onion, peeled and chopped	½ small onion, peeled and chopped
1 × 15 ml. spoon chili sauce	1 tablespoon chili sauce
150 ml. olive, corn or nut oil	¼ pint olive, corn or nut oil
3 × 15 ml. spoons lemon juice	3 tablespoons lemon juice
1 × 5 ml. spoon sugar	1 teaspoon sugar
1 × 2.5 ml. spoon salt	½ teaspoon salt
Pinch of cayenne pepper	Pinch of cayenne pepper

Put all the ingredients in an electric blender and blend until the dressing is smooth. Taste for seasoning.

Mustard dressing

A sharp, tangy dressing, excellent for salads to serve with cold roast beef, pork or ham.

METRIC	IMPERIAL
1 × 15 ml. spoon Dijon-style mustard	1 tablespoon Dijon-style mustard
2 × 15 ml. spoons boiling water	2 tablespoons boiling water
150 ml. olive oil	¼ pint olive oil
2 × 15 ml. spoons freshly chopped parsley	2 tablespoons freshly chopped parsley
Salt and freshly ground black pepper	Salt and freshly ground black pepper

Put the mustard in a mixing bowl and beat in the water gradually. Then add the oil, drop by drop, beating until the dressing is thick. Stir in the chopped parsley, and salt and pepper to taste.

Aïoli (Garlic mayonnaise)

Traditionally, Aïoli is served in France with boiled fish or *crudités*, raw vegetables. Put the prepared Aïoli in a serving bowl and surround with bowls of raw carrot sticks, scrubbed celery stalks, small new potatoes, boiled and halved, and raw cauliflower flowerets. Guests dip these in the Aïoli.

METRIC	IMPERIAL
3 garlic cloves, crushed	*3 garlic cloves, crushed*
1 slice of white bread, crusts removed, soaked in water and squeezed dry	*1 slice of white bread, crusts removed, soaked in water and squeezed dry*
1 egg yolk	*1 egg yolk*
150 ml. olive oil	*¼ pint olive oil*
1 × 15 ml. spoon lemon juice	*1 tablespoon lemon juice*
Salt and freshly ground black pepper	*Salt and freshly ground black pepper*
1 × 15 ml. spoon boiling water to finish	*1 tablespoon boiling water to finish*

Put the crushed garlic cloves in a mixing bowl with the bread and mash together with a pestle or wooden spoon until thoroughly combined. Beat in the egg yolk with a fork.

Add the oil to this mixture, drop by drop at first, beating until the mixture begins to thicken. The oil may then be added in a thin steady stream. When all the oil is incorporated, stir in the lemon juice and add salt and pepper to taste. Finish by stirring in the boiling water.

(clockwise) Yogurt dressing; Devilled dressing; Vinaigrette dressing; Mustard dressing; Blender mayonnaise; Aïoli; French dressing(centre)

Snacks and suppers

From simple toasted savouries to meaty evening meals, the choice of snacks and suppers is enormous. With very little extra time and trouble it is possible to provide tasty, nourishing and different meals for your family and friends.

Try to ring the changes as much as possible, varying dishes from one day to another. In this Chapter you will find over 30 recipes to choose from – savoury omelets and soufflés, quiches, flans, stuffed potatoes and pancakes, and dishes using sausages and minced beef, many of them with an international flavour.

French (savoury) omelets

The beauty of the French omelet is that it is so versatile – and relatively quick to make. Once the art of making a good omelet has been mastered, there is no limit to the variations on the omelet theme, and a nourishing, wholesome meal can be made in minutes. The choice is endless, from plain and *fines herbes* omelets to the more fancy omelets filled with such delicacies as chicken livers or lobster.

For best results when making omelets, a heavy-based pan should be used, ideally made of cast iron or aluminium. If possible, reserve one pan for omelet making and do not use it for anything else. Wipe it clean with kitchen paper after use and rub a little salt into it. Wipe off salt when ready to use again. Do not wash it or use detergent or scouring agents of any kind as this will cause the omelets to stick.

The recipes below are for 3 to 4 egg quantities, enough for 2 people, using a 17.5–20 cm/7–8 in. pan.

Plain omelet

METRIC	IMPERIAL
3–4 eggs	*3–4 eggs*
1 × 15 ml. spoon cold water	*1 tablespoon cold water*
Salt and freshly ground	*Salt and freshly ground*
black pepper	*black pepper*
25 g. butter	*1 oz. butter*

Beat the eggs lightly in a mixing bowl, then stir in the water and add salt and pepper to taste.

Melt the butter over medium heat in the omelet pan. When foaming, pour in the egg mixture. Using a palette knife, smooth over the surface of the omelet, lifting up the edge of the omelet to allow any unset omelet mixture to flow around the sides into the hot butter. Cook for about 20 seconds or until the mixture is creamy, then tilt the pan away from you and fold the omelet over with the palette knife. Press down with the knife, then tip the omelet onto a hot platter. Serve immediately.

Omelet aux fines herbes

Add 2 × 15 ml. spoons/2 tablespoons freshly chopped mixed herbs (parsley, thyme, snipped chives, marjoram) to the egg mixture before cooking. Cook as for plain omelet above.

Ham and cheese omelet

Add 50 g./2 oz. grated Gruyère or Cheddar cheese, 50 g./2 oz. finely chopped cooked ham and a pinch of cayenne pepper to the egg mixture before cooking. Cook as for plain omelet above.

French onion stuffing

METRIC
Butter for frying
*1 large onion, peeled and
  sliced into rings*
*1 garlic clove, crushed
  (optional)*
50 g. Gruyère cheese, grated
*Salt and freshly ground
  black pepper*

IMPERIAL
Butter for frying
*1 large onion, peeled and
  sliced into rings*
*1 garlic clove, crushed
  (optional)*
2 oz. Gruyère cheese, grated
*Salt and freshly ground
  black pepper*

Melt a knob of butter in a small pan. Add the onion and garlic (if using) and fry gently over very low heat for 10 to 15 minutes or until soft and golden. Remove from the heat and stir in the grated Gruyère. Add salt to taste and plenty of black pepper. Use to fill a plain omelet as above.

Mushroom stuffing

METRIC
1 × 15 ml. spoon butter
*100 g. button mushrooms,
  cleaned and sliced*
2 × 5 ml. spoons flour
*3–4 × 15 ml. spoons
  chicken stock or water*
*Salt and freshly ground
  black pepper*

IMPERIAL
1 tablespoon butter
*4 oz. button mushrooms,
  cleaned and sliced*
2 teaspoons flour
*3–4 tablespoons chicken
  stock or water*
*Salt and freshly ground
  black pepper*

Melt the butter in a small pan. When foaming, add the mushrooms. Sauté for 2 minutes, then stir in the flour and cook for a further 1 to 2 minutes. Add the stock or water gradually, stirring constantly until the mixture thickens. Season to taste with salt and pepper and use to fill a plain omelet as above.

Spanish omelet

A Spanish omelet is quite different from a French omelet in that it is not folded over. The filling is cooked in a frying pan and the egg mixture is poured over; it is then cooked on both sides and served like a pancake, sometimes cut into wedges. The fillings used in Spanish omelets vary tremendously, depending on the region from which they originate. This is a fairly simple, Catalan version.

METRIC
Olive oil for frying
*1 large onion, peeled and
  finely chopped*
*1 garlic clove, crushed with 1
  × 2.5 ml. spoon salt*
*2 medium-sized potatoes,
  boiled in their skins and
  diced*
*Freshly ground black
  pepper*
6 eggs, beaten

IMPERIAL
Olive oil for frying
*1 large onion, peeled and
  finely chopped*
*1 garlic clove, crushed with
  ½ teaspoon salt*
*2 medium-sized potatoes,
  boiled in their skins and
  diced*
*Freshly ground black
  pepper*
6 eggs, beaten

Heat 2 spoons of oil in a large frying pan. Add the onion and garlic and fry gently until golden. Add the potatoes and season with black pepper. Cook until the potatoes are golden, stirring occasionally.

Pour the eggs into the pan and cook until the bottom sets and is lightly browned when lifted with a palette knife. Transfer the pan to a preheated hot grill and cook for 3 to 4 minutes or until the top of the omelet is browned and bubbling. Slide onto a hot platter and serve immediately.

137

Welsh rarebit

More substantial than simple cheese on toast, a well-made Welsh rarebit is truly delicious, especially if brown ale is used. Serve with grilled tomatoes and a glass of beer.

METRIC	IMPERIAL
25 g. butter	1 oz. butter
225 g. Cheddar cheese, grated	½ lb. Cheddar cheese, grated
1 × 1.25 ml. spoon dry English mustard	¼ teaspoon dry English mustard
Dash of Worcestershire sauce	Dash of Worcestershire sauce
3 × 15 ml. spoons brown ale or milk	3 tablespoons brown ale or milk
Salt and freshly ground black pepper	Salt and freshly ground black pepper
4 slices hot buttered toast	4 slices hot buttered toast

Melt the butter in a heavy-based saucepan. Stir in the remaining ingredients, and heat through gently over low heat until the cheese has melted, stirring constantly with a wooden spoon.

Taste for seasoning, then spread onto toast. Serve immediately.

NOTE: Buck rarebit is made as for Welsh rarebit but with a poached egg on top of each slice of toast.

Scotch woodcock

Traditionally, Scotch woodcock used to be served as a savoury at the end of a meal, but in these less formal times it is more likely to be served as a snack.

METRIC	IMPERIAL
1 × 50 g. can anchovies in olive oil, drained and soaked in milk for 30 minutes	1 × 2 oz. can anchovies in olive oil, drained and soaked in milk for 30 minutes
25 g. butter	1 oz. butter
4 slices hot toast	4 slices hot toast
3 eggs, beaten with 2 × 15 ml. spoons milk	3 eggs, beaten with 2 tablespoons milk
Freshly ground black pepper	Freshly ground black pepper
Cayenne pepper to finish	Cayenne pepper to finish

Drain the anchovies and pound half in a mortar and pestle with the butter, reserving a little butter for scrambling the eggs.

Spread the anchovy butter onto hot toast and keep hot. Melt the reserved butter in a saucepan and add the beaten eggs. Season to taste with black pepper. Stir over gentle heat until scrambled. Pile onto the buttered toast. Cut the remaining anchovy fillets in half lengthways and use to decorate in a lattice pattern on top of the scrambled egg. Sprinkle with cayenne pepper and serve immediately.

Buck rarebit; Welsh rarebit; Scotch woodcock

Cauliflower cheese special

A substantial meal can be made out of cauliflower cheese, if it has such mouth-watering ingredients as sautéed mushrooms and onions added to it.

METRIC	IMPERIAL
1 large cauliflower, washed and divided into flowerets	1 large cauliflower, washed and divided into flowerets
Salt	Salt
Butter for frying	Butter for frying
1 medium-sized onion, peeled and finely chopped	1 medium-sized onion, peeled and finely chopped
175 g. button mushrooms, cleaned and sliced	6 oz. button mushrooms, cleaned and sliced
Freshly ground black pepper	Freshly ground black pepper

For the cheese sauce:	For the cheese sauce:
25 g. butter	1 oz. butter
2 × 15 ml. spoons flour	2 tablespoons flour
350 ml. hot milk	12 fl. oz. hot milk
150 g. Cheddar cheese, grated	5 oz. Cheddar cheese, grated
Pinch of cayenne pepper	Pinch of cayenne pepper

Cook the cauliflower in boiling salted water for 10 to 15 minutes or until just tender. Meanwhile, melt a knob of butter in a small frying pan. Add the onion and fry until golden. Add the sliced mushrooms and continue to fry for a further 2 to 3 minutes, stirring constantly. Remove from the pan with a slotted spoon and drain on absorbent kitchen paper.

To prepare the cheese sauce, melt the butter in a pan. Stir in the flour and cook for 1 to 2 minutes, stirring constantly. Remove the pan from heat and gradually add the hot milk, stirring vigorously. When all the milk is incorporated, return

Cauliflower cheese special

Devilled mushroom toasties; Kidney toasties

the pan to the heat and bring slowly to the boil, stirring constantly. Lower the heat, add 100 g./4 oz. of the cheese, the cayenne pepper, and salt and pepper to taste. Simmer for a further 2 minutes. Stir in the onion and mushrooms.

When the cauliflower is tender, drain well and put in a shallow flameproof dish. Pour over the cheese sauce mixture and sprinkle with the remaining 50 g./2 oz. cheese. Put under a preheated hot grill for 5 minutes or until browned and bubbling. Serve immediately.

Toasties

Toast can make a meal in moments out of the simplest ingredients: all that is needed is a little ingenuity and a few basic store-cupboard items. Crusts should be removed from bread before toasting.

Quantities given are enough for 4 slices from a large loaf.

Kidney toasties

METRIC	IMPERIAL
25 g. butter	1 oz. butter
8 lambs' kidneys, cleaned and finely chopped	8 lambs' kidneys, cleaned and finely chopped
2 × 5 ml. spoons garam masala or curry powder	2 teaspoons garam masala or curry powder
Juice of ½ lemon	Juice of ½ lemon
1 × 15 ml. spoon freshly chopped parsley	1 tablespoon freshly chopped parsley
Dash of Tabasco sauce	Dash of Tabasco sauce
Salt and freshly ground black pepper	Salt and freshly ground black pepper
4 slices hot buttered toast	4 slices hot buttered toast
1 × 15 ml. spoon freshly chopped parsley to finish	1 tablespoon freshly chopped parsley to finish

Melt the butter in a small pan. Add the kidneys and garam masala or curry powder and fry gently until golden-brown and cooked through. Stir in the remaining ingredients with salt and pepper to taste. Pile onto hot, buttered toast, sprinkle with parsley and serve immediately.

Devilled mushroom toasties

METRIC	IMPERIAL
1 × 15 ml. spoon butter	1 tablespoon butter
175 g. button mushrooms, cleaned and sliced	6 oz. button mushrooms, cleaned and sliced
Juice of ½ lemon	Juice of ½ lemon
Scant 1 × 15 ml. spoon flour	Scant 1 tablespoon flour
4 × 15 ml. spoons top of the milk	4 tablespoons top of the milk
1 × 5 ml. spoon horseradish sauce	1 teaspoon horseradish sauce
2 × 5 ml. spoons Worcestershire sauce	2 teaspoons Worcestershire sauce
1 × 5 ml. spoon French Dijon-style mustard	1 teaspoon French Dijon-style mustard
1 × 5 ml. spoon tomato purée	1 teaspoon tomato purée
Salt and freshly ground black pepper	Salt and freshly ground black pepper
4 slices hot buttered toast	4 slices hot buttered toast
1 × 15 ml. spoon freshly chopped parsley to finish	1 tablespoon freshly chopped parsley to finish

Melt the butter in a small pan. Add the mushrooms and fry gently for 2 minutes, stirring constantly. Sprinkle in the lemon juice. Stir in the flour and cook for 1 minute, then stir in the milk and the remaining ingredients with salt and pepper to taste. Pile onto hot buttered toast, sprinkle with parsley and serve immediately.

Jacket baked potatoes

A potato baked in its skin can be a meal in itself, even more so if the cooked potato is scooped out and mixed with eggs, cheese, bacon, ham, or what you will. There is nothing easier to cook for a light lunch – the potato is simply put in the oven and forgotten about until the time comes to eat it.

Potatoes with eggs

METRIC	IMPERIAL
4 large potatoes, scrubbed	4 large potatoes, scrubbed
50 g. butter	2 oz. butter
2 × 15 ml. spoons top of the milk	2 tablespoons top of the milk
Salt and freshly ground black pepper	Salt and freshly ground black pepper
4 eggs	4 eggs

Prick the potatoes all over with a skewer and put onto the middle shelf of a fairly hot oven (200°C/400°F or Gas Mark 6). Bake for about 1 hour or until soft. Remove from the oven. Allow to cool slightly, then slice off one-third, lengthways. Scoop out the potato flesh with a teaspoon and mash in a bowl with the butter, milk, and salt and pepper to taste. Press this mixture into the potato skins, smoothing out a hollow in the centre of each. Break an egg into each hollow and return the potatoes to the oven for 10 to 15 minutes or until the eggs have set. Serve immediately.

Cream cheese and pepper stuffing

METRIC	IMPERIAL
4 large potatoes, scrubbed	4 large potatoes, scrubbed
100 g. cream cheese	4 oz. cream cheese
4 × 15 ml. spoons top of the milk	4 tablespoons top of the milk
1 green pepper, cored, seeded and finely chopped	1 green pepper, cored, seeded and finely chopped
Salt and freshly ground black pepper	Salt and freshly ground black pepper
1 × 15 ml. spoon snipped chives or freshly chopped parsley to finish	1 tablespoon snipped chives or freshly chopped parsley to finish

Prick the potatoes and bake until soft as for Potatoes with eggs above. Remove from the oven. Allow to cool slightly, then slice off one-third, lengthways. Scoop out the potato flesh with a teaspoon and mash in a bowl with the cream cheese, milk and green pepper. Season to taste and mix well. Spoon the mixture into the potato skins. Sprinkle the tops with chives or parsley and serve immediately.

Potatoes with eggs; with mushroom and ham stuffing; with cream cheese and pepper stuffing

Mushroom and ham stuffing

METRIC	IMPERIAL
4 large potatoes, scrubbed	4 large potatoes, scrubbed
75 g. butter	3 oz. butter
100 g. button mushrooms, cleaned and sliced	4 oz. button mushrooms, cleaned and sliced
50 g. cooked ham, chopped	2 oz. cooked ham, chopped
1 × 1.25 ml. spoon dry English mustard	¼ teaspoon dry English mustard
Salt and freshly ground black pepper	Salt and freshly ground black pepper
2 × 15 ml. spoons top of the milk	2 tablespoons top of the milk

To serve:

4 × 15 ml. spoons soured cream	4 tablespoons soured cream
Snipped chives or freshly chopped parsley	Snipped chives or freshly chopped parsley

Prick the potatoes and bake until soft as for Potatoes with eggs above. Meanwhile, melt 1 × 15 ml. spoon/1 tablespoon of the butter in a small frying pan. Add the mushrooms and fry gently for 2 minutes. Add the chopped ham and heat through. Stir in the mustard, and salt and pepper to taste. Keep hot.

When the potatoes are cooked, remove from the oven. Allow to cool slightly, then slice off one-third, lengthways. Scoop out the potato flesh with a teaspoon and mash in a bowl with the remaining butter, the hot mushroom and ham mixture and the milk. Spoon into potato skins. Top with soured cream and sprinkle with chives or parsley to taste. Serve immediately.

Quiches and flans

Pastry-based quiches, flans and tarts make ideal lunchtime dishes as they are easy to prepare, quick to cook, light in texture and delicious. The pastry case can be filled with different ingredients, depending on what is available – and personal preference, of course. Serve them with a green, mixed or tomato salad and French bread. Never serve straight from the oven – the flavour of all quiches or flans is much improved if they are allowed to 'rest' for 10 minutes or so before eating.

Shortcrust pastry flan case

METRIC	IMPERIAL
Scant 175 g. flour	*6 oz. flour*
Pinch of salt	*Pinch of salt*
50 g. butter	*2 oz. butter*
25 g. lard	*1 oz. lard*
2–3 × 15 ml. spoons cold water to mix	*2–3 tablespoons cold water to mix*

Sift the flour and salt into a mixing bowl. Add the butter and lard in pieces and rub into the flour until the mixture resembles fine breadcrumbs. Stir in enough cold water to draw the mixture together. Form into a ball, wrap in foil or grease-proof paper and chill in the refrigerator for at least 30 minutes before using.

Roll out the dough on a floured board and use to line a 20 cm./8 in. flan dish or flan ring placed on a baking sheet. Chill in the refrigerator for 15 minutes, then use for one of the following quiches or flans.

Quiche Lorraine

The classic French egg and bacon tart, Quiche Lorraine has numerous variations. This version includes cheese among its ingredients to add flavour.

METRIC	IMPERIAL
100–175 g. unsmoked streaky bacon, rinds removed and chopped	*4–6 oz. unsmoked streaky bacon, rinds removed and chopped*
Shortcrust pastry flan case	*Shortcrust pastry flan case*
2 whole eggs	*2 whole eggs*
2 egg yolks	*2 egg yolks*
150 ml. fresh single cream	*¼ pint fresh single cream*
Approx. 150 ml. milk	*Approx. ¼ pint milk*
Salt and freshly ground black pepper	*Salt and freshly ground black pepper*
50 g. Gruyère cheese, grated	*2 oz. Gruyère cheese, grated*

Fry the bacon over gentle heat in a small frying pan until the fat runs and the bacon becomes golden-brown. Put the bacon into the flan case. Beat the whole eggs, egg yolks and cream together lightly in a bowl and pour over the bacon. Stir in enough milk almost to fill the case. Season to taste with salt and pepper and sprinkle with the grated Gruyère.

Bake in a fairly hot oven (190°C/375°F or Gas Mark 5) for 25 to 30 minutes or until the filling is set and the pastry is golden. Remove from the oven and leave to rest for 10 minutes before serving.

Quiche Lorraine

Pissaladière
Cheese and courgette flan

Pissaladière

Original recipes for Pissaladière come from the South of France – and the ingredients used in this rich, tasty quiche are typical of the cuisine of that region.

METRIC	IMPERIAL
Olive oil for frying	Olive oil for frying
2 large onions, peeled and sliced	2 large onions, peeled and sliced
1 garlic clove, crushed with 1 × 2.5 ml. spoon salt	1 garlic clove, crushed with ½ teaspoon salt
1 × 226 g. can tomatoes, drained	1 × 8 oz. can tomatoes, drained
1 × 15 ml. spoon tomato purée	1 tablespoon tomato purée
1 × 5 ml. spoon freshly chopped basil or 1 × 2.5 ml. spoon dried basil	1 teaspoon freshly chopped basil or ½ teaspoon dried basil
1 × 5 ml. spoon sugar	1 teaspoon sugar
Freshly ground black pepper	Freshly ground black pepper
Shortcrust pastry flan case (see previous page)	Shortcrust pastry flan case (see previous page)
4 tomatoes, skinned and thinly sliced	4 tomatoes, skinned and thinly sliced
50 g. Gruyère or Cheddar cheese, grated	2 oz. Gruyère or Cheddar cheese, grated
1 × 50 g. can anchovies in olive oil, drained and soaked in milk for 30 minutes	1 × 2 oz. can anchovies in olive oil, drained and soaked in milk for 30 minutes
25 g. black olives, stoned and halved	1 oz. black olives, stoned and halved

Heat 2 spoons of oil in a frying pan. Add the onions and garlic and fry gently until golden. Stir in the canned tomatoes, tomato purée, basil, sugar and pepper to taste. Stir well, pulping the tomatoes with a wooden spoon, and bring to the boil. Cool slightly, then transfer to the flan case. Arrange tomato slices in a circle on top, sprinkle with the cheese then arrange drained anchovies in a lattice pattern on top. Put halved olives in each 'window' of the lattice.

Bake in a fairly hot oven (190°C/375°F or Gas Mark 5) for 25 to 30 minutes or until the pastry is golden-brown. Remove from the oven and leave to rest for 10 minutes before serving.

Cheese and courgette flan

A superbly flavoured flan, this should be made in late summer when courgettes are at their most plentiful.

METRIC	IMPERIAL
Vegetable oil for frying	Vegetable oil for frying
1 medium-sized onion, peeled and sliced	1 medium-sized onion, peeled and sliced
Approx. ½ kg. courgettes, washed and sliced	Approx. 1 lb. courgettes, washed and sliced
Shortcrust pastry flan case (see previous page)	Shortcrust pastry flan case (see previous page)
3 eggs, beaten with 150 ml. milk	3 eggs, beaten with ¼ pint milk

METRIC	IMPERIAL
Salt and freshly ground black pepper	*Salt and freshly ground black pepper*
100 g. Cheddar cheese, grated	*4 oz. Cheddar cheese, grated*

Heat 2 spoons of oil in a frying pan. Add the onion and fry gently until golden. Add the courgettes and continue cooking for about 10 minutes or until the courgettes are lightly coloured, stirring occasionally. Remove from the pan with a slotted spoon and place in the flan case. Pour over the eggs and milk and season to taste with salt and pepper. Sprinkle with the grated cheese.

Bake in a fairly hot oven (190°C/375°F or Gas Mark 5) for 25 to 30 minutes or until the filling is set and the pastry is golden. Remove from the oven and leave to rest for 10 minutes before serving.

Scotch eggs

Homemade Scotch eggs are really delicious served with a crisp green or tomato salad.

METRIC	IMPERIAL
½ kg. pork sausagemeat	*1 lb. pork sausagemeat*
1 small onion, peeled and finely chopped	*1 small onion, peeled and finely chopped*
1 × 5 ml. spoon dried mixed herbs	*1 teaspoon dried mixed herbs*
4 eggs, hard-boiled and shelled	*4 eggs, hard-boiled and shelled*
Flour for coating	*Flour for coating*
1 egg, beaten	*1 egg, beaten*
Approx. 175 g. dried breadcrumbs	*Approx. 6 oz. dried breadcrumbs*
Oil for deep-fat frying	*Oil for deep-fat frying*

Put the sausagemeat, onion and mixed herbs together in a bowl and mix well. Divide the mixture into four and press firmly around the hard-boiled eggs. Roll in flour, then dip in the beaten egg. Coat with the breadcrumbs, making sure that the sausagemeat is evenly covered. Chill in the refrigerator for at least 1 hour before frying.

Heat the oil gently in a deep-fat fryer until it is hot enough to turn a stale bread cube golden in 20 to 30 seconds (180–190°C/350–375°F on a deep-frying thermometer). Fry the Scotch eggs two at a time for about 10 minutes until crisp and golden-brown. Drain on absorbent kitchen paper and keep warm while frying the remaining two Scotch eggs. Drain. Transfer to a hot serving platter and serve.

Oeufs Florentine

Eggs and spinach together make a very nutritious light luncheon dish. If possible fresh spinach should be used for the best flavour and texture, but if not available frozen chopped spinach will make a good substitute.

METRIC	IMPERIAL
¾ kg. spinach, stalks removed	*1½ lb. spinach, stalks removed*
Salt	*Salt*
25 g. butter	*1 oz. butter*

Oeufs Florentine; Scotch eggs

METRIC	IMPERIAL
Pinch of grated nutmeg	*Pinch of grated nutmeg*
Freshly ground black pepper	*Freshly ground black pepper*
4 eggs	*4 eggs*
50 g. Cheddar or Cheshire cheese, grated	*2 oz. Cheddar or Cheshire cheese, grated*

Wash the spinach and put in a large saucepan with salt to taste. Heat gently until juices flow from the spinach, then cover the pan and cook gently for 5 to 10 minutes or until the spinach is tender. Drain and chop. Return to the rinsed-out pan with the butter, nutmeg, and pepper to taste, and allow to dry out for a few minutes over gentle heat.

Meanwhile, lightly poach the eggs in gently simmering water. Put the chopped spinach into four individual gratin dishes or one large flameproof serving dish. Place the drained, poached eggs on top. Sprinkle with the cheese and brown under a preheated hot grill for 2 to 3 minutes. Serve immediately.

Cheese soufflé

Convent eggs

Convent eggs

Rich and creamy, Convent eggs look most attractive if served in individual cocottes or ramekin dishes.

METRIC	IMPERIAL
1 × 15 ml. spoon butter, softened	1 tablespoon butter, softened
4 eggs	4 eggs
Salt and freshly ground black pepper	Salt and freshly ground black pepper
4 × 15 ml. spoons fresh double cream	4 tablespoons fresh double cream

Brush the insides of the cocottes or ramekins with the butter. Break in the eggs, season to taste with salt and pepper, then carefully spoon 1 × 15 ml. spoon/1 tablespoon cream over each egg.

Place in a roasting tin half-full of hot water and cover with buttered greaseproof paper or foil. Bake in a moderate oven (180°C/350°F or Gas Mark 4) for 10 to 15 minutes or until the eggs are set. Serve immediately.

Soufflés

Soufflés make ideal lunch dishes as they should be quickly made and quickly eaten. Many cooks are wary of making soufflés as they are commonly thought of as being difficult, but this is not so if a few basic rules are followed and the cook keeps a cool head.

1. Whisk the egg whites (see recipe) until very stiff and standing in peaks (turn the bowl upside down – if the egg whites do not drop, then they are stiff enough). Fold 1 × 15 ml. spoon/1 tablespoon of egg white into the sauce before folding in the bulk. This helps to soften the sauce.
2. Preheat the oven to the required temperature with the baking sheet on the centre shelf of the oven – this ensures that when the soufflé is put on the baking sheet in the hot oven, it will start cooking immediately. Remove shelves above the centre shelf to allow room to rise.
3. Time the cooking of the soufflé accurately, and be prepared to serve and eat immediately the soufflé is ready.

Cheese soufflé

This is most popular savoury soufflé of all. Use a sharp cheese with plenty of flavour.

METRIC	IMPERIAL
25 g. butter	1 oz. butter
6 × 5 ml. spoons flour	6 teaspoons flour
150 ml. hot milk	¼ pint hot milk
50 g. Cheddar cheese, grated	2 oz. Cheddar cheese, grated
1 × 1.25 ml. spoon dry English mustard	¼ teaspoon dry English mustard
Salt and freshly ground black pepper	Salt and freshly ground black pepper
3 egg yolks	3 egg yolks
4 egg whites	4 egg whites

Melt the butter in a saucepan. Stir in the flour and cook for 1 to 2 minutes, stirring constantly. Remove from the heat and gradually add the hot milk, stirring vigorously. When all the milk is incorporated, return to the heat and bring slowly to the boil, stirring constantly. Simmer gently until the sauce thickens. Lower the heat, stir in the grated cheese, mustard, and salt and pepper to taste. Remove from the heat and allow to cool slightly. When cool, beat in the egg yolks.

Whisk the egg whites in a clean bowl until stiff. Fold 1 × 15 ml. spoon/1 tablespoon of the egg whites into the cooled sauce with a metal spoon, then fold in the remainder, making a figure of eight pattern with the spoon and bringing the sauce up from the bottom of pan with the spoon.

Spoon the mixture lightly into the prepared soufflé dish and bake in the oven preheated to fairly hot (190°C/375°F or Gas Mark 5) for 30 to 35 minutes or until set and golden-brown. Serve immediately.

Haddock soufflé

Prepare and bake as for Cheese soufflé, substituting 100 g./4 oz. cooked, flaked smoked haddock for the cheese.

Cider sausages

Cider makes a rich, flavoursome sauce in which to bake sausages. Serve with creamed potatoes for a tasty supper meal.

METRIC	IMPERIAL
Pork or beef dripping for frying	Pork or beef dripping for frying
½ kg. pork or beef chipolatas	1 lb. pork or beef chipolatas
1 onion, peeled and sliced into rings	1 onion, peeled and sliced into rings
2 celery stalks, scrubbed and chopped	2 celery stalks, scrubbed and chopped
2 carrots, peeled and chopped	2 carrots, peeled and chopped
2 × 15 ml. spoons flour	2 tablespoons flour
300 ml. medium-dry cider	½ pint medium-dry cider
150 ml. beef stock	¼ pint beef stock
1 bouquet garni	1 bouquet garni
Salt and freshly ground black pepper	Salt and freshly ground black pepper
2 × 15 ml. spoons freshly chopped parsley to finish	2 tablespoons freshly chopped parsley to finish

Melt a knob of dripping in a flameproof casserole. Add the sausages and fry until browned on all sides. Remove from the casserole and set aside. Put the vegetables into casserole and fry gently, stirring constantly, until lightly coloured. Stir in the flour and cook, stirring, for 1 to 2 minutes. Pour in the cider and stock, stir well and bring to the boil.

Lower the heat, return the sausages to the casserole and add the bouquet garni, and salt and pepper to taste. Cover and cook for 45 minutes, stirring occasionally. Remove the bouquet garni, taste for seasoning and sprinkle with chopped parsley.

Toad in the hole

Toad in the hole is quick and makes a filling supper meal out of a few ingredients. Serve with baked beans if in a hurry, or with Chinese-style cabbage.

METRIC	IMPERIAL
8 large pork or beef sausages	8 large pork or beef sausages
25 g. pork or beef dripping or lard	1 oz. pork or beef dripping or lard
100 g. flour	4 oz. flour
1 × 1.25 ml. spoon salt	¼ teaspoon salt
2 eggs, beaten	2 eggs, beaten
300 ml. milk	½ pint milk
1 × 5 ml. spoon dried mixed herbs	1 teaspoon dried mixed herbs
Freshly ground black pepper	Freshly ground black pepper

Put the sausages in a shallow ovenproof dish or baking tin with the dripping or lard and bake in a hot oven (220°C/425°F or Gas Mark 7) for 5 to 10 minutes, turning the sausages occasionally to brown on all sides.

Meanwhile, make the batter. Sift the flour and salt into a mixing bowl. Make a well in the centre and put in the beaten eggs and half the milk. Mix the flour into the eggs and milk, gradually drawing flour in from the sides. Stir in remaining milk and beat vigorously with a wooden spoon or wire whisk to make the batter smooth. Stir in the dried herbs, and pepper to taste.

Pour the batter into the dish or tin with the sausages and continue to bake in a hot oven for a further 40 to 45 minutes or until the batter has risen and is brown and crisp. Serve immediately.

Cider sausages

Toad in the hole

Bangers with lentils

Pungent and spicy lentil purée goes well with sausages, especially the continental varieties such as bratwürst or Frankfurters. Serve this protein-packed dish on its own – with a simple salad tossed in French dressing.

METRIC	IMPERIAL
¼ kg. lentils, soaked overnight	½ lb. lentils, soaked overnight
Salt	Salt
Pork or beef dripping for frying	Pork or beef dripping for frying
1 medium-sized onion, peeled and finely chopped	1 medium-sized onion, peeled and finely chopped
2 garlic cloves, crushed with 1 × 2.5 ml. spoon salt	2 garlic cloves, crushed with ½ teaspoon salt
100 g. unsmoked streaky bacon, rinds removed and chopped	4 oz. unsmoked streaky bacon, rinds removed and chopped
Freshly ground black pepper	Freshly ground black pepper
½ kg. German bratwürst or Frankfurters	1 lb. German bratwürst or Frankfurters

Drain the lentils and rinse under cold running water. Put in a saucepan with a little salt, cover with water and bring to the boil. Simmer for 30 minutes or until the lentils are soft.

Meanwhile, melt a knob of dripping in a frying pan. Add the onion, garlic and bacon and fry until the onion is golden and the bacon is crisp. Add to the lentils and season with plenty of black pepper. Continue cooking until the liquid reduces in the pan and the lentils are almost a purée.

If using bratwürst melt another knob of dripping in the pan. Fry these until golden-brown and cooked through. Frankfurters should be put in a pan of cold water, brought to the boil, taken off the heat and left to warm through for 5 minutes.

Taste the lentil mixture for seasoning and transfer to a hot serving platter. Arrange the sausages over the lentils and serve immediately.

Moussaka

Popular all over the Middle East, but particularly in Greece, Cyprus and Turkey, Moussaka is a delicious combination of minced lamb, onion and aubergines with a topping of thick creamy sauce. As it is a fairly substantial dish, serve with a simple dressed green or tomato salad.

METRIC	IMPERIAL
2 medium-sized aubergines (approx. ½ kg.), cleaned, sliced and dégorgé	2 medium-sized aubergines, (approx. 1 lb.), cleaned, sliced and dégorgé
Vegetable or cooking oil and butter for frying	Vegetable or cooking oil and butter for frying
1 large onion, peeled and chopped	1 large onion, peeled and chopped
1 garlic clove, crushed with 1 × 2.5 ml. spoon salt	1 garlic clove, crushed with ½ teaspoon salt
½ kg. cooked lamb, minced	1 lb. cooked lamb, minced
1 × 5 ml. spoon ground allspice or cinnamon	1 teaspoon ground allspice or cinnamon

Bangers with lentils

2 × 15 ml. spoons freshly chopped parsley	2 tablespoons freshly chopped parsley
Freshly ground black pepper	Freshly ground black pepper
3 × 15 ml. spoons tomato purée	3 tablespoons tomato purée
½ kg. potatoes, parboiled, peeled and thinly sliced	1 lb. potatoes, parboiled, peeled and thinly sliced

For the sauce:	For the sauce:
25 g. butter	1 oz. butter
40 g. flour	1½ oz. flour
400 ml. hot milk	¾ pint hot milk
Pinch of ground allspice	Pinch of ground allspice
Salt and freshly ground black pepper	Salt and freshly ground black pepper
1 egg yolk	1 egg yolk

Dry the aubergines thoroughly on a clean tea-towel or absorbent kitchen paper. Heat some oil and butter in a large frying pan and, when foaming, add enough aubergine slices to cover the bottom of the pan. Fry until browned on both sides. Remove from the pan with a slotted spoon and drain on absorbent kitchen paper. Fry the remaining aubergine slices in this way, adding more oil and butter when necessary. Fry the onion and garlic until golden in the same pan. Stir in the lamb and fry until browned. Add the allspice or cinnamon, parsley, and pepper to taste, then stir in the tomato purée and a little water to moisten.

In a large ovenproof casserole dish or earthenware cooking pot, put alternate layers of meat and aubergines, starting and ending with a meat layer. Put a layer of potatoes on top of this.

Moussaka

Stuffed peppers

To prepare the sauce, melt the butter in a saucepan. Stir in the flour and cook for 1 to 2 minutes, stirring constantly. Remove from the heat and gradually add the hot milk, stirring vigorously. When all the milk is incorporated, return to the heat and bring to the boil, stirring constantly. Lower the heat, add the seasonings and simmer gently until the sauce thickens. Remove from the heat and allow to cool slightly. Beat the egg yolk in a mixing bowl then beat a few spoons of the sauce into the egg. Stir this mixture into the pan of sauce and taste for seasoning. Spoon the sauce over the potatoes in the baking dish.

Bake in a fairly hot oven (190°C/375°F or Gas Mark 5) for 25 to 30 minutes when the sauce topping will have risen and become golden. Remove from the oven, allow to cool for a few minutes, then serve straight from the cooking dish.

Stuffed peppers

Stuffed peppers make a colourful and economical supper meal during the late summer when peppers are plentiful. They can also be served as a first course, in which case small peppers should be used and the quantity of stuffing halved.

METRIC	IMPERIAL
4 large green or red peppers, cored and seeded, tops reserved	*4 large green or red peppers, cored and seeded, tops reserved*
Salt	*Salt*
Vegetable or cooking oil for frying	*Vegetable or cooking oil for frying*
1 small onion, peeled and finely chopped	*1 small onion, peeled and finely chopped*

100 g. minced beef	*4 oz. minced beef*
1 × 15 ml. spoon tomato purée	*1 tablespoon tomato purée*
2 tomatoes, skinned, seeded and chopped	*2 tomatoes, skinned, seeded and chopped*
1 × 5 ml. spoon freshly chopped basil or 1 × 2.5 ml. spoon dried basil	*1 teaspoon freshly chopped basil or ½ teaspoon dried basil*
1 × 15 ml. spoon freshly chopped parsley	*1 tablespoon freshly chopped parsley*
Salt and freshly ground black pepper	*Salt and freshly ground black pepper*
100 g. long-grain rice, cooked and drained	*4 oz. long-grain rice, cooked and drained*
1 × 15 ml. spoon butter	*1 tablespoon butter*

Blanch the peppers and tops by bringing to the boil in salted water. Drain and refresh under cold running water. Pat dry with absorbent kitchen paper.

Heat a spoon of oil in a frying pan. Add the onion and fry until golden. Add the minced beef and fry until browned, stirring constantly. Stir in the tomato purée, tomatoes, basil, parsley and salt and pepper to taste and cook for 5 minutes. Remove the pan from the heat, stir in the boiled rice and mix well.

Stand the peppers in a deep ovenproof casserole dish. Spoon the stuffing into them. If there is too much stuffing for the peppers, spoon it around them. Put a knob of butter on top of each and place the reserved tops on the peppers. Cover with foil and bake in a moderate oven (180°C/350°F or Gas Mark 4) for 40 minutes or until the peppers are tender and soft when pierced with a skewer. Serve straight from the casserole.

Chilli con carne

Spaghetti Bolognese

This is the ever-popular English version of Spaghetti Bolognese – ideal for family evening meals and impromptu weekday supper parties. Serve with a crisp green salad and a glass of red Italian wine.

METRIC	IMPERIAL
Olive oil for frying	*Olive oil for frying*
1 large onion, peeled and finely chopped	*1 large onion, peeled and finely chopped*
1 garlic clove, crushed with 1 × 2.5 ml. spoon salt	*1 garlic clove, crushed with ½ teaspoon salt*
¾ kg. minced beef	*1½ lb. minced beef*
2 × 15 ml. spoons tomato purée	*2 tablespoons tomato purée*
1 × 396 g. can tomatoes	*1 × 14 oz. can tomatoes*
Approx. 300 ml. chicken stock	*Approx. ½ pint chicken stock*
1 × 5 ml. spoon sugar	*1 teaspoon sugar*
1 × 15 ml. spoon red or white wine vinegar	*1 tablespoon red or white wine vinegar*
1 × 5 ml. spoon freshly chopped basil or 1 × 2.5 ml. spoon dried basil	*1 teaspoon freshly chopped basil or ½ teaspoon dried basil*
1 × 5 ml. spoon freshly chopped oregano or 1 × 2.5 ml. spoon dried oregano	*1 teaspoon freshly chopped oregano or ½ teaspoon dried oregano*
Freshly ground black pepper to taste	*Freshly ground black pepper to taste*

To serve:	**To serve:**
350 g. spaghetti	*12 oz. spaghetti*
Salt	*Salt*
1 × 15 ml. spoon butter	*1 tablespoon butter*
50 g. Parmesan cheese, grated	*2 oz. Parmesan cheese, grated*

Heat 2 spoons of oil in a large pan. Add the onion and garlic and fry until golden. Add the beef and fry until browned, stirring constantly. Stir in the tomato purée, tomatoes and stock and mix until well blended. Stir in the remaining ingredients with salt and black pepper to taste and bring to the boil. Lower the heat and simmer gently for 20 minutes, stirring occasionally, and adding a little more stock or water if the sauce becomes dry.

Meanwhile, cook the spaghetti in boiling salted water for 12 to 15 minutes or until 'al dente' (tender, but firm to the bite). Drain, return to pan with the butter and heat through over gentle heat.

Arrange the spaghetti in a circle on a hot serving platter. Taste the meat sauce for seasoning and spoon into the centre. Serve immediately with grated Parmesan handed separately.

Chilli con carne

As its name suggests, Chilli con carne is a hot, spicy dish. Originally from Mexico, it is a tasty stew of minced beef, onions, red kidney beans and spices. Serve with plain boiled rice. Chilli powder can vary considerably in strength, so add to taste.

METRIC	IMPERIAL
Vegetable or cooking oil for frying	*Vegetable or cooking oil for frying*
1 large onion, peeled and sliced	*1 large onion, peeled and sliced*
1 garlic clove, crushed with 1 × 2.5 ml. spoon salt	*1 garlic clove, crushed with ½ teaspoon salt*
¾ kg. minced beef	*1½ lb. minced beef*
1 × 5 ml. spoon chilli powder or to taste	*1 teaspoon chilli powder or to taste*
1 × 396 g. can tomatoes	*1 × 14 oz. can tomatoes*
150 ml. beef stock	*¼ pint beef stock*
1 × 5 ml. spoon sugar	*1 teaspoon sugar*
2 × 15 ml. spoons tomato purée	*2 tablespoons tomato purée*
Freshly ground black pepper	*Freshly ground black pepper*
1 × 432 g. can red kidney beans, drained and rinsed in cold running water	*1 × 15¼ oz. can red kidney beans, drained and rinsed in cold running water*

Heat 2 spoons of oil in a large pan. Add the onion and garlic and fry gently until golden. Add the beef and chilli powder and fry until the meat is well-browned, stirring constantly. Stir in the tomatoes, stock, sugar, tomato purée and pepper to taste and bring to the boil. Lower the heat, cover and simmer gently for 30 minutes, adding the drained kidney beans 5 minutes before the end of the cooking time. Adjust seasoning and serve immediately on a bed of freshly boiled rice.

Lasagne al forno; Spaghetti Bolognese

Lasagne al forno

There are numerous variations of this delicious Italian dish with its layers of meat, pasta and cheese sauce.

METRIC
Olive oil for frying
1 large onion, peeled and chopped
1 garlic clove, crushed with 1 × 2.5 ml. spoon salt
2 celery stalks, scrubbed and finely chopped
100 g. unsmoked streaky bacon, rinds removed and chopped
½ kg. minced beef
1 × 396 g. can tomatoes
150 ml. beef stock
2 × 15 ml. spoons tomato purée
1 × 5 ml. spoon sugar
2 × 5 ml. spoons freshly chopped oregano or 1 × 5 ml. spoon dried oregano
Freshly ground black pepper
175 g. lasagne verde
50 g. Parmesan cheese, grated, to finish

For the sauce:
25 g. butter
50 g. flour
600 ml. hot milk
Pinch of grated nutmeg
Salt and freshly ground black pepper
1 × 226 g. carton cottage cheese, sieved

IMPERIAL
Olive oil for frying
1 large onion, peeled and chopped
1 garlic clove, crushed with ½ teaspoon salt
2 celery stalks, scrubbed and finely chopped
4 oz. unsmoked streaky bacon, rinds removed and chopped
1 lb. minced beef
1 × 14 oz. can tomatoes
¼ pint beef stock
2 tablespoons tomato purée
1 teaspoon sugar
2 teaspoons freshly chopped oregano or 1 teaspoon dried oregano
Freshly ground black pepper
6 oz. lasagne verde
2 oz. Parmesan cheese, grated, to finish

For the sauce:
1 oz. butter
2 oz. flour
1 pint hot milk
Pinch of grated nutmeg
Salt and freshly ground black pepper
1 × 8 oz. carton cottage cheese, sieved

Heat a spoon of oil in a large pan. Add the onion, garlic and celery and fry until golden. Add the chopped bacon and continue to fry until crisp. Add the minced beef to the pan and fry until browned, stirring constantly. Stir in the tomatoes, stock, tomato purée, sugar, oregano and black pepper to taste. Bring to the boil, stirring constantly, then lower the heat, half cover and simmer gently for 20 minutes or until the sauce is well reduced and thick.

Meanwhile, cook the lasagne. Bring a large pan of salted water to the boil and stir in a spoonful of oil. Cook the pasta, a few sheets at a time, for 8 to 10 minutes or until 'al dente' (tender but firm to the bite). Drain and pat dry with a clean tea-towel or absorbent kitchen paper. Add more oil to the water for each batch of lasagne.

To prepare the sauce, melt the butter in a pan. Stir in the flour and cook for 1 to 2 minutes, stirring constantly. Remove from the heat and gradually add the milk, stirring vigorously. When all the milk is incorporated, return to the heat and bring to the boil, stirring constantly. Lower the heat, add the seasonings and simmer gently for a few minutes until the sauce thickens. Remove from heat, leave to cool slightly, then stir in the cottage cheese.

Arrange the meat, pasta and prepared sauce in layers in a buttered shallow baking dish, starting with a layer of meat, then pasta, then sauce. Sprinkle the top layer of sauce with the Parmesan.

Bake in a moderately hot oven (190°C/375°F or Gas Mark 5) for 30 minutes or until browned and bubbling. Serve straight from the baking dish.

Keema curry

American-style hamburgers

Keema curry

Keema curry is a spicy mixture of minced beef, onions, garlic, tomatoes and yogurt. Serve with freshly boiled rice and sweet mango chutney for a quickly prepared family supper.

METRIC	IMPERIAL
Vegetable or cooking oil for frying	Vegetable or cooking oil for frying
1 medium-sized onion, peeled and finely chopped	1 medium-sized onion, peeled and finely chopped
1 garlic clove, crushed with 1 × 2.5 ml. spoon salt	1 garlic clove, crushed with ½ teaspoon salt
2 × 5 ml. spoons ground ginger	2 teaspoons ground ginger
¾ kg. minced beef	1½ lb. minced beef
1 × 15 ml. spoon garam masala or curry powder	1 tablespoon garam masala or curry powder
1 × 2.5 ml. spoon chilli powder	½ teaspoon chilli powder
6 tomatoes, skinned, seeded and chopped	6 tomatoes, skinned, seeded and chopped
2 × 15 ml. spoons tomato purée	2 tablespoons tomato purée
150–300 ml. beef stock	¼–½ pint beef stock
2 × 141 g. cartons natural unsweetened yogurt	2 × 5 oz. cartons natural unsweetened yogurt

Heat 2 spoons of oil in a large frying pan. Add the onion, garlic and ginger and fry until golden. Stir in the minced beef, garam masala or curry powder and chilli powder and fry until the meat is browned, stirring constantly. Add the tomatoes, tomato purée, 150 ml./¼ pint of the stock and half the yogurt and mix well. Cover and simmer gently for about 30 minutes or until the beef is cooked, adding more stock if the mixture becomes dry. Taste for seasoning, stir in the remaining yogurt and transfer to a hot serving platter.

American-style hamburgers

To be eaten in true American style, hamburgers must be served with tomato ketchup, mayonnaise, a selection of spicy relishes, cola or lager and French fries or potato crisps.

METRIC	IMPERIAL
¾ kg. minced beef	1½ lb. minced beef
50 g. fresh white breadcrumbs	2 oz. fresh white breadcrumbs
1 × 5 ml. spoon dried mixed herbs	1 teaspoon dried mixed herbs
Salt and freshly ground black pepper	Salt and freshly ground black pepper
1 egg, beaten	1 egg, beaten
To serve:	**To serve:**
4 soft hamburger buns or picnic rolls	4 soft hamburger buns or picnic rolls
25 g. butter	1 oz. butter
4 large lettuce leaves	4 large lettuce leaves
2 tomatoes, sliced	2 tomatoes, sliced
1 small onion, peeled and sliced into rings	1 small onion, peeled and sliced into rings

Put the beef, breadcrumbs and herbs in a large mixing bowl and mix well together. Season to taste with salt and pepper and bind the mixture with the egg. Shape the mixture into four thick hamburgers and chill for at least 30 minutes.

Preheat the grill until very hot, then grill the hamburgers for about 8 minutes on each side or until well-browned and cooked through. If they are becoming too brown, turn down the grill to moderate or low and cook for a longer time.

Meanwhile, split the buns or rolls in half and butter both halves. Reshape and put in a slow oven to warm through.

When the hamburgers are ready, remove the buns or rolls from the oven, put lettuce, tomato and onion on one half of each, top with the hamburgers and other half of the bread.

Savoury stuffed pancakes

Pancakes make a versatile supper dish as they can be stuffed or layered with practically any sort of filling. They can be made well in advance (cooked pancakes keep very well in the freezer) and the chosen filling can be put in at the last minute. If made in advance, stack the pancakes, interleaving them with greaseproof paper. Special pancake pans are available which, like omelet pans, should be kept for frying pancakes only. See the notes on omelet pans for proving and cleaning these pans.

METRIC	IMPERIAL
For the batter:	**For the batter:**
100 g. flour	*4 oz. flour*
1 × 1.25 ml. spoon salt	*¼ teaspoon salt*
1 egg, beaten	*1 egg, beaten*
300 ml. milk	*½ pint milk*
2 × 15 ml. spoons vegetable or cooking oil	*2 tablespoons vegetable or cooking oil*
Mushroom and ham filling:	**Mushroom and ham filling:**
Butter for frying	*Butter for frying*
1 small onion, peeled and finely chopped	*1 small onion, peeled and finely chopped*
225 g. mushrooms, cleaned and finely chopped	*½ lb. mushrooms, cleaned and finely chopped*
3 tomatoes, skinned, seeded and chopped	*3 tomatoes, skinned, seeded and chopped*
100 g. cooked ham, diced	*4 oz. cooked ham, diced*
1 × 2.5 ml. spoon freshly chopped marjoram or 1 × 1.25 ml. spoon dried marjoram	*½ teaspoon freshly chopped marjoram or ¼ teaspoon dried marjoram*
Pinch of cayenne pepper	*Pinch of cayenne pepper*
Salt and freshly ground black pepper	*Salt and freshly ground black pepper*
For the cheese sauce:	**For the cheese sauce:**
25 g. butter	*1 oz. butter*
25 g. flour	*1 oz. flour*
300 ml. hot milk	*½ pint hot milk*
Pinch of grated nutmeg	*Pinch of grated nutmeg*
50 g. Cheddar cheese, grated	*2 oz. Cheddar cheese, grated*
To finish:	**To finish:**
25 g. Parmesan cheese, grated	*1 oz. Parmesan cheese, grated*
Knob of butter	*Knob of butter*

Sift the flour and salt into a mixing bowl. Make a well in the centre and put in the egg. Gradually add half the milk, beating in the flour vigorously with a wooden spoon until a thick creamy batter is formed. Pour in the remaining milk and 1 × 5 ml. spoon/1 teaspoon of the oil and beat until quite smooth. Transfer to a jug for easy pouring.

Heat a little of the remaining oil in a 25cm./10in. frying or pancake pan and, when very hot, pour in a little of the batter from the jug. Tip the pan quickly so that the batter runs over the bottom of the pan. Cook over high heat until the underneath is golden-brown, then turn the pancake over, either by tossing it, or with the help of a palette knife. Cook the other side for about 15 seconds or until golden-brown. Slide out of the pan onto a hot plate and keep warm while the remaining

Savoury stuffed pancakes

pancakes are made in the same way. Keep them warm.

To prepare the filling, melt a knob of butter in a frying pan. Add the onion and fry until golden. Add the mushrooms and fry for 1 to 2 minutes, then stir in the tomatoes and diced ham. Sprinkle with the marjoram and cayenne and season to taste with salt and pepper. Simmer gently for 5 minutes, then use to fill the prepared pancakes, taking from the pan with a slotted spoon.

Spoon some of the filling onto the centre of each pancake. Roll up and put in a flameproof dish.

To prepare the cheese sauce, melt the butter in a saucepan. Stir in the flour and cook for 1 to 2 minutes, stirring constantly. Remove from the heat and gradually add the hot milk, stirring vigorously. When all the milk is incorporated, return to the heat and bring to the boil, stirring constantly. Lower the heat, add the nutmeg, salt and pepper to taste, and the grated cheese. Simmer gently until the sauce is thick, stirring constantly.

Coat the pancakes with the sauce and sprinkle with Parmesan cheese. Dot with butter and put under a preheated hot grill for a few minutes or until the top is golden-brown.

Makes approx. 12 pancakes.

Desserts and puddings

In this country we have an immense range of desserts and puddings. Homely substantial sponge- and suet-based puds and pastries compete with the lighter milk puddings and the extra-special ices, soufflés and fresh fruit sweets.

Do not neglect the last course of any meal, however simple it may be. For most family meals, when only two courses are to be served, choose the more substantial puddings which are relatively easy and inexpensive to make. If the dessert is the third course of a dinner party meal, more planning is required. Choose a dessert that contrasts well in colour, flavour and texture with the previous two courses and, if possible, one that can be made in advance. Many dinner party desserts are served cold and can therefore be left to chill in the refrigerator until serving time, giving you time to concentrate on the rest of the meal.

Rhubarb and ginger crumble

The flavour of rhubarb is greatly improved by the addition of a spice such as ginger. Serve hot with sweetened whipped cream or cold with vanilla ice-cream.

METRIC	IMPERIAL
For the topping:	**For the topping:**
175 g. flour	*6 oz. flour*
75 g. butter or margarine	*3 oz. butter or margarine*
75 g. caster sugar	*3 oz. caster sugar*
For the filling:	**For the filling:**
¾ kg. rhubarb, trimmed, cleaned and cut into 2.5 cm. slices	*1½ lb. rhubarb, trimmed, cleaned and cut into 1 in. slices*
100 g. demerara sugar	*4 oz. demerara sugar*
Juice and finely grated rind of 1 orange	*Juice and finely grated rind of 1 orange*
1 × 5 ml. spoon ground ginger	*1 teaspoon ground ginger*

To prepare the topping, sift the flour into a mixing bowl. Add the butter or margarine in pieces and rub into the flour until the mixture resembles fine breadcrumbs. Mix in the sugar.

Put the rhubarb slices in a medium-sized deep pie dish and stir in the remaining ingredients with a large metal spoon. Sprinkle the prepared topping over the rhubarb and bake in a fairly hot oven (200°C/400°F or Gas Mark 6) for 30 minutes or until the topping is golden-brown and the filling soft when pierced with a skewer.

Old English apple pie

There are few more delicious puddings than Old English apple pie with its filling of apples, dried fruit and spices. Serve with custard sauce, or sweetened whipped cream. Cheddar cheese is also good with apple pie.

METRIC	IMPERIAL
For the pastry:	**For the pastry:**
225 g. flour	*8 oz. flour*
Pinch of salt	*Pinch of salt*
2 × 5 ml. spoons caster sugar	*2 teaspoons caster sugar*
100 g. butter	*4 oz. butter*
2–3 × 15 ml. spoons cold water	*2–3 tablespoons cold water*
For the filling:	**For the filling:**
¾ kg. cooking apples, peeled, cored and sliced	*1½ lb. cooking apples, peeled, cored and sliced*
4 × 15 ml. spoons sultanas or raisins	*4 tablespoons sultanas or raisins*
175 g. soft brown sugar	*6 oz. soft brown sugar*
1 × 2.5 ml. spoon ground cinnamon	*½ teaspoon ground cinnamon*
1 × 1.25 ml. spoon grated nutmeg	*¼ teaspoon grated nutmeg*
Finely grated rind and juice of ½ lemon	*Finely grated rind and juice of ½ lemon*
To finish:	**To finish:**
Milk	*Milk*
Caster sugar	*Caster sugar*

To prepare the pastry, sift the flour and salt into a mixing bowl, then stir in the sugar. Add the butter in pieces and rub into the flour with the fingertips until the mixture resembles fine breadcrumbs. Stir in enough water to hold the mixture together, then form into a smooth ball. Wrap in foil or greaseproof paper and chill in the refrigerator for 30 minutes.

Divide the dough in two and roll out one half on a floured board to a circle to fit the base of a 20 cm./8 in. pie dish.

Put the apples in a mixing bowl, then stir in the remaining filling ingredients. Spoon into the dough-lined pie dish. Roll out the remaining dough to a circle for the lid. Lay over the filling, pressing down and sealing the edge with water. Flute the edge with your fingers or crimp with the prongs of a fork. Brush with a little milk and dredge with caster sugar. Make a slit in the centre of the pie for the steam to escape.

Bake on a baking sheet in the centre of a fairly hot oven (200°C/400°F or Gas Mark 6) for 15 minutes, then reduce the heat to moderate (180°C/350°F or Gas Mark 4) and continue baking for 20 minutes.

Allow to cool for 5 minutes before serving.

Lemon meringue pie

A popular favourite, Lemon meringue pie is a versatile dessert suitable for family and guests. Serve warm or cold.

METRIC	IMPERIAL
For the rich shortcrust pastry:	**For the rich shortcrust pastry:**
175 g. flour	6 oz. flour
Pinch of salt	Pinch of salt
2 × 5 ml. spoons caster sugar	2 teaspoons caster sugar
75 g. butter	3 oz. butter
1 egg yolk	1 egg yolk
1–2 × 15 ml. spoons cold water	1–2 tablespoons cold water
For the filling:	**For the filling:**
3 × 15 ml. spoons cornflour	3 tablespoons cornflour
150 ml. water	¼ pint water
Finely grated rind of 2 lemons	Finely grated rind of 2 lemons
Scant 150 ml. lemon juice	Scant ¼ pint lemon juice
75 g. caster sugar	3 oz. caster sugar
2 egg yolks	2 egg yolks
For the topping:	**For the topping:**
2 egg whites	2 egg whites
100 g. caster sugar	4 oz. caster sugar

To make the pastry, sift the flour and salt into a mixing bowl. Stir in the sugar. Add the butter in pieces and rub into the flour until the mixture resembles fine breadcrumbs. Mix the egg yolk with 1 spoon of the water and stir into the dry mixture with a palette knife until it draws together. Add more water if necessary. Form the dough into a smooth ball, then wrap in foil or greaseproof paper and chill in the refrigerator for 30 minutes.

Roll out the chilled dough on a floured board to a circle large enough to line a 20 cm./8 in. flan ring placed on a baking sheet. Prick the base of the dough with a fork. Chill in the refrigerator for a further 15 minutes.

Line the dough with crumpled greaseproof paper and three-quarters fill with rice or baking beans. Bake in a fairly hot oven (190°C/375°F or Gas Mark 5) for 15 minutes, then remove the rice or beans and greaseproof paper and bake for a further 5 minutes. Take from the oven and remove the flan ring.

To prepare the filling, mix the cornflour and water together in a saucepan. Add the lemon rind and juice and bring slowly to the boil, stirring constantly with a wooden spoon. Simmer gently until the mixture thickens, then remove from the heat and stir in the sugar. Leave to cool slightly, then beat in the egg yolks. Pour this mixture into the cooked pastry case.

In a clean bowl whisk the egg whites until stiff with a wire whisk, rotary or electric beater. Whisk in 1 × 15 ml. spoon/1 tablespoon of the sugar, then carefully fold in the remainder, reserving a little for dredging. Spoon or pipe the meringue onto the lemon filling to cover it and dredge with the reserved sugar.

Bake in a very cool oven (140°C/275°F or Gas Mark 1) for 30 minutes or until the meringue is crisp and golden.

Apricot tart

This is a rich French flan to be served cold with sweetened whipped cream. It makes an ideal dinner party dessert.

METRIC	IMPERIAL
For the French flan pastry:	**For the French flan pastry:**
100 g. flour	4 oz. flour
Pinch of salt	Pinch of salt
50 g. butter	2 oz. butter
2 egg yolks	2 egg yolks
1 × 15 ml. spoon caster sugar	1 tablespoon caster sugar
For the filling:	**For the filling:**
½ kg. fresh apricots, halved and stoned, or 1 × 425 g. can apricots	1 lb. fresh apricots, halved and stoned, or 1 × 15 oz. can apricots
50 g. caster sugar	2 oz. caster sugar
1 vanilla pod or 1 × 2.5 ml. spoon vanilla essence	1 vanilla pod or ½ teaspoon vanilla essence
For the glaze:	**For the glaze:**
1 × 15 ml. spoon arrowroot	1 tablespoon arrowroot
1 × 15 ml. spoon sieved apricot jam	1 tablespoon sieved apricot jam

Sift the flour and salt onto a marble slab or board. Make a well in the centre, then put in the butter in pieces, the egg yolks and sugar. With your fingertips, draw the flour into the centre and work all ingredients together until a soft dough is formed. Form into a smooth ball and wrap in foil or grease-proof paper. Chill in the refrigerator for 30 minutes.

Press the chilled dough into a 20 cm./8 in. flan ring placed on a baking sheet. Prick the base with a fork. Chill in the refrigerator for a further 15 minutes.

Line the dough with crumpled greaseproof paper and three-quarters fill with rice or baking beans. Bake in a fairly hot oven (190°C/375°F or Gas Mark 5) for 15 minutes, then remove the rice or beans and greaseproof paper and bake for a further 5 minutes. Take from the oven and remove the flan ring. Leave to cool.

Put fresh apricots in a saucepan. Just cover with water, add the sugar and vanilla pod, if using, and heat very slowly until the sugar dissolves, stirring gently with a wooden spoon. Simmer for 15 to 20 minutes or until the apricots are soft and tender. Leave to cool in the juices, then lift out with a slotted spoon, reserving the juice. Discard the vanilla pod. If using canned apricot halves, drain well and reserve the juice. Mix with the vanilla essence. Arrange the apricot halves in the flan case.

To prepare the apricot glaze, put the reserved juice (there should be 300 ml./½ pint so make up to this amount with water if necessary) in a small pan and heat through. Dissolve the arrowroot in a little water, then stir into the juice with the apricot jam. Bring to the boil and simmer until thick. Cool slightly, then pour over the apricots. Cool completely before serving.

Jam turnovers

Rough-puff pastry, crisp yet light in texture, is perfect for Jam turnovers. If the dough seems very sticky and difficult to handle, make sure that your hands, rolling pin and board are well floured.

METRIC	IMPERIAL
For the pastry:	**For the pastry:**
225 g. flour	*8 oz. flour*
1 × 1.25 ml. spoon salt	*¼ teaspoon salt*
150 g. butter	*5 oz. butter*
25 g. lard	*1 oz. lard*
150 ml. cold water	*¼ pint cold water*
For the filling:	**For the filling:**
Approx. 225 g. red fruit or apricot jam	*Approx. 8 oz. red fruit or apricot jam*
To finish:	**To finish:**
Milk	*Milk*
Caster sugar	*Caster sugar*

Sift the flour and salt into a mixing bowl. Add the butter and lard in walnut-sized pieces, then add the water. Press the dough gently together with floured hands, then roll out on a well-floured board into a long thin oblong shape with a floured rolling-pin, keeping the edges as straight as possible with a palette knife. Fold this oblong strip into three with the open edge facing you. Turn the dough a quarter turn clockwise, and roll out to an oblong shape again. Repeat this folding and rolling process three times more, turning the dough a quarter turn each time it is folded. Fold into three, wrap in polythene or foil and chill in the refrigerator for 30 minutes.

Roll out the chilled dough very thinly into a square shape. Cut into 12 × 10 cm./4 in. squares. Put 2 × 5 ml. spoons/2 teaspoons jam in one corner of each square of dough, leaving a margin. Dampen the edges with water. Fold the dough over the jam to form a triangular shape and press the edges together to seal. Brush with a little milk and dredge with caster sugar. Place on a greased baking sheet. Bake in the oven preheated to fairly hot (200°C/400°F or Gas Mark 6) for 20 minutes or until the pastry is puffed and golden-brown. **Makes approx. 12 turnovers.**

Lemon meringue pie; Apricot tart; Jam turnovers

Jam roly-poly

Jam roly-poly makes a marvellous warming pud for the family and, apart from the long steaming, is very quick to prepare. Serve with hot custard.

METRIC	IMPERIAL
100 g. self-raising flour	4 oz. self-raising flour
Pinch of salt	Pinch of salt
50 g. shredded beef suet	2 oz. shredded beef suet
2–3 × 15 ml. spoons hot water	2–3 tablespoons hot water
8 × 15 ml. spoons jam	8 tablespoons jam

Sift the flour and salt into a mixing bowl. Stir in the suet, then gradually stir in the hot water until the dough comes together and leaves the sides of the bowl. Knead until smooth, then roll out on a floured board to an oblong about .75 cm./¼ in. thick.

Spread half of the jam along the dough, leaving a margin round the sides. Roll up like a Swiss roll from one of the short sides, pinching and sealing the edges with a little water. Wrap loosely in greased foil or a double thickness of greaseproof paper. Seal well.

Place in the top of a steamer over rapidly boiling water and steam for 1½ to 2 hours, topping up the water level from time to time during cooking.

Just before serving the roly-poly, heat the remaining jam in a small pan. When the roly-poly is cooked, remove from the steamer, unwrap the foil or greaseproof paper and transfer the pudding to a hot serving dish. Pour over the warmed jam and serve immediately. **Serves 3 to 4.**

Jam roly-poly

Treacle sponge pudding

An old-fashioned English steamed pud, Treacle sponge pudding is light and fluffy in texture, with a hint of ginger to its flavour. Traditionally, it is served with hot custard.

METRIC	IMPERIAL
100 g. flour	4 oz. flour
Pinch of salt	Pinch of salt
100 g. fresh white breadcrumbs	4 oz. fresh white breadcrumbs
Scant 1 × 5 ml. spoon bicarbonate of soda	Scant 1 teaspoon bicarbonate of soda
100 g. shredded beef suet	4 oz shredded beef suet
1 × 5 ml. spoon ground ginger	1 teaspoon ground ginger
50 g. soft brown sugar	2 oz. soft brown sugar
3 × 15 ml. spoons black treacle	3 tablespoons black treacle
4 × 15 ml. spoons golden syrup	4 tablespoons golden syrup
1 egg, beaten	1 egg, beaten
Milk to mix	Milk to mix

Sift the flour and salt into a mixing bowl. Stir in the breadcrumbs, bicarbonate of soda, suet, ginger and sugar.

Warm the treacle and half the golden syrup and stir into the dry ingredients. Stir in the egg and enough milk to make a soft dropping consistency.

Grease the inside of a 900 ml./1½ pint pudding basin and put the remaining 2 × 15 ml. spoons/2 tablespoons of golden

Treacle sponge pudding

syrup into the bottom. Pour in the pudding mixture and cover the top with greased greaseproof paper or foil. Make a pleat in the centre and tie on with string around the rim.

Place the basin in the top of a steamer or double boiler, or in a large pan of gently bubbling water, cover and steam for 1½ to 2 hours, topping up the water level from time to time during cooking. Remove the basin carefully from the pan. Discard the greaseproof paper or foil and turn the pudding out onto a hot serving plate or dish. Serve immediately.

Christmas pudding

This Christmas pudding does not need time to mature; in fact it is best made just two days before Christmas.

METRIC	IMPERIAL
225 g. dark molasses sugar	½ lb. dark molasses sugar
400 g. fresh white breadcrumbs	14 oz. fresh white breadcrumbs
225 g. shredded beef suet	½ lb. shredded beef suet
1 × 2.5 ml. spoon salt	½ teaspoon salt
1 × 5 ml. spoon mixed spice	1 teaspoon mixed spice
350 g. sultanas	¾ lb. sultanas
350 g. raisins	¾ lb. raisins
225 g. currants	½ lb. currants
100 g. candied peel, chopped	4 oz. candied peel, chopped
50 g. blanched almonds, finely chopped	2 oz. blanched almonds, finely chopped
2 large cooking apples, peeled, cored and finely chopped	2 large cooking apples, peeled, cored and finely chopped
Finely grated rind and juice of ½ lemon	Finely grated rind and juice of ½ lemon
2 eggs, beaten	2 eggs, beaten
300 ml. Guinness or milk stout	½ pint Guinness or milk stout
Approx. 150 ml. milk	Approx. ¼ pint milk
2 silver threepenny or sixpenny pieces, wrapped in foil	2 silver threepenny or sixpenny pieces, wrapped in foil

Christmas pudding

Put the dry ingredients, dried fruit, candied peel and chopped almonds in a large mixing bowl and stir well to mix. Add the apples with the lemon rind and juice, eggs and Guinness or milk stout. Stir well to mix. Stir in enough milk to make a soft dropping consistency.

Pour the mixture into two greased 1 l./2 pint pudding basins. Bury one silver coin in each pudding. Cover the tops of the puddings with circles of greased greaseproof paper, then with foil. Fold a pleat in the centre and tie string around the rim. Leave overnight.

Place the basins in the top of a steamer or double boiler, or in a large pan of gently bubbling water, and steam for 4 to 5 hours, topping up the water level from time to time during cooking.

Remove the basins carefully from the pan and leave until quite cold. Discard the foil and greaseproof paper and replace with fresh greaseproof paper and foil before storing.

Steam again for about 2 hours before serving, with Brandy butter.

Brandy butter

Traditional with Christmas pudding, Brandy butter adds a little touch of luxury to the festivities of the Christmas meal.

METRIC	IMPERIAL
75 g. unsalted butter, softened	3 oz. unsalted butter, softened
75 g. icing sugar, sifted	3 oz. icing sugar, sifted
Finely grated rind and juice of ½ orange	Finely grated rind and juice of ½ orange
2 × 15 ml. spoons brandy	2 tablespoons brandy

Put the butter in a mixing bowl and beat until light and fluffy with an electric or rotary beater or wooden spoon. Gradually beat in the icing sugar until all is incorporated, then beat in the orange rind and juice and the brandy.

Pile into a serving bowl and chill in the refrigerator until quite firm. Use straight from the refrigerator.

Crème caramel

There is nothing quite so versatile as Crème caramel – it is equally at home for a family supper as it is for a dinner party.

METRIC	IMPERIAL
For the custard:	**For the custard:**
600 ml. milk	1 pint milk
2 eggs, beaten	2 eggs, beaten
2 egg yolks, beaten	2 egg yolks, beaten
2 × 15 ml. spoons caster sugar	2 tablespoons caster sugar
150 ml. evaporated milk	¼ pint evaporated milk
For the caramel:	**For the caramel:**
100 g. sugar	4 oz. sugar
150 ml. water	¼ pint water

Put the milk in a saucepan and heat gently until lukewarm. Meanwhile, put the remaining ingredients for the custard in a mixing bowl and stir with a fork until the sugar dissolves. Stir in the warmed milk and set aside.

Put the sugar and water for the caramel in a saucepan and let the sugar dissolve slowly over gentle heat. When dissolved increase the heat and boil, without stirring, until the syrup turns a golden-brown caramel colour. Immediately pour the caramel into a warm 900 ml./1½ pint cake tin or mould. Tip the tin or mould from side to side to ensure that the base and sides are thoroughly coated with the caramel.

Strain the custard mixture into the tin or mould. Cover with foil, then put in a roasting tin half full of hot water. Bake in a moderate oven (180°C/350°F or Gas Mark 4) for 50 minutes to 1 hour or until the custard is set. Test by shaking it gently from side to side.

When set, remove from the tin and leave to cool. Chill in the refrigerator for several hours, preferably overnight, then carefully turn out onto a flat serving dish.

Custard tart

Traditional English Custard tart is a great favourite and well worth making at home.

METRIC	IMPERIAL
For the shortcrust pastry:	**For the shortcrust pastry:**
100 g. flour	4 oz. flour
Pinch of salt	Pinch of salt
1 × 15 ml. spoon caster sugar	1 tablespoon caster sugar
50 g. butter	2 oz. butter
1–2 × 15 ml. spoons water	1–2 tablespoons water
For the custard:	**For the custard:**
2 eggs, beaten	2 eggs, beaten
25 g. caster sugar	1 oz. caster sugar
300 ml. milk	½ pint milk
1 × 2.5 ml. spoon grated nutmeg	½ teaspoon grated nutmeg

To prepare the pastry, sift the flour and salt into a mixing bowl, then stir in the sugar. Add the butter in pieces and rub into the flour until the mixture resembles fine breadcrumbs. Gradually stir in enough water to form a soft dough. Form the dough into a ball and wrap in foil or greaseproof paper. Chill in the refrigerator for 30 minutes.

Roll out the chilled dough on a floured board to a circle large enough to line a 17.5 cm./7 in. flan dish placed on a

Crème caramel

Custard tart

baking sheet. Prick the bottom of the dough. Chill in the refrigerator for a further 15 minutes.

Meanwhile, make the custard. Put the eggs and sugar in a mixing bowl and beat in the milk with a fork until the sugar dissolves. Strain the custard into the chilled flan case. Sprinkle with the grated nutmeg and bake in a fairly hot oven (200°C/400°F or Gas Mark 6) for 10 minutes. Lower the heat to moderate (180°C/350°F or Gas Mark 4) and bake for a further 20 to 25 minutes or until the pastry is golden and the filling is set. Serve warm or cold.

Crème brûlée

This is a magnificently sumptuous dessert which is at its best served chilled with fresh raspberries or strawberries steeped in vanilla sugar – these contrast well with the richness of the Crème brûlée.

METRIC	IMPERIAL
600 ml. fresh double cream	1 pint fresh double cream
4 egg yolks	4 egg yolks
75 g. caster sugar	3 oz. caster sugar
1 × 5 ml. spoon vanilla essence	1 teaspoon vanilla essence

Put the cream in the top of a double boiler or in a heatproof bowl over a pan of hot water and bring to just below boiling point.

Meanwhile, put the egg yolks, 50 g./2 oz. of the caster sugar and the vanilla essence in a mixing bowl and beat thoroughly. Pour in the cream and stir to combine. Pour the mixture into a shallow baking dish and place in a roasting tin

half full of hot water. Bake in a cool oven (150°C/300°F or Gas Mark 2) for 1 hour or until set.

When set, remove from the tin and leave to go cold. Chill in the refrigerator for several hours, preferably overnight.

Sprinkle the top of the Crème brûlée with the remaining sugar and put under a preheated hot grill until the sugar turns to caramel. Leave to cool before serving.

Rice pudding

Rice pudding is a basic and it's easy, once you know how. The texture should be soft and creamy and the flavour subtly sweet with only a hint of spice.

METRIC	IMPERIAL
3 × 15 ml. spoons pudding rice	3 tablespoons pudding rice
50 g. sugar	2 oz. sugar
600 ml. milk	1 pint milk
1 cinnamon stick or 1 × 2.5 ml. spoon grated nutmeg	1 cinnamon stick or ½ teaspoon grated nutmeg
Knob of butter	Knob of butter

Put the rice and sugar in a shallow ovenproof dish. Pour on the milk and add the cinnamon or nutmeg with the butter.

Bake in a very hot oven (230°C/450°F or Gas Mark 8) for 10 to 15 minutes or until the pudding is bubbling and a skin has formed. Lower the heat to very cool (140°C/275°F or Gas Mark 1) and bake for a further 1 hour or until the pudding is soft and creamy and the skin is golden in colour. Remove the cinnamon stick, if used. Serve straight from the baking dish.

Creme brûlée

Rice pudding

American refrigerator cheesecake

Meanwhile, make the filling. Put the cheese, sugar, egg yolks and three-quarters of the raspberries in a bowl and beat together. Whip the cream until it holds its shape, then fold into the cream cheese mixture. Set aside.

Sprinkle the gelatine over the water in a small heatproof bowl and leave until spongy, then place the bowl in a pan of hot water and stir over low heat until the gelatine has dissolved. Remove the bowl from the pan and leave to cool slightly. Stir into the cheese mixture. Pour into the prepared base and chill in the refrigerator for 4 hours or overnight, until set.

Take the cheesecake carefully out of the tin (the base may be left on if difficult to move) and place on a serving platter. Top with the reserved raspberries, sprinkle with vanilla sugar and serve. **Serves 8 to 10.**

Easy ice-cream

This vanilla-flavoured ice-cream is made in the freezing compartment of the refrigerator. Home-made ice-cream is not like the commercial varieties; it has a different, softer texture – and more flavour.

METRIC	IMPERIAL
1 × 15 ml. spoon custard powder	*1 tablespoon custard powder*
50 g. caster sugar	*2 oz. caster sugar*
1 × 5 ml. spoon vanilla essence	*1 teaspoon vanilla essence*
1 egg, separated	*1 egg, separated*
600 ml. milk	*1 pint milk*
1 × 15 ml. spoon gelatine powder	*1 tablespoon gelatine powder*
2 × 15 ml. spoons water	*2 tablespoons water*
150 ml. fresh double cream	*¼ pint fresh double cream*

Turn the refrigerator to its coldest setting. Put the custard powder, sugar, vanilla essence and egg yolk in a mixing bowl and stir in a little of the milk. Mix to a smooth cream.

Scald the remaining milk (bring to just under boiling point) and pour onto the custard mixture, stirring constantly. Return to the rinsed-out pan and heat gently until thick, stirring constantly with a wooden spoon.

Sprinkle the gelatine over the water in a small heatproof bowl. Leave until spongy, then place the bowl in a pan of hot water and stir over low heat until the gelatine has dissolved. Remove from the heat and stir into the custard mixture. Leave to cool, then chill in the refrigerator, stirring occasionally, for about 1 hour.

Beat the egg white until stiff and fold into the custard mixture. Pour into a shallow freezer tray or polythene container that will fit into the freezing compartment of the refrigerator. Freeze for about 30 minutes or until mushy.

Take from the freezing compartment, empty into an ice-cold mixing bowl and beat vigorously with an electric whisk or rotary beater. Whip the cream until thick and fold into the ice-cream. Return to the freezing compartment and freeze until quite firm. This could take several hours, depending on the refrigerator.

Before serving, the ice-cream should be transferred to the body of the refrigerator to allow it to soften. Leave for about 1 hour, then scoop into serving bowls and serve immediately.

American refrigerator cheesecake

With its raspberry filling, this cheesecake makes an impressive-looking dessert. Fresh raspberries are excellent for making cheesecakes and therefore this makes a lovely summer dessert. If you like, decorate the base of the cheesecake with rosettes of whipped cream.

METRIC	IMPERIAL
225 g. digestive biscuits	*8 oz. digestive biscuits*
100 g. butter, melted	*4 oz. butter, melted*
450 g. cream cheese	*1 lb. cream cheese*
50 g. caster sugar	*2 oz. caster sugar*
2 egg yolks	*2 egg yolks*
225 g. fresh raspberries	*8 oz. fresh raspberries*
150 ml. double cream	*¼ pint double cream*
1 sachet gelatine powder	*1 sachet gelatine powder*
4 × 15 ml. spoons water	*4 tablespoons water*
25 g. vanilla sugar to finish	*1 oz. vanilla sugar to finish*

Put the biscuits between two sheets of greaseproof paper and crush finely with a rolling pin. Put in a mixing bowl. Pour in the melted butter and stir to combine. Using a metal spoon, press into the base of a 20 cm./8 in. loose-bottomed cake tin. Chill in the refrigerator for 30 minutes or until quite firm.

NOTE: remember to turn the refrigerator back to normal setting once the ice-cream is made.

Strawberry soufflé

A chilled fruit soufflé always makes a spectacular dessert – it looks so attractive in the soufflé dish with the soufflé mixture decorated above the rim.

METRIC	IMPERIAL
350 g. fresh strawberries, hulled and washed	¾ lb. fresh strawberries, hulled and washed
150 g. caster sugar	5 oz. caster sugar
3 eggs, separated	3 eggs, separated
1 × 15 ml. spoon gelatine powder	1 tablespoon gelatine powder
2 × 15 ml. spoons lemon juice	2 tablespoons lemon juice
Red food colouring (optional)	Red food colouring (optional)
150 ml. fresh double cream	¼ pint fresh double cream
25 g. finely chopped hazelnuts or walnuts or crushed ratafias to finish	1 oz. finely chopped hazelnuts or walnuts or crushed ratafias to finish

First prepare a 600 ml./1 pint or 12.5 cm./5 in. soufflé dish: cut a strip of doubled greaseproof paper long enough to go around the outside of the soufflé dish (overlapping by 2.5–5 cm./1–2 in.) and 5–8 cm./2–3 in. higher than the dish. Tie this securely around the outside of the dish with string. Brush the inside of the greaseproof paper above the rim with melted butter.

Purée the strawberries in an electric blender or work through a sieve, reserving a few whole ones for decoration. Stir in 50 g./2 oz. of the sugar.

Put the egg yolks and remaining sugar in a heatproof bowl and stand over a pan of hot water. Beat with a rotary beater or whisk until thick. Remove from the pan and continue beating until the mixture is cold. Fold in the strawberry purée.

Sprinkle the gelatine over the lemon juice in a small heatproof bowl. Leave until spongy, then place the bowl in a pan of hot water and stir over low heat until the gelatine has dissolved. Leave to cool slightly, then stir into the strawberry mixture. Add a few drops of red food colouring if the mixture seems rather pale. Whip the cream until it is thick and stir into the strawberry mixture, making sure that it is thoroughly blended.

Beat the egg whites until stiff then fold into the strawberry mixture. Spoon into the prepared soufflé dish and chill in the refrigerator for at least 4 hours or until set.

Before serving, carefully remove the greaseproof paper. Decorate the top of the soufflé with the reserved strawberries and press the nuts or ratafias around the edge.

Easy ice-cream
Strawberry soufflé

Raspberry water ice

Pommes Bristol

Raspberry water ice

Water ices make super summer desserts as they are cool, light and refreshing, and make use of plentiful summer fruits. If liked, strawberries or blackberries can be used instead of raspberries.

METRIC	IMPERIAL
100 g. caster sugar	4 oz. caster sugar
300 ml. water	½ pint water
Juice of ½ lemon	Juice of ½ lemon
¼ kg. fresh raspberries, hulled and washed, or frozen raspberries, thawed	½ lb. fresh raspberries, hulled and washed, or frozen raspberries, thawed
2 egg whites	2 egg whites

Turn the refrigerator to its coldest setting.

Put the sugar and water in a saucepan and heat gently until the sugar dissolves. Bring to the boil, add the lemon juice and simmer gently for 10 minutes. Remove from the heat and leave to cool.

Meanwhile, purée the raspberries in an electric blender or work through a sieve. When the sugar syrup is cool, stir in the raspberry purée and transfer to a shallow freezer tray or polythene container that will fit into the freezer compartment of the refrigerator. Freeze until mushy: the length of time this takes will depend on the refrigerator.

Beat the egg whites until stiff, then fold into the mushy fruit mixture, making sure that they are thoroughly mixed. Return to the freezer compartment and freeze until quite firm, stirring occasionally. This will take several hours depending on the refrigerator. Scoop out into individual serving bowls and serve immediately.

NOTE: remember to turn the refrigerator back to normal setting once the water ice is made.

Pommes Bristol

A dessert made with relatively simple ingredients, Pommes Bristol is delicious. Choose a firm-textured apple such as Cox's Orange Pippin and serve with whipped cream.

METRIC	IMPERIAL
100 g. sugar	4 oz. sugar
300 ml. water	½ pint water
1 × 5 ml. spoon vanilla essence	1 teaspoon vanilla essence
4 large eating apples, peeled, cored and sliced	4 large eating apples, peeled, cored and sliced
3 oranges	3 oranges

For the caramel:	For the caramel:
75 g. sugar	3 oz. sugar
75 ml. water	3 fl. oz. water

Put the sugar and water in a saucepan with the vanilla essence and let the sugar dissolve slowly over gentle heat. When dissolved, increase the heat slightly and simmer until a fairly thick syrup forms.

Add the apples to the pan. Simmer very gently for about 10 minutes or until tender, taking care that the apples do not break. Remove from the heat, cover with a lid until quite cold; the apples should be transparent.

Meanwhile, remove the outer rind from one of the oranges with a sharp knife and cut into thin matchstick strips. Put in a small pan of water, bring to the boil and simmer for 5 minutes. Drain, refresh under cold running water and set aside.

Remove the peel and pith from the oranges and slice into rounds. Discard any pips.

Put the apples and syrup into a large serving bowl or divide between individual bowls. Arrange the orange rounds on top.

Gooseberry fool

Chocolate mousse

To prepare the caramel, put the sugar and water in a saucepan and let the sugar dissolve slowly over gentle heat. When dissolved, increase the heat and boil until the syrup turns a rich-brown, caramel colour. Pour into a greased shallow baking tin and leave until set. Crush with a pestle, wooden mallet or rolling pin and sprinkle over the oranges with the orange rind strips. Chill in the refrigerator for at least 3 hours before serving.

Gooseberry fool

A superb summer dessert, Gooseberry fool is creamy yet light, ideal after a rich main course.

METRIC	IMPERIAL
½ kg. fresh gooseberries, topped, tailed and washed	1 lb. fresh gooseberries, topped, tailed and washed
Approx. 100 g. caster sugar	Approx. 4 oz. caster sugar
150 ml. thick custard made with 2 × 5 ml. spoons custard powder and 150 ml. milk	¼ pint thick custard made with 2 teaspoons custard powder and ¼ pint milk
150 ml. fresh double cream	¼ pint fresh double cream
Approx. 12 ratafias to finish	Approx. 12 ratafias to finish

Put the gooseberries and sugar in a saucepan. Stir in a little water and simmer gently until the gooseberries are tender. Remove from the heat and rub through a sieve into a mixing bowl. Stir in the thick custard until thoroughly mixed and allow to cool.

Whip the cream until it is thick, then fold into the gooseberry purée. Taste for sweetness and add more caster sugar if liked. Spoon into a large serving bowl or individual glasses and chill in the refrigerator for at least 3 hours. Decorate with ratafias before serving.

Chocolate mousse

A very popular dessert, Chocolate mousse is rich and creamy, with just a hint of rum. It can be served in a large bowl with cream piped around the edge.

METRIC	IMPERIAL
175 g. plain chocolate, broken into pieces	6 oz. plain chocolate, broken into pieces
2 × 15 ml. spoons strong black coffee	2 tablespoons strong black coffee
4 eggs, separated	4 eggs, separated
1 × 15 ml. spoon rum	1 tablespoon rum

To finish:	To finish:
150 ml. fresh double cream	¼ pint fresh double cream
1 × 15 ml. spoon grated chocolate	1 tablespoon grated chocolate

Put the chocolate pieces and coffee in a heatproof bowl over a pan of hot water and heat gently until the chocolate melts, stirring occasionally. Remove from the heat and leave to cool for 1 to 2 minutes.

Beat the egg yolks and gradually stir into the chocolate mixture. Stir in the rum. Beat the egg whites until stiff in a clean mixing bowl with an electric or rotary beater. Carefully fold into the chocolate mixture until thoroughly combined.

Spoon into four individual glasses and chill in the refrigerator for several hours, preferably overnight.

Before serving, whip the cream until thick, then pipe a rosette of cream on each mousse. Sprinkle with the grated chocolate.

Cherry compôte

Cherries, like most other soft fruit, have a very short season. To enjoy them at their best they should be served as simply as possible, so their unique flavour will not be spoilt. For a more economical version of this recipe, omit the red wine and use water instead.

METRIC	IMPERIAL
150 ml. red wine	¼ pint red wine
Approx. 50 g. caster sugar	Approx. 2 oz. caster sugar
¾ kg. fresh cherries, stoned	1½ lb. fresh cherries, stoned
1 cinnamon stick	1 cinnamon stick
2 × 5 ml. spoons arrowroot	2 teaspoons arrowroot

Put the red wine and sugar in a saucepan and heat gently until the sugar dissolves. Add the cherries to the pan with the cinnamon stick and a little water if the sugar syrup does not quite cover the cherries.

Simmer the cherries very gently for 8 to 10 minutes or until just soft, being careful not to overcook. Take the pan off the heat. Taste for sweetness ·and add more sugar if necessary.

Dissolve the arrowroot in a little water, then stir into the pan. Return to the heat and bring slowly to the boil, stirring constantly. The juices should be thick and syrupy. Discard the cinnamon stick and transfer the compôte to a serving bowl. Serve hot or cold.

Pears in red wine

Small Conference pears are perfect for this luscious dessert as they have very little core and can be poached whole. Serve with fresh pouring cream.

METRIC	IMPERIAL
100 g. sugar	4 oz. sugar
150 ml. red wine (Burgundy-type)	¼ pint red wine (Burgundy-type)
150 ml. water	¼ pint water
1 strip of lemon rind	1 strip of lemon rind
1 × 1.25 ml. spoon ground cinnamon	¼ teaspoon ground cinnamon
8–10 small Conference pears	8–10 small Conference pears
50 g. blanched almonds, split and toasted, to finish	2 oz. blanched almonds, split and toasted, to finish

Put the sugar, wine, water, lemon rind and cinnamon in a large saucepan and heat gently until the sugar dissolves.

Peel the pears, cutting off the core at the base and leaving the stalks on. Add to the pan, cover and simmer gently for 20 to 25 minutes or until soft and coloured by the wine. Remove the pears carefully from the pan with a slotted spoon and place, standing upright, in a heatproof glass serving bowl. Set aside.

Increase the heat and boil the liquid in the pan rapidly until it thickens and is syrupy. Take off the heat and allow to cool slightly. Remove the lemon rind, then pour over the pears. When the pears and syrup are quite cold, chill in the refrigerator for several hours, spooning the syrup over the pears from time to time. Just before serving, sprinkle over the almonds.

Summer pudding

One of the most delicious of all summer desserts, Summer pudding is probably most-loved because it is least-made. It is only for a very short period in late summer that at least three of the soft fruits are in season – and to make a really good summer pudding at least three fruits must be used.

METRIC	IMPERIAL
¾ kg. mixed soft fruits (blackcurrants,	1½ lb. mixed soft fruits (blackcurrants,

redcurrants, raspberries
or blackberries), hulled
and washed
100 g. caster sugar
100–150 g. crustless stale
white bread, cut into
1.25 cm.-thick slices

redcurrants, raspberries
or blackberries), hulled
and washed
4 oz. caster sugar
4–6 oz. crustless stale white
bread, cut into ½ in.-thick
slices

Put the soft fruits in a saucepan with the sugar and cook gently for 5 minutes or until the juices run and the fruits soften.

Line the base and sides of a 900 ml./1½ pint pudding basin or soufflé dish with the bread, making sure that there are no gaps between the slices. Reserve two slices for the top.

Put the fruit and all but 2 × 15 ml. spoons/2 tablespoons of the juice into the bread-lined basin or dish. Cover with the reserved bread slices, put a plate over the top and weigh down with weights or a heavy tin. Chill overnight.

To unmould, hold a serving plate, inverted, over the top and turn the pudding over. Use the reserved fruit juice to pour over any parts of the bread that have not been coloured.

Summer pudding; Pears in red wine; Cherry compôte

Bramble mousse

Lemon honeycomb mould

Bramble mousse

A deliciously rich dessert, Bramble mousse is made with fresh blackberries, sugar and double cream.

METRIC	IMPERIAL
½ kg. blackberries, stalks removed and washed	1 lb. blackberries, stalks removed and washed
100 g. caster sugar	4 oz. caster sugar
1 × 15 ml. spoon gelatine powder	1 tablespoon gelatine powder
2 × 15 ml. spoons water	2 tablespoons water
1 × 15 ml. spoon lemon juice	1 tablespoon lemon juice
150 ml. fresh double cream	¼ pint fresh double cream
2 egg whites	2 egg whites

Put the blackberries in a saucepan, reserving a few whole ones for decoration. Stir in the sugar and simmer over gentle heat for 10 to 15 minutes or until the blackberries are soft and juicy.

Meanwhile, sprinkle the gelatine over the water in a small heatproof bowl. Leave until spongy, then place the bowl in a pan of hot water and stir over low heat until the gelatine has dissolved. Remove the bowl from the pan and stir in the lemon juice.

Remove the blackberries from the heat and rub through a sieve into a mixing bowl. Stir in the gelatine mixture and leave the blackberry purée until it is beginning to set.

Whip the cream until thick and fold into the blackberry purée. Beat the egg whites until stiff and fold into the mousse until thoroughly combined. Spoon into a large serving bowl or individual glasses and chill in the refrigerator until set. Decorate with the reserved blackberries before serving.

Lemon honeycomb mould

This is a very attractive dessert as the boiling of the custard after the egg whites are added makes it separate into layers.

METRIC	IMPERIAL
Finely grated juice and rind of 2 lemons	Finely grated juice and rind of 2 lemons
1 envelope (1¼ × 15 ml. spoons) gelatine powder	1 envelope (1¼ tablespoons) gelatine powder
3 eggs, separated	3 eggs, separated
50 g. caster sugar	2 oz. caster sugar
600 ml. milk	1 pint milk

To decorate (optional):
Frosted mint leaves
Lemon slices

To decorate (optional):
Frosted mint leaves
Lemon slices

Put the lemon juice in a small heatproof bowl. Sprinkle over the gelatine and leave until spongy, then place the bowl in a pan of hot water and stir over low heat until the gelatine has dissolved. Remove from the heat and keep warm.

Mix together the egg yolks and sugar. Scald the milk (bring to just under boiling point) and pour into the egg yolk and sugar mixture, stirring constantly. Strain the mixture back into the rinsed-out pan and cook gently over low heat, stirring constantly with a wooden spoon, until the custard thickens enough to coat the back of the spoon. Remove the pan from the heat and allow the custard to cool slightly.

Strain the gelatine and lemon juice mixture into the custard and add the lemon rind. Stir well and leave until quite cold, stirring occasionally.

Beat the egg whites until stiff, then stir them into the cold custard mixture. Return the pan to the heat and bring just to boiling point. Immediately pour the mixture into a dam-

Plum charlotte

Oranges in caramel

pened 900 ml./1½ pint mould. Allow to cool to room temperature, then chill in the refrigerator until set.

To unmould the dessert, dip the mould into warm water for a few seconds, then turn out onto a serving plate. Decorate with mint leaves and lemon slices around the edge if you like. **Serves 4 to 6.**

Plum charlotte

Plums are an ideal fruit for a charlotte as they become soft and juicy in cooking and so blend into the bread.

METRIC	IMPERIAL
Approx. 50 g. butter	*Approx. 2 oz. butter*
175 g. fresh white breadcrumbs	*6 oz. fresh white breadcrumbs*
¾ kg. ripe fresh plums, halved and stoned	*1½ lb. ripe fresh plums, halved and stoned*
100 g. soft brown sugar	*4 oz. soft brown sugar*
Finely grated rind and juice of ½ lemon	*Finely grated rind and juice of ½ lemon*
225 ml. fresh or diluted frozen orange juice	*7½ fl. oz. fresh or diluted frozen orange juice*

Brush the base and sides of a shallow baking dish with some of the butter. Cover the base with some of the breadcrumbs. Put a layer of plums in the dish, sprinkle with some of the sugar and a little lemon rind and juice. Dot with more butter. Continue with these layers until all the ingredients are used up, finishing with a layer of breadcrumbs and dotting with butter. Pour over the orange juice and bake in a fairly hot oven (190°C/375° F or Gas Mark 5) for 40 to 45 minutes or until the charlotte feels tender when pierced with a skewer and the top layer of breadcrumbs is golden-brown. Serve straight from the baking dish. **Serves 4 to 6.**

Oranges in caramel

Although a fairly economical dessert to prepare, Oranges in caramel always look impressive. For added effect the orange slices can be re-assembled in the shape of the orange, securing with cocktail sticks. Serve with fresh pouring cream.

METRIC	IMPERIAL
8 juicy oranges	*8 juicy oranges*
225 g. sugar	*½ lb. sugar*
300 ml. water	*½ pint water*

Remove the outer rind from two of the oranges with a sharp knife and cut into thin matchstick strips. Put in a small pan of water, bring to the boil and simmer for 5 minutes. Drain and refresh under cold running water. Set aside.

Remove the peel and pith from the oranges and slice into rounds. Discard any pips. Put in a large glass serving bowl and set aside.

Put the sugar and half the water in a saucepan and let the sugar dissolve slowly over gentle heat. When dissolved, increase the heat and boil until the syrup turns a rich brown, caramel colour. Remove the pan from the heat and immediately pour in the remaining water, being careful to avoid any splashing of hot caramel. Return the pan to the heat and dissolve the caramel over very gentle heat. Remove from the heat and leave to cool before pouring over the oranges. Sprinkle with the orange rind and chill in the refrigerator before serving.

Breads, scones, cakes and biscuits

Making bread is a very satisfying experience and there is nothing quite like the smell and taste of home baking.

For successful results when bread-making work in a warm, draught-free kitchen with warm hands, mixing bowl, utensils, etc., and put the dough to rise and prove in a warm draught-free place (an airing cupboard is ideal). Fresh yeast should be used whenever possible and will keep for a few days in the refrigerator, or up to one year in the freezer. If fresh yeast is not available, dried yeast can be substituted and this will keep up to six months in a cool dry place. In general, use half as much dried yeast as fresh, but check with directions on the tin before using as quantities may vary. Strong plain flour should also be used for breadmaking as its high gluten content combined with the yeast makes the bread rise and keep its shape when risen. Strong flour is normally available at some supermarkets and most health food shops.

Bread is only one small part of baking; from this you can progress to other yeast-based recipes including deep-fried Doughnuts and rich fruity Hot Cross Buns.

Cakes and bakes make super teatime treats; you can be sure family and friends will always appreciate your homemade fare. There is simply no comparison between these and the commercial varieties.

White bread

Homemade White bread has a firmer and more substantial texture than its commercial counterpart, and it has far more flavour – two good reasons why more bread should be baked at home. For a crunchier bite, try mixing half wholemeal flour, half strong plain flour and sprinkling the loaves with a few wholemeal husks before baking.

METRIC	IMPERIAL
700 g. strong plain flour	*1½ lb. strong plain flour*
2 × 5 ml. spoons salt	*2 teaspoons salt*
1 × 15 ml. spoon lard	*1 tablespoon lard*
12.5 g. fresh yeast, or 3 × 5 ml. spoons dried yeast and 1 × 5 ml. spoon sugar	*½ oz. fresh yeast, or 3 teaspoons dried yeast and 1 teaspoon sugar*
Scant 400 ml. warm milk and water, mixed	*Scant ¾ pint warm milk and water, mixed*

Sift the flour and salt into a warm mixing bowl and rub in the lard. Cream the fresh yeast with a little of the milk and water mixture. (If using dried yeast, stir the sugar into the milk and water mixture then sprinkle over the dried yeast. Leave in a warm place for about 10 minutes or until frothy.)

Make a well in the centre of the flour and pour in the yeast and liquid. Mix together with your hands until a thick dough is formed. Knead on a floured board for 10 minutes, then put in a greased bowl and cover with a damp cloth. Leave in a warm place for 1 to 1½ hours or until doubled in bulk.

Knead the dough again on a floured board for a further 5 minutes or until smooth and elastic, then divide into two. Shape and put into two warm greased 1 kg./2 lb. loaf tins. Cover and leave to prove (rise again) in a warm place for about ¾ hour or until the dough has risen to the tops of the tins.

Bake in a hot oven (220°C/425°F or Gas Mark 7) for 30 to 35 minutes or until loaves are brown on top.

Remove from the tins and knock the bottoms with your knuckles – if the loaves sound hollow they are ready. If not, return the loaves to the oven without the tins and continue baking a few minutes more. Transfer to a wire rack and leave to cool before slicing.

White buns

Proceed as for White bread as above until the second kneading, then cut and shape into 12 to 18 bun shapes. Cover and place on a greased baking sheet, leaving room for expansion. Prove in a warm place for ½ to ¾ hour or until doubled in bulk.

Bake in a hot oven (220°C/425°F or Gas Mark 7) for 15 to 20 minutes. Transfer to a wire rack and leave to cool.

Wholemeal bread

One of the easiest of breads to bake at home, Wholemeal bread has an interesting texture. Eat it quickly, preferably on the day it is made, as it does not keep very well.

METRIC	IMPERIAL
450 g. wholemeal flour	*1 lb. wholemeal flour*
1 × 5 ml. spoon salt	*1 teaspoon salt*
12.5 g. fresh yeast, or 3 × 5 ml. spoons dried yeast and 1 × 5 ml. spoon sugar	*½ oz. fresh yeast, or 3 teaspoons dried yeast and 1 teaspoon sugar*
Approx. 300 ml. warm milk and water, mixed	*Approx ½ pint warm milk and water, mixed*

Mix the flour and salt together in a warm mixing bowl. Cream the fresh yeast with a little of the milk and water mixture. (If using dried yeast, stir the sugar into the milk and water mixture then sprinkle over the dried yeast. Leave in a warm place for about 10 minutes or until frothy.)

Make a well in the centre of the flour and pour in the yeast and liquid. With your hands mix the flour and liquid together, kneading until a soft dough is formed. Shape the dough and put into a warm greased 1 kg./2 lb. loaf tin. Cover with a damp cloth and leave to rise in a warm place for about ¾ to 1 hour or until the dough reaches the top of the tin.

Bake in a fairly hot oven (200°C/400°F or Gas Mark 6) for 35 to 40 minutes or until the bread is brown on top and hollow when tapped. (See recipe for White bread.)

Quick brown bread

This is a quick bread for cooks in a hurry who have no yeast. It also keeps well; in fact, it improves with keeping!

METRIC	IMPERIAL
225 g. wholemeal flour	*½ lb. wholemeal flour*
225 g. plain flour	*½ lb. plain flour*
1 × 5 ml. spoon salt	*1 teaspoon salt*
1 × 5 ml. spoon bicarbonate of soda	*1 teaspoon bicarbonate of soda*
1 × 5 ml. spoon cream of tartar	*1 teaspoon cream of tartar*
150 ml. warm milk	*¼ pint warm milk*
300 ml. warm water	*½ pint warm water*
1 × 15 ml. spoon golden syrup	*1 tablespoon golden syrup*
1 ×5 ml. spoon malt vinegar	*1 teaspoon malt vinegar*

Put the wholemeal flour in a warm mixing bowl. Sift the plain flour and salt into the bowl, then stir in the remaining dry ingredients. Mix the milk and water together in a jug and stir in the golden syrup and vinegar.

Make a well in the centre of the dry ingredients. Pour in the liquid and stir quickly with a spoon to mix thoroughly.

Turn the mixture into a warm greased 1 kg./2 lb. loaf or cake tin and bake in a fairly hot oven (200°C/400°F or Gas Mark 6) for 20 minutes. Reduce the heat to moderate (180°C/350°F or Gas Mark 4) and bake for a further 30 minutes or until the bread is brown on top and hollow when tapped. (See recipe for White bread.)

Doughnuts; Hot cross buns

Hot cross buns

Although an Easter speciality, traditionally eaten on Good Friday, there is no reason why these delicious spicy buns should not be eaten at other times of the year.

METRIC	IMPERIAL
450 g. strong plain flour	1 lb. strong plain flour
1 × 5 ml. spoon salt	1 teaspoon salt
1 × 5 ml. spoon mixed spice	1 teaspoon mixed spice
1 × 2.5 ml. spoon grated nutmeg	½ teaspoon grated nutmeg
50 g. sugar	2 oz. sugar
50 g. butter, margarine or lard	2 oz. butter, margarine or lard
18 g. fresh yeast, or 4½ × 5 ml. spoons dried yeast and 1 × 5 ml. spoon sugar	¾ oz. fresh yeast, or 4½ teaspoons dried yeast and 1 teaspoon sugar
Scant 300 ml. warm milk and water, mixed	Scant ½ pint warm milk and water, mixed
50 g. currants	2 oz. currants
50 g. chopped mixed peel	2 oz. chopped mixed peel

To glaze:
50 g. sugar
2 × 15 ml. spoons water

To glaze:
2 oz. sugar
2 tablespoons water

Sift the flour, salt, mixed spice, nutmeg and sugar into a warm mixing bowl. Rub in the fat. Cream the fresh yeast with a little of the milk and water mixture. (If using dried yeast, stir the sugar into the milk and water mixture, then sprinkle over the dried yeast. Leave in a warm place for about 10 minutes or until frothy.)

Make a well in the centre of the flour and pour in the yeast and liquid. Mix together with your hands until a thick dough is formed. Knead on a floured board for 10 minutes, then put in a greased bowl and cover with a damp cloth. Leave in a warm place for 1 to 1½ hours or until doubled in bulk.

Mix in the currants and mixed peel, then knead on a floured board for a further 5 minutes or until smooth and elastic. Roll the dough into a long piece the shape of a sausage and cut into 12 pieces of equal size. Shape into 12 bun shapes with floured hands and place on greased baking sheets, leaving room for expansion. With a sharp knife, mark the tops of the buns with a cross. Cover and prove in a warm place for ½ to ¾ hour or until doubled in bulk.

Bake in a hot oven (220°C/425°F or Gas Mark 7) for 15 to 20 minutes or until browned on top. Transfer to a wire rack. Leave to cool slightly before slicing and spreading with butter.

To prepare the glaze, put the sugar and water in a small pan and dissolve the sugar over gentle heat. Bring to the boil and boil rapidly for a few minutes until a syrup is formed. Brush the hot syrup over the buns and cool before serving.

NOTE: the crosses can be made with shortcrust pastry dough, if preferred. **Makes 12.**

Doughnuts

Deep-fried Doughnuts rolled in sugar and cinnamon are a favourite teatime treat with adults and children alike. Serve these on the day they are made to enjoy them at their best.

Soda scones

METRIC	IMPERIAL
225 g. strong plain flour	½ lb. strong plain flour
1 × 2.5 ml. spoon salt	½ teaspoon salt
50 g. caster sugar	2 oz. caster sugar
1 × 15 ml. spoon butter or margarine	1 tablespoon butter or margarine
4 × 15 ml. spoons warm milk	4 tablespoons warm milk
2 × 5 ml. spoons dried yeast	2 teaspoons dried yeast
1 egg, beaten	1 egg, beaten
Oil for deep-fat frying	Oil for deep-fat frying

To finish:

3 × 15 ml. spoons caster sugar	3 tablespoons caster sugar
1 × 2.5 ml. spoon ground cinnamon	½ teaspoon ground cinnamon

Sift the flour and salt into a warm mixing bowl. Stir in the sugar, reserving 1 × 5 ml. spoon/1 teaspoon, and rub in the fat. Stir the reserved sugar into the milk, then sprinkle over the dried yeast. Leave in a warm place for about 10 minutes or until frothy.

Make a well in the centre of the flour and pour in the yeast mixture, with the egg. Mix together to form a soft dough, adding a little more warm milk if necessary. Do not allow the dough to become sticky. Cover the bowl with a damp cloth and leave in a warm place for about 1 hour or until doubled in bulk.

Transfer the dough to a floured board and knead lightly. Roll out to 1.25 cm./ ½ in. thick and cut with a 6.25 cm./2½ in. pastry cutter into about 14 rounds. Cut a hole in the middle of each round with a 1.25 cm./½ in. pastry cutter. Put the doughnuts on a greased baking sheet, leaving room for expansion, and prove in a warm place for ½ hour.

Heat the oil gently in a deep-fat fryer until it is hot enough to turn a stale bread cube golden in 20 to 30 seconds (180–190°C/350–375°F on a deep-frying thermometer). Lower the doughnuts into the hot oil one at a time, until there are three or four in the fryer, then increase the heat and fry for about 1 to 2 minutes or until golden and crisp, turning once during cooking. Drain on absorbent kitchen paper and keep hot while the remaining doughnuts are cooked. Coat in the sugar mixed with the cinnamon and leave to cool before serving. **Makes approx. 14.**

Soda scones

Warm, buttered scones, spread with plenty of homemade jam and topped with whipped fresh or clotted cream, are everyone's idea of an English cream tea. If buttermilk is not available, use fresh milk with 1 × 2.5 ml. spoon/½ teaspoon lemon juice.

METRIC	IMPERIAL
225 g. plain flour	½ lb. plain flour
1 × 5 ml. spoon bicarbonate of soda	1 teaspoon bicarbonate of soda
1 × 5 ml. spoon cream of tartar	1 teaspoon cream of tartar
25 g. butter	1 oz. butter
150 ml. buttermilk	¼ pint buttermilk

Sift the flour with the bicarbonate of soda and cream of tartar into a mixing bowl. Rub in the butter. Make a well in the centre of the flour and pour in the buttermilk, mixing quickly to a soft dough with a palette knife.

Turn the dough onto a floured board and knead lightly until smooth. Roll out until approx. 1.75 cm./¾ in. thick. Stamp out into approx. 12 rounds with a 5 cm./2 in. pastry cutter. Leave to stand for 15 minutes before baking.

Put the rounds on a heated greased baking sheet and bake in a hot oven (220°C/425°F or Gas Mark 7) for about 10 minutes or until the scones are well-risen and golden. Transfer to a wire rack to cool slightly. Serve warm.

Makes approx. 12.

Girdle scones; Scots pancakes

Girdle scones

Girdle scones, as their name suggests, should be cooked on a girdle, but as for Scots pancakes they can equally well be cooked in a heavy-based pan or on the hot plate of an electric cooker. To serve, split in two and spread thickly with butter.

METRIC	IMPERIAL
225 g. flour	½ lb. flour
Pinch of salt	Pinch of salt
1 × 15 ml. spoon baking powder	1 tablespoon baking powder
1 × 5 ml. spoon caster sugar	1 teaspoon caster sugar
50 g. butter	2 oz. butter
150 ml. milk	¼ pint milk

Sift the flour with the salt and baking powder into a mixing bowl. Stir in the sugar. Rub in the butter. Make a well in the centre of the flour and stir in the milk gradually until a stiff dough is formed.

Divide the dough in half and roll out on a floured board into two rounds approx. 1.25 cm./½ in. thick. Cut each round into four triangles. Dust with a little flour.

Heat the girdle or frying pan until hot. Wrap a small piece of suet in a piece of kitchen paper and use to grease girdle. Cook the scones for about 5 minutes on each side or until risen and golden-brown. Serve immediately. **Makes 8.**

Scots pancakes

Sometimes also called drop scones, these are traditionally cooked on a girdle. If a girdle is not available, a heavy-based frying pan can be used, or the pancakes can be cooked directly on the hot plate of an electric cooker.

METRIC	IMPERIAL
100 g. flour	4 oz. flour
1 × 2.5 ml. spoon bicarbonate of soda	½ teaspoon bicarbonate of soda
1 × 5 ml. spoon cream of tartar	1 teaspoon cream of tartar
1 × 15 ml. spoon sugar	1 tablespoon sugar
2 × 5 ml. spoons cooking oil	2 teaspoons cooking oil
1 egg, beaten	1 egg, beaten
Approx. 150 ml. milk	Approx. ¼ pint milk

Sift the flour with the bicarbonate of soda and cream of tartar into a mixing bowl. Stir in the sugar and oil, then beat in the egg and milk gradually until a thick batter is formed.

Heat the girdle or frying pan until hot. Wrap a small piece of suet in a piece of kitchen paper and use to grease girdle between frying each batch of pancakes. Drop batter onto the hot girdle, a spoonful at a time, leaving room for the batter to run. Cook until golden-brown on the underside and bubbles rise on the surface. Turn over and cook the other side.

Keep the pancakes hot in a warm tea-towel while cooking the remaining batter. Serve with maple or golden syrup and fresh pouring cream. **Makes approx. 16.**

Chocolate cake

Chocolate cake is one of the most popular of all cakes. This recipe makes a rich, moist cake with a puddingy texture.

METRIC	IMPERIAL
275 g. soft brown sugar	10 oz. soft brown sugar
25 g. cocoa powder	1 oz. cocoa powder
90 ml. water	3 fl. oz. water
225 g. flour	½ lb. flour
2 × 5 ml. spoons baking powder	2 teaspoons baking powder
1 × 2.5 ml. spoon bicarbonate of soda	½ teaspoon bicarbonate of soda
1 × 2.5 ml. spoon salt	½ teaspoon salt
100 g. butter	4 oz. butter
1 × 5 ml. spoon vanilla essence	1 teaspoon vanilla essence
2 eggs, separated	2 eggs, separated
150 ml. soured cream	¼ pint soured cream

For the icing:	For the icing:
100 g. butter, softened	4 oz. butter, softened
225 g. icing sugar, sifted	8 oz. icing sugar, sifted
100 g. plain chocolate, broken into pieces	4 oz. plain chocolate, broken into pieces
1 × 15 ml. spoon milk	1 tablespoon milk
25 g. chopped nuts (hazelnuts, almonds, walnuts), to finish	1 oz. chopped nuts (hazelnuts, almonds, walnuts), to finish

Put 75 g./3 oz of the sugar in a pan with the cocoa powder and water. Bring to the boil and simmer gently for a few minutes until smooth, stirring constantly. Leave to cool.

Sift the flour and remaining dry ingredients into a mixing bowl. Cream together the remaining sugar and the butter until fluffy, then beat in the vanilla essence and the egg yolks until the mixture is light. Stir in the cooled cocoa mixture and fold in the dry ingredients alternately with the soured cream. Beat the egg whites until stiff, then fold into the cake mixture until evenly mixed.

Pour the mixture into a deep 17.5 cm./7 in. round greased cake tin. Bake in a moderate oven (180°C/350°F or Gas Mark 4) for about 1¼ hours or until a skewer inserted in the centre comes out clean. Remove the cake from the oven and leave to cool for about 5 minutes. Transfer to a wire rack to cool completely.

To prepare the icing, beat the butter with an electric or rotary beater or wooden spoon until light and fluffy. Gradually beat in the icing sugar until thoroughly mixed. Put the chocolate pieces in a heatproof bowl with the milk and stand over a pan of hot water until melted, stirring occasionally. Stir into the butter and icing sugar mixture.

Cut the cake into two layers. Spread the bottom layer with three-quarters of the icing and re-shape the cake. Spread the top with the remaining icing and sprinkle around the edge with the chopped nuts.

Spicy tea bread; Chocolate cake

Spicy tea bread

Tea bread is a very popular teatime treat – it is sweet, spicy and moist, and is particularly good when spread with butter. It will become more moist if wrapped in foil and stored in an airtight tin for a day or two before eating.

METRIC	IMPERIAL
450 g. self-raising flour	1 lb. self-raising flour
1 × 5 ml. spoon salt	1 teaspoon salt
1 × 5 ml. spoon mixed spice	1 teaspoon mixed spice
1 × 2.5 ml. spoon cinnamon	½ teaspoon cinnamon
175 g. soft brown sugar	6 oz. soft brown sugar
100 g. butter	4 oz. butter
2 eggs, beaten	2 eggs, beaten
2 × 15 ml. spoons black treacle	2 tablespoons black treacle
approx. 175 ml. milk	approx. 6 fl. oz. milk
½ egg, beaten, to glaze	½ egg, beaten, to glaze

Sift the flour, salt, spice and cinnamon into a mixing bowl. Stir in the sugar. Rub in the butter. Mix the eggs, treacle and half of the milk together and stir into the flour mixture. Gradually stir in the remaining milk until the mixture drops easily from the spoon when it is shaken.

Spoon the mixture into a 1 kg./2 lb. loaf tin lined with greased greaseproof paper. Bake in a fairly hot oven (190°C/375°F or Gas Mark 5) for ¾ to 1 hour or until well-risen and brown, or when a skewer inserted in the centre comes out clean. Brush with the beaten egg after 30 minutes. Cool on a wire rack before slicing.

Christmas cake

Rich fruit mixtures like this one are best made at least one month in advance; this gives the cake a chance to mature. When the cake has cooled after baking, wrap in foil and store in an airtight tin. If liked, a few holes may be pricked in the top of the cake and brandy or rum can be poured over from time to time during storing.

METRIC	IMPERIAL
275 g. flour	10 oz. flour
Pinch of salt	Pinch of salt
1 × 2.5 ml. spoon baking powder	½ teaspoon baking powder
1 × 5 ml. spoon ground cinnamon	1 teaspoon ground cinnamon
1 × 5 ml. spoon mixed spice	1 teaspoon mixed spice
1 × 15 ml. spoon cocoa powder	1 tablespoon cocoa powder
450 g. mixed dried fruit	1 lb. mixed dried fruit
350 g. sultanas	12 oz. sultanas
225 g. currants	½ lb. currants
225 g. glacé cherries, chopped	½ lb. glacé cherries, chopped
100 g. blanched almonds, chopped	4 oz. blanched almonds, chopped
225 g. butter, softened	½ lb. butter, softened
225 g. dark soft brown sugar	½ lb. dark soft brown sugar
4 eggs, beaten	4 eggs, beaten
Finely grated rind and juice of 1 lemon	Finely grated rind and juice of 1 lemon
1 × 15 ml. spoon black treacle	1 tablespoon black treacle
3 × 15 ml. spoons brandy or rum	3 tablespoons brandy or rum
A little milk, if necessary	A little milk, if necessary

Sift the flour and salt into a large mixing bowl and stir in the baking powder, cinnamon. mixed spice and cocoa. Add the dried fruit, sultanas, currants, glacé cherries and nuts and stir to mix. Set aside.

In another mixing bowl, cream together the butter and sugar until fluffy, then beat in the eggs a little at a time. Fold in half of the flour and fruit mixture, then fold in the remainder. Stir in the lemon rind and juice, black treacle and brandy or rum. Stir the mixture until well-mixed, adding a little milk if it seems too dry.

Pour the mixture into a greased deep 20 cm./8 in. or 22.5 cm./9 in. round or square cake tin, double-lined with greased greaseproof paper. Make a slight indentation in the centre of the mixture. Bake in a cool oven (150°C/300°F or Gas Mark 2) for 1 hour, then reduce the heat to very cool (140°C/275°F or Gas Mark 1) and continue baking for a further 3 to 3½ hours or until a skewer inserted in the centre of the cake comes out clean. If the top of the cake becomes too brown during the cooking, cover with greaseproof paper or foil.

When cooked, remove from the oven and leave to cool in the tin before turning out and carefully peeling off the greaseproof paper.

Almond paste (marzipan)

METRIC	IMPERIAL
225 g. ground almonds	½ lb. ground almonds
225 g. icing sugar, sifted	½ lb. icing sugar, sifted
225 g. caster sugar	½ lb. caster sugar
1 egg, beaten	1 egg, beaten
2 × 5 ml. spoons lemon juice	2 teaspoons lemon juice
1 × 1.25 ml. spoon vanilla essence	¼ teaspoon vanilla essence
1 × 1.25 ml. spoon almond essence	¼ teaspoon almond essence
4 × 15 ml. spoons apricot jam, sieved	4 tablespoons apricot jam, sieved

Put the almonds, icing and caster sugars into a large mixing bowl and stir well to mix. Beat in the remaining ingredients, except the jam, until the paste is soft but not sticky. Turn onto a board or table sprinkled with icing sugar and knead the paste lightly until smooth. Use immediately or wrap in polythene.

Divide the prepared almond paste in half and roll out one half to a 20 cm./8 in. or 22.5 cm./9 in. round or square. Brush the top of the cake with half of the sieved jam, then place the cake upside-down on the almond paste and press down firmly.

Roll the remaining almond paste into a strip long enough to go around the sides of the cake. Cut in half for a round cake, or in four equal pieces if the cake is square. Brush one side of the almond paste pieces with the remaining jam and press onto the sides of the cake, making the joins as neat as possible. Leave to dry for 2 to 3 days.

Royal icing

If a soft, not brittle, icing is preferred, add 2 × 5 ml. spoons/2 teaspoons glycerine.

METRIC	IMPERIAL
2 egg whites	2 egg whites
450 g. icing sugar, sifted	1 lb. icing sugar, sifted
2 × 5 ml. spoons lemon juice	2 teaspoons lemon juice
2 × 5 ml. spoons glycerine (optional)	2 teaspoons glycerine (optional)

Put the egg whites in a large mixing bowl and beat until lightly frothy. Beat in the icing sugar gradually until all is incorporated and the icing is stiff enough to stand in peaks. Beat well to remove any lumps. Beat in the lemon juice, and glycerine if using. Use immediately, or cover the bowl with a damp cloth or polythene.

To rough ice, put the prepared icing on top of the cake placed on a cake board. Work with a palette knife over the top of the cake, using a to-and-fro motion. Gradually work the icing down the sides of the cake until entirely covered. Using the tip of the palette knife, quickly rough up the surface of the icing with short, sharp movements. This will create a traditional snow-scene effect that can be decorated with ornaments, etc.

To flat ice, put three-quarters of the prepared icing on top of the cake (cover remaining icing as above) placed on a cake board. Work with a steel ruler or palette knife over the top of the cake using a to-and-fro motion. Continue with this motion, smoothing out the icing and breaking any air bubbles that appear on the surface.

When quite smooth, draw the ruler or palette knife in one movement across the top of the cake, making the surface completely smooth. Scrape off any icing from the sides, return to the mixing bowl and keep covered. Leave the cake until the icing on the top is set before icing the sides with the reserved icing in the same way – smoothing round the cake with the steel ruler or palette knife and making the joins as smooth as possible.

Fruity gingerbread

Gingerbreads always improve and become moist and soft if kept for a while before eating. When cooled, place in an airtight tin and leave for one week. Cut into squares.

METRIC	IMPERIAL
100 g. butter	4 oz. butter
100 g. soft brown sugar	4 oz. soft brown sugar
100 g. black treacle	4 oz. black treacle
1 egg, beaten	1 egg, beaten
100 g. plain flour	4 oz. plain flour
2 × 5 ml. spoons ground ginger	2 teaspoons ground ginger
2 × 5 ml. spoons ground cinnamon	2 teaspoons ground cinnamon
100 g. wholewheat flour	4 oz. wholewheat flour
Approx. 150 ml. warm milk	Approx. ¼ pint warm milk
1 × 5 ml. spoon bicarbonate of soda	1 teaspoon bicarbonate of soda
50 g. mixed dried fruit	2 oz. mixed dried fruit

Put the butter, sugar and treacle in a saucepan and heat gently until melted, stirring constantly. Allow to cool slightly, then beat in the egg.

Sift the plain flour and spices into a mixing bowl, then stir in the wholewheat flour and melted mixture and beat well to combine. Mix the milk with the bicarbonate of soda and add this to the mixture in the bowl. Stir in the fruit. The mixture should have a soft dropping consistency; more milk can be added at this stage if it seems too dry.

Spoon the mixture into a greased oblong tin, 22.5 × 15 cm./ 9 × 6 in. lined with greased greaseproof paper. Bake in a cool oven (150°C/300°F or Gas Mark 2) for about 1 hour or until a skewer inserted in the centre comes out clean. Leave to cool in the tin, then remove from the tin and discard the greaseproof paper.

Farmhouse fruit cake

A country recipe using some wholewheat flour, Farmhouse fruit cake is a popular cake to bake as it keeps well and even improves with age – if given the chance!

METRIC	IMPERIAL
100 g. plain flour	4 oz. plain flour
Pinch of salt	Pinch of salt
125 g. wholewheat flour	5 oz. wholewheat flour
2 × 5 ml. spoons baking powder	2 teaspoons baking powder
1 × 5 ml. spoon mixed spice	1 teaspoon mixed spice
1 × 2.5 ml. spoon ground cinnamon	½ teaspoon ground cinnamon
100 g. soft brown sugar	4 oz. soft brown sugar
100 g. butter or margarine	4 oz. butter or margarine
225 g. mixed dried fruit	½ lb. mixed dried fruit
50 g. chopped mixed peel	2 oz. chopped mixed peel
2 eggs, beaten	2 eggs, beaten
2 × 15 ml. spoons marmalade	2 tablespoons marmalade
A little milk (if necessary)	A little milk (if necessary)

Date and walnut loaf; Farmhouse fruit cake; Fruity gingerbread

Sift the plain flour and salt into a mixing bowl, then stir in the wholewheat flour, baking powder, mixed spice, cinnamon and sugar. Rub in the butter or margarine. Stir in the remaining ingredients and mix well. Stir in a little milk if the mixture seems too stiff.

Spoon into a greased 20 cm./8 in. round cake tin lined with greased greaseproof paper. Bake in a warm oven (160°C/325°F or Gas Mark 3) for about 1½ hours or until a skewer inserted in the centre comes out clean. Cover the top of the cake with greaseproof paper if it begins to become too brown during the cooking.

Remove from the oven, take out of the tin and discard the greaseproof paper. Cool on a wire rack, then store in an airtight tin.

Date and walnut loaf

Sliced and spread with butter, Date and walnut loaf makes an excellent teatime treat. This recipe makes a fairly large-sized loaf that keeps well – and even improves with age if stored in an airtight tin.

METRIC	IMPERIAL
225 g. stoned dates, chopped	8 oz. stoned dates, chopped
1 × 5 ml. spoon bicarbonate of soda	1 teaspoon bicarbonate of soda
Pinch of salt	Pinch of salt
300 ml. hot water	½ pint hot water
275 g. self-raising flour	10 oz. self-raising flour
100 g. butter or margarine	4 oz. butter or margarine
50 g. shelled walnuts, chopped	2 oz. shelled walnuts, chopped
100 g. dark soft brown sugar	4 oz. dark soft brown sugar
1 egg, beaten	1 egg, beaten

Put the dates, bicarbonate of soda and salt in a bowl and pour over the hot water. Set aside until cool.

Meanwhile, sift the flour into a mixing bowl. Add the butter or margarine in pieces and rub into the flour. Stir in the walnuts and sugar until thoroughly combined.

Mix the dry ingredients into the cooled date mixture and beat in the egg. Pour into a greased 1 kg./2 lb. loaf tin and bake in a moderate oven (180°C/350°F or Gas Mark 4) for 1 to 1¼ hours or until a skewer inserted in the centre comes out clean.

Turn out on to a wire rack and leave to cool. Store in an airtight tin.

Walnut Victoria sandwich

The secret of making a good Victoria sandwich lies in the creaming and beating – if sufficient air is not incorporated into the mixture the cake will not be light and spongy.

METRIC	IMPERIAL
175 g. caster sugar	6 oz. caster sugar
175 g. butter, softened	6 oz. butter, softened
3 eggs, beaten	3 eggs, beaten
175 g. self-raising flour	6 oz. self-raising flour
Pinch of salt	Pinch of salt
Approx. 2 × 15 ml. spoons warm water	Approx. 2 tablespoons warm water

Walnut Victoria sandwich

Jam for spreading	Jam for spreading
Approx. 8 walnut halves, to finish	Approx. 8 walnut halves, to finish
For the glacé icing:	**For the glacé icing:**
150 g. icing sugar	5 oz. icing sugar
1–2 × 15 ml. spoons warm water	1–2 tablespoons warm water

Cream together the sugar and butter in a mixing bowl until light and fluffy, using an electric or rotary beater or wooden spoon. Gradually beat in the eggs.

Sift the flour and salt. Stir 1 × 15 ml. spoon/1 tablespoon of flour into the butter mixture until well mixed. Gradually fold in the remaining flour. Add enough water to give the mixture a soft dropping consistency. Pour into two greased 5 cm./7 in. round sandwich tins, the bases lined with greased greaseproof paper.

Bake just above centre in a fairly hot oven (190°C/375°F or Gas Mark 5) for about 20 minutes or until well-risen and golden and the cakes have shrunk away from the sides of the tins.

Turn out onto a wire rack and leave to cool. Spread the jam evenly over one cake and place the remaining cake on top.

To prepare the icing, sift the icing sugar into a mixing bowl and gradually mix in the water until a smooth paste is formed which coats the back of the spoon. Quickly beat out any lumps. Spread over the cake before the icing is set, and decorate around the edge with the walnut halves.

Caramel cakes

Caramel cakes

Everyone, especially the children, will love these delicious layers of rich shortbread, caramel and chocolate. Cut them into easy-to-handle portions and serve with morning coffee. It is essential to use sweetened condensed milk in this recipe, *not* evaporated milk.

METRIC
For the shortbread:
150 g. butter
100 g. caster sugar
275 g. flour
100 g. plain chocolate,
  broken into pieces, for
  topping

For the filling:
100 g. butter
100 g. caster sugar
2 × 15 ml. spoons golden
  syrup
1 large can condensed milk
  (equivalent to approx. 1 l.
  125 ml. of skimmed milk)

IMPERIAL
For the shortbread:
5 oz. butter
4 oz. caster sugar
10 oz. flour
4 oz. plain chocolate,
  broken into pieces, for
  topping

For the filling:
4 oz. butter
4 oz. caster sugar
2 tablespoons golden syrup
1 large can condensed milk
  (equivalent to 1⅞ pints of
  skimmed milk)

To prepare the shortbread, cream the butter and sugar together in a mixing bowl. Work in the flour with a wooden spoon or electric or rotary beater. Press into a greased 30 × 22.5 cm./12 × 9 in. Swiss roll tin and bake in a moderate oven (180°C/350°F or Gas Mark 4) for 15 to 20 minutes or until the shortbread is golden in colour. Remove from the oven and leave to cool.

To prepare the filling, put all the ingredients in a saucepan and heat gently until the sugar has dissolved, stirring occasionally. Increase the heat and boil the mixture for 5 minutes, stirring continuously. Remove from the heat, leave to cool for 1 minute, then pour onto the cooled shortbread base. Leave to set.

Melt the chocolate in a small heatproof bowl over a pan of hot water. Spread over the set filling. Mark into serving portions, fingers or squares, and leave until quite cold and set before removing from the tin.

Choux buns

Choux pastry can be used in a number of different ways, for both sweet and savoury dishes, and it is not difficult to make. Use this quantity and coat with icing to make Chocolate Éclairs for tea, or coat with hot chocolate sauce for Profiteroles to serve as a dessert.

Éclairs

<table>
<tr><td>

METRIC
For the choux pastry:
150 ml. water
50 g. butter or margarine
Pinch of salt
65 g. flour
2 eggs, beaten

For the chocolate icing:
50 g. plain chocolate,
* broken into pieces*
Knob of butter
2 × 15 ml. spoons water
175 g. icing sugar, sifted

For the filling:
150 ml. fresh double cream
* whipped with 1 × 15 ml.*
* spoon caster sugar*

</td><td>

IMPERIAL
For the choux pastry:
¼ pint water
2 oz. butter or margarine
Pinch of salt
2½ oz. flour
2 eggs, beaten

For the chocolate icing:
2 oz. plain chocolate,
* broken into pieces*
Knob of butter
2 tablespoons water
6 oz. icing sugar, sifted

For the filling:
¼ pint fresh double cream,
* whipped with 1*
* tablespoon caster sugar*

</td></tr>
</table>

To prepare the pastry, put the water, butter or margarine and salt in a saucepan and heat gently until the fat has melted. Bring to the boil and, when bubbling vigorously, remove the pan from the heat. Quickly beat in the flour all at once. Continue beating until the mixture draws away from the sides of the pan and forms a ball: do not overbeat or the mixture will become fatty. Leave to cool slightly. Beat in the eggs gradually until the pastry is smooth and glossy.

Put the mixture into a forcing bag fitted with a 1.25 cm./½ in. plain pipe. Pipe onto greased baking sheets, either in finger shapes approx. 7.5 cm./3 in. long for éclairs or in rounds approx. 5 cm./2 in. in diameter for profiteroles. Allow room between each shape for expansion during cooking.

Bake just above the centre of a fairly hot oven (200°C/400°F or Gas Mark 6) for 25 to 30 minutes or until the pastry is well-risen and crisp.

Remove from the oven and make a slit along the sides of the éclairs, or in the base of the profiteroles. Leave to cool on a wire rack.

To prepare the chocolate icing, put the chocolate pieces, butter and 1 × 15 ml./1 tablespoon water in a heatproof bowl over a pan of hot water and heat gently until melted. Remove from the heat and gradually beat in the icing sugar until the icing is thick and smooth. If the icing is too thick, add the rest of the water.

Fill the pastry with the sweetened cream, then ice the tops of éclairs with the chocolate icing. (If making profiteroles, pile onto a serving dish or in individual serving bowls and pour over hot chocolate sauce.) **Makes approx. 8.**

179

English madeleines

These individual little cakes look so pretty on the tea table, yet they're simple to make with the basic Victoria sandwich mix.

METRIC	IMPERIAL
100 g. butter, softened	4 oz. butter, softened
100 g. caster sugar	4 oz. caster sugar
2 eggs, beaten	2 eggs, beaten
100 g. self-raising flour	4 oz. self-raising flour
Pinch of salt	Pinch of salt
Approx. 1 × 15 ml. spoon warm water	Approx. 1 tablespoon warm water

To finish:

4–6 × 15 ml. spoons red fruit jam, sieved	4–6 tablespoons red fruit jam, sieved
4 × 15 ml. spoons desiccated coconut	4 tablespoons desiccated coconut
Approx. 6 glacé cherries, halved	Approx. 6 glacé cherries, halved
Few snips candied angelica	Few snips candied angelica

Cream together the butter and sugar in a mixing bowl until light and fluffy, using an electric or rotary beater or wooden spoon. Beat in the eggs.

Sift the flour and salt. Stir 1 × 15 ml. spoon/1 tablespoon of flour into the butter mixture until well mixed. Gradually fold in the remaining flour. Add enough water to give the mixture a soft dropping consistency.

Divide the mixture equally between 10 to 12 dariole or castle pudding moulds, greased and dusted with flour. Bake just above centre in a moderate oven (180°C/350°F or Gas Mark 4) for 15 to 20 minutes or until well risen and golden.

Turn the madeleines carefully out of the moulds, upside down, and leave to cool. Trim the bases if they do not stand up well. When cool, brush with the sieved jam, then roll in the coconut. Stand upright on a serving plate and decorate the top of each with a halved glacé cherry and two angelica 'leaves'. **Makes 10 to 12.**

Coconut macaroons

For lovers of coconut, these macaroons are so simple to make. They're soft and sugary, and children adore them.

METRIC	IMPERIAL
1 egg, beaten	1 egg, beaten
50 g. caster sugar	2 oz. caster sugar
175 g. desiccated coconut	6 oz. desiccated coconut

Put the egg in a mixing bowl. Beat in the sugar with a fork, then stir in the coconut. Press the mixture, a few spoonfuls at a time, into a small egg cup, then turn upside down and tap out onto a greased baking sheet to form little mounds.

Bake in a moderate oven (180°C/350°F or Gas Mark 4) for about 20 minutes or until golden-brown. Remove from the oven and leave to cool for a few minutes before transferring to a wire rack to cool completely. **Makes 8.**

English madeleines

Coconut macaroons

Brownies

Immensely popular in the United States, Brownies are squares of chocolate and nut cake which become soft and moist if stored in an airtight tin for 1 to 2 days before eating.

METRIC	IMPERIAL
100 g. butter	4 oz. butter
100 g. plain chocolate, broken into pieces	4 oz. plain chocolate, broken into pieces
100 g. soft brown sugar	4 oz. soft brown sugar
100 g. self-raising flour	4 oz. self-raising flour
Pinch of salt	Pinch of salt
2 eggs, beaten	2 eggs, beaten
50 g. walnuts, coarsely chopped	2 oz. walnuts, coarsely chopped
1–2 × 15 ml. spoons milk	1–2 tablespoons milk

Put the butter and chocolate pieces in a heatproof bowl and stand over a pan of hot water until melted, stirring occasionally. Remove the bowl from the heat. Stir in the sugar and mix thoroughly. Leave to cool.

Sift the flour and salt into a mixing bowl. Make a well in the centre and pour in the cooled chocolate mixture. Mix together, gradually drawing in the flour from the sides of the bowl. Beat in the eggs and walnuts and stir thoroughly to combine, adding enough milk to make a soft dropping consistency.

Pour into a greased 20 cm./8 in. square cake tin and bake in the centre of a moderate oven (180°C/350°F or Gas Mark 4) for about 30 minutes or until a skewer inserted in the centre comes out clean. Leave to cool in the tin before cutting into squares. **Makes approx. 16.**

Brownies

Meringues

Perfect meringues are easy to make if a few basic rules are followed: make sure all equipment is grease-free; use 50 g./2 oz. caster sugar to every egg white; refrigerate the egg whites for 24 hours before use; do not overbeat once the sugar is added; bake at the very lowest temperature.

METRIC	IMPERIAL
2 egg whites	2 egg whites
100 g. caster sugar	4 oz. caster sugar
A little caster sugar for dredging	A little caster sugar for dredging
150 ml. fresh double cream whipped with 1 × 15 ml. spoon caster sugar	¼ pint fresh double cream whipped with 1 tablespoon caster sugar

Put the egg whites in a large mixing bowl and beat until stiff with a balloon whisk or rotary or electric beater. Fold in 1 × 15 ml. spoon/1 tablespoon caster sugar, then beat again until smooth and satiny and standing in peaks. Fold in the remaining sugar with a large metal spoon.

Put the meringue mixture into a forcing bag fitted with a 1.25 cm./½ in. plain pipe. Pipe into small rounds on foil, or non-stick silicone or parchment paper placed on a baking sheet. Dredge with a little caster sugar.

Bake in a very cool oven (120°C/225°F or Gas Mark ¼) for 3 to 4 hours or until the meringues are crisp and firm to the touch. If the meringues begin to turn brown, open the oven door slightly.

Remove from the oven and leave to cool on a wire rack. Peel off the foil or paper when the meringues are completely cold and sandwich together with the sweetened whipped cream just before serving. **Makes approx. 8.**

Meringues

Chocolate chip cookies

Homemade biscuits always taste more fresh and crisp than the bought variety. If a nutty cookie is preferred, substitute 50 g./2 oz. chopped hazelnuts for the chocolate.

METRIC	IMPERIAL
225 g. self-raising flour	½ lb. self-raising flour
Pinch of salt	Pinch of salt
150 g. butter or margarine	5 oz. butter or margarine
100 g. caster sugar	4 oz. caster sugar
1 egg, beaten	1 egg, beaten
50 g. plain chocolate, coarsely grated	2 oz. plain chocolate, coarsely grated

Sift the flour and salt into a mixing bowl. Add the butter or margarine in pieces and rub in. Stir in the sugar, then mix to a stiff dough with the beaten egg.

Turn the dough onto a floured board and knead until smooth. Add the grated chocolate and work it quickly into the dough until evenly distributed, then form into a ball. Wrap in foil or polythene and chill in the refrigerator for about 30 minutes.

Roll out the chilled dough thinly on a floured board or table, then cut into approx. 30 × 5 cm./2 in. rounds with a fluted pastry cutter. Place the biscuits on greased baking sheets, leaving room between each to allow for spreading during cooking. Prick the biscuits with a fork and bake in a moderate oven (180°C/350°F or Gas Mark 4) for 10 to 12 minutes or until golden.

Remove from the oven and leave to cool for a few minutes before transferring to a wire rack to cool completely. Store in an airtight tin. **Makes approx. 30.**

Flapjacks

Moist and munchy, Flapjacks are a great favourite with everyone, especially the children. They are particularly good spread with butter.

METRIC	IMPERIAL
100 g. demerara sugar	4 oz. demerara sugar
100 g. butter or margarine	4 oz. butter or margarine
3 × 15 ml. spoons golden syrup	3 tablespoons golden syrup
175 g. porridge oats	6 oz. porridge oats
50 g. desiccated coconut	2 oz. desiccated coconut
1 × 5 ml. spoon baking powder	1 teaspoon baking powder
1 × 2.5 ml. spoon salt	½ teaspoon salt
1 egg, beaten	1 egg, beaten

Put the sugar, butter or margarine and golden syrup in a saucepan and heat gently until melted. Remove from the heat and stir in the remaining ingredients.

Press the mixture into a shallow greased 20 cm./8 in. square baking tin and bake in a moderate oven (180°C/350°F or Gas Mark 4) for 20 to 30 minutes or until golden and firm to the touch.

Remove from the oven and leave for 5 minutes, then cut into squares and leave to cool. When completely cold, loosen with a palette knife and lift each square carefully from the tin. **Makes approx. 16.**

Florentine slices

Rich, luscious biscuits, these Florentine slices are lovely with coffee, either morning or after dinner.

METRIC	IMPERIAL
225 g. block chocolate, broken into pieces	8 oz. block chocolate, broken into pieces
50 g. butter	2 oz. butter
100 g. demerara sugar	4 oz. demerara sugar
1 egg, beaten	1 egg, beaten
50 g. mixed dried fruit	2 oz. mixed dried fruit
100 g. sweetened coconut	4 oz. sweetened coconut
50 g. chopped mixed peel or glacé cherries, quartered	2 oz. chopped mixed peel or glacé cherries, quartered

Put the chocolate pieces in a heatproof bowl and stand over a pan of hot water until melted, stirring occasionally. Spoon the chocolate into a greased 19 cm./7½ in. square cake tin. Spread it out over the bottom and leave to set.

Meanwhile, cream together the butter and sugar until the mixture is light and fluffy. Beat in the egg thoroughly. Mix together the remaining ingredients and add to the creamed mixture. Spoon into the tin and spread over the set chocolate.

Bake in the centre of a cool oven (150°C/300°F or Gas Mark 2) for 40 to 45 minutes, or until golden-brown. Remove from the oven and leave for 5 minutes, then carefully mark into 12 to 16 squares with a sharp knife. The mixture will be quite sticky at this stage.

Leave until cold, then loosen with a palette knife and lift each square carefully from the tin. **Makes 12 to 16.**

Rum truffles

Rum truffles are just right to hand round with the coffee after a dinner party. They can also make a very pretty gift packed in an attractive sweet box. In hot weather they should be chilled in the refrigerator before packing into sweet cases.

METRIC	IMPERIAL
100 g. plain chocolate, broken into pieces	4 oz. plain chocolate, broken into pieces
50 g. icing sugar, sifted	2 oz. icing sugar, sifted
50 g. seedless raisins, finely chopped	2 oz. seedless raisins, finely chopped
50 g. stale sponge cake, crumbled and soaked in 2 × 15 ml. spoons rum	2 oz. stale sponge cake, crumbled and soaked in 2 tablespoons rum
1–2 × 15 ml. spoons apricot jam, sieved	1–2 tablespooons apricot jam, sieved
50 g. chocolate vermicelli	2 oz. chocolate vermicelli

Put the chocolate pieces in a heatproof bowl over a pan of hot water and heat gently until the chocolate melts, stirring occasionally. Remove from the heat and beat in the sugar, raisins and cake. Knead lightly until smooth.

Shape the mixture into approx. 18 balls the size of walnuts. Brush with the sieved apricot jam, then roll in the chocolate vermicelli. Leave until firm, then pack in sweet cases. **Makes approx. 18.**

Shortbread; Florentine slices; Chocolate chip cookies; Rum truffles; Flapjacks

Shortbread

Although plain and simple, the beauty of homemade Shortbread lies in its buttery richness and its short, crispy texture.

METRIC	IMPERIAL
150 g. flour	*5 oz. flour*
Pinch of salt	*Pinch of salt*
25 g. ground rice	*1 oz. ground rice*
50 g. caster sugar	*2 oz. caster sugar*
100 g. butter, chilled	*4 oz. butter, chilled*
Caster sugar for dredging	*Caster sugar for dredging*

Sift the flour, salt and ground rice into a mixing bowl and stir in the sugar. Add the butter, in one piece, and gradually rub into the dry ingredients. Knead until well mixed, but do not allow the dough to become sticky. Wrap in foil or polythene and chill in the refrigerator for about 30 minutes.

Press the chilled dough into a 17.5 cm./7 in. round in a fluted edge flan ring placed on a greased baking sheet. Prick all over the dough with a fork and mark into triangular portions with a knife. Chill in the refrigerator for a further 15 minutes.

Bake in the centre of a warm oven (160°C/325°F or Gas Mark 3) for 40 to 45 minutes or until pale-golden in colour. If the shortbread becomes too brown during the cooking time, cover with foil.

Remove from the oven, leave to cool slightly, then transfer to a wire rack to cool completely. Dredge with sugar. Break or cut into slices for serving. **Makes approx. 8.**

Index

Acknowledgments

The publishers would like to thank the following companies for the loan of accessories for all the photography in this book:

Laura Ashley
John Barker & Co. Ltd.
Craftsmen Potters
Elizabeth David
General Trading Company
Graham & Green
Habitat
The House of Hardy
Stephen Long
David Mellor
C. Rassell Ltd.
The Russian Shop
The Scotch House
The Tile Mart

Photography by: Rex Bamber: 16, 17 left, 18–27, 30–39, 48–61, 155–167, 170–183; Melvin Grey: 70–73, 74 above, 81–85, 87 above, 88–89, 96–115, 120–151; Paul Kemp: 17 right, 94–95; Michael Leale: 74 below, 75–77, 80, 86, 87 below, 90–93; Roger Phillips: endpapers, 4–15, 28–29, 40–43, 62–65, 78–79, 152–153, 168–169.

Notes

Notes

Notes

Notes

Notes